**Based On A True Story**

# SO, WHAT'S YOUR PLAN?

**By Boy Oh Boy**

AN ADVENTURE FULL OF LIFE-CHANGING STORIES,
TRUE LOVE, JOY, SELF-DOUBT, FAILURES AND
THE DESIRE TO BECOME AN ARTIST

Pre-editing by Aldo Ventresca, Conor Fitzpatrick
Editing by The Pro Book Editor
Interior and Cover Design by IAPS.rocks
Artworks painted by Anne Veiser, Anika Schnabel, Rafael Schnabel, Marco Wagner

eBook ISBN: 978-3-00-073842-5
paperback ISBN: 978-3-00-073843-2

Main category—Fiction
Other category—Biographical

First Edition

This book is dedicated to the woman who
taught me what love is really about.

I would like to thank her, her entire family, and all my friends in New
Zealand who made this adventure so unique and unforgettable.

Your life advice and infectious spirit of encouraging others to
become who you truly want to be will never be forgotten.

There will always be a special place for you in my heart.


Marco Wagner
(Boy Oh Boy)

# PREFACE

**M**any in this lifetime strive for a better, happier, more fulfilling life. They have dreams (that they don't dare to reach for), wishes (that they don't dare to voice), all due to a fear of the risks involved in bringing these to fruition. They have a comfort zone and they're already in it. They have shelter and a sense of relative security, but often a dull day-to-day existence is part and parcel of the experience.

Their biggest fear is losing all that they currently have and so they end up playing things on the safe side—"I'll just live like everyone else around me and hope that I strike it lucky somehow! Maybe my saviour will come along and discover the talents I've so expertly hidden! Maybe they'll spur me along, forcing me to grab my passion by the horns and ride!"

This is all well and good...as long as you're able to accept the potential scenario in which you look back on your achievements, in say "five years" time, and realise that not a lot has really happened.

I wasn't necessarily afraid of looking back and seeing nothing—I really felt that I had no other choice but to take a risk. I just had to, and even though the proverbial shit hit the proverbial fan, I can look in the mirror today and say, "at least I tried." Try I most certainly did, and what emanated from trying was a journey that will forever be etched in my memory.

This was a journey filled with self-doubt, breakthroughs, true love and setbacks, and the realisation that although you seemingly have things all figured out, the possibility of losing everything within a matter of seconds remains ever-present. One second you could be living out the most glittering moments once dreamt up in your psyche, the next the rug could be pulled out from under your feet.

Even if the brightest and shiniest moments that you were always thinking of become true—just be prepared for your mind to play another trick on you: a trap that sits deeper than you think, a simple mechanism that always starts doubting your little paradise once you've arrived. The constant thought of growing bigger and growing faster, or of being something or someone, such desires will never stop unless you confront yourself with their underlying source. Otherwise, you will keep chasing this little paradise, and you might actually end up happy and fulfilled without realising it, and only upon losing it, you may notice that you actually might have had all these things you've ever asked for, a few years ago.

This story is based on true events that have happened far away on the other side of the world (depending on where you are, of course): a place that gifted me a life beyond marvellous, since I had the courage to leave old thought patterns behind and to take risks. However, if you take the risks, you also have to consider and accept that those fears may become reality someday. If they do, your mind may suddenly be overtaken by waves of emotion stronger than you have ever felt, you may lose the ability to think rationally and the truth may be shrouded in plumes of smoke that your eyes won't be able to see through.

You may not even want to see it, but may rather sink into the quicksand of the moment, eventually getting stuck. I was stuck in such quicksand, and now it's time to tell you the why and the how of my ending up there, in a situation where I couldn't bear the weight of the question, "What's your plan?"

# 1.
# HITTING ROCK BOTTOM

"So, what's your plan, then?" asked Aunty Anne.

"Pardon?" My thoughts had been drifting off again while the sunlight shone as it so rarely does through the orange leaves on the trees above me.

"What's your plan, Ben? What do you want to do when you go back to Germany tomorrow?" she asked more precisely.

Ahhhh my plan, that perfect life plan, she meant. That master plan that carries you throughout life, one that you can always attach yourself to when things don't turn out the way you had planned them to. The rock that gives you that feeling of security and stability in life. Oh yeah, right, this plan.

"That's a good question, Aunty Anne," I muttered as I attempted to evade her query.

It was a rather cold Sunday morning in late autumn. The whole family had gone out for a walk; thick coats were necessary to keep us warm while we walked along the path that meandered its way around the lake. It was the usual Sunday walk where everyone came together to relax from their hard, long and stressful work weeks. Such walks afford time to reflect upon the past few days, as well as time to look forward to what might be ahead. The birds were singing, the dogs chasing each other and nothing was amiss—a classic Sunday vibe.

"I had a meeting with my boss last week to discuss my promotion," I heard George saying in front of me as he walked ahead with Uncle Joe. George is in his early forties and is the husband of my girlfriend's sister.

"How did it go?" asked Uncle Joe.

"He promised me a better position as a product manager within the next six months," responded George.

"That sounds great," Joe replied, congratulating him.

George reacted determinedly, "He better stick to his words or I'm off applying to a position in another company." *That sounds like a plan right there*, I thought.

"Haven't heard back from any jobs yet?" Aunty Anne threw my way, while I was still listening to the guys ahead of us. I tried to snap out of it and repeated her question in my head. "Any jobs yet?"

No, I haven't, because I really didn't want to. I don't like the notion of working in the corporate world, following someone else's vision to help them get rich and to grow the country's economy.

"No, unfortunately, nothing yet," I replied quietly.

"Ah well, fingers crossed you will find something soon so at least you'll have a backup plan," she said. While I was still processing her wishes of good fortune, it was Joe's turn to tell George about his latest experience at work.

"I just found out that if I reach my targets for next year, I'll get the same bonus every single year until I retire. I'm really going to focus on performing now," he said.

"That's great. You better try your hardest!" said George excitedly.

I don't know why I have literally nothing to contribute to this kind of conversation—do I just not care at all, or is it a matter of never wanting to end up in this "alluring" corporate rat race?

"Hey, my name is Ben. I'm twenty-eight years old and I think I just hit rock bottom."

They make a beautiful family, Aunty Anne, Uncle Joe, George, Ally and her mum Jay. There's just one little caveat—it's not mine. It's Emma's family. My girlfriend, twenty-eight years old as well, and the Sunday walk is their family tradition.

I wouldn't say that she's also hit rock bottom, but her life was up in the air just like mine. Lots of people have a midlife crisis, but what constitutes the "quarter-life crisis"? To me (who may be in the midst of one), it seems to boil down to two choices, swimming with or against the current. Going against it is accompanied by the risk of failure and disappointment, but you give yourself that chance of a more fulfilling and memorable life. Travelling with the current is a somewhat safe bet— so many others have travelled down that stream before you and know exactly where the hidden rocks beneath the surface are located.

Either way, upstream or downstream, there's one commonality. You need a plan. What's yours?

# 2.
# SUNDAY WALK

"It's a shame about what happened to you, Ben," said Uncle Joe. He had just finished his conversation with George, who was running after his son, wee Alex, who was beginning his next round of hide-and-seek in the woods. George and Ally have three kids; Alex is four years old—younger than his sisters Amy, nine, and Lilly, eleven. Both sisters stopped playing hide-and-seek a few years ago.

*Such a shame*, I thought. I used to love playing hide-and-seek and felt somewhat jealous of Alex, who was hiding behind a tree thinking no one could see him (pretty much the whole family knew where he was). George played along and looked behind two other trees first, before slowly coming around the other side where Alex couldn't see him.

"Gotcha!" he shouted, making Alex jump. His fright remained emblazoned across his face for a brief moment, before morphing into a smile and then a big laugh.

"Again!" Alex shouted. Watching them having fun, I noticed a smile invade my lips. I then turned to Joe and said,

"Oh yeah, it's a bummer, but there isn't anything I can do, unfortunately." Joe was referring to my life a few months ago—a life on the other side of the world, where I was never once asked this specific question: "What is your plan?" The opposite was the case. Back in that life, I was the one who sometimes asked others that stupid, little question.

I don't actually know exactly why I never got asked this question over there. Maybe because it didn't matter, or perhaps I looked more like someone who would actually have a plan. I hardly doubt the second option though. Three months ago, I was living in New Zealand with Emma, where we had met each other two years previously. I worked in a café during the day, and in the evening, I would head to my studio to paint abstract art.

I used to call myself an artist. I like to paint, and I like very abstract art—a picture or a painting that you could get lost in. Something that might present itself as a random assortment of colours to one person, but which another might regard as a masterpiece.

I'd like to make a proper living from selling my own paintings one day, but up until now, this is just a dream that has drifted progressively further across the horizon. I had a good network in New Zealand; my artwork had been displayed at a few exhibitions. I sold a couple of my paintings and, ironically, that is exactly what killed the vibes eventually.

"How much money did you make from your paintings in New Zealand?" Uncle Joe had asked.

"Not a lot to be honest," I retorted, and that makes the whole ordeal even worse.

One of my best friends in New Zealand had begun an art collective many years ago. Sam was his name and he'd managed to assemble a lovely group of like-minded people. Sam is a full-on New Zealander. He says, "Sweet As" more often as "Hello." He once told me something that has truly stuck with me over the years.

"Ben, there are dreamers and realists, and I'll tell you right away, the magic is somewhere in the middle. You're just a dreamer the moment when you wouldn't be able to realise that making your dreams come true and chasing a happy and fulfilling life can be freaking difficult, full of just as many good as bad experiences, experiences that push you forward or pull you back. If the bad ones make you give up on your dream, then you will always be a dreamer!"

"People need to realise that you need all those bad experiences in order to have this chance of fulfilment. The most important thing is that you need to believe in it, because otherwise you would end up as a realist and would always find an excuse as to why you shouldn't take the risk."

I took the risk, but unfortunately, I ended up back down at the bottom, at the very bottom to be precise. I now feel like I belong to that latter group of people once again, those who are just dreaming of escaping a life that is dictated by someone else's previous experiences. However, can we really put the blame on others though? Even if we'd try to blame someone else, like those people who are just passing on potential experiences, we have to admit that we can't really be mad at them. They have told us that a career, money and security result in a happy life. That is something we have heard often from our parents, grandparents, teachers or even close friends sometimes. People who got brought up this way usually try their best to pass it on to the next generation. If it's not the life lessons they would like to teach you, then it's at least their worries about you and the fact that you shouldn't make the same mistakes they did, or that they have to protect you from all the terrible stuff that's on the news every day. After all, there is always a positive intention behind it and I am convinced none of these people ever wanted to harm you, but some of them do harm you, unintentionally.

"I'm surprised they found out about you selling your paintings. I always thought New Zealanders were a bit backwards compared to us," Joe surmised.

As with most things in life, there is always more than one perspective. Saying that someone, or a whole society, is behind, implies that another society is ahead. I wasn't quite sure how to take it, but what he probably meant is that New Zealand is rather laid-back, and work does not take centre stage for most. In my experience, they don't see the human being revolving around work.

Sure, someone who works for their whole life to secure that bright future that is called the pension—someone like Joe or George—might consider the Kiwi mindset "backwards." Personally, I consider it genius and a relief to the pressure that lies on every single one of us. We put that pressure on ourselves, along with the pressure we take on from those who initially wanted to help and guide us through this little adventure called life.

"Yeah, they can be a bit behind sometimes," I heard myself say. *Why did I just say that?* I thought in the same second. It had almost become routine now—I had stopped saying the things I truly believed in. It felt more like I lost faith in trying to widen people's narrow minds by sharing my honest opinions with them, or that I might not even be able to handle the eventual confrontation that would erupt. Sometimes I even think that I am not getting taken seriously by those who are convinced that the career-driven life is the true way to happiness.

# 3.
# I AM EASY

It was already past midday, and I was watching the raindrops run horizontally across the backseat window, while Jay, Emma's mum, was driving us back home to her place. I don't really have a place that I can call my home right now. I am usually not the couch surfer type of guy, but at the moment I didn't have a choice.

The main reason I'm here is Emma. She's visiting from New Zealand, and since our relationship was forced into the most arduous possible long-distance relationship a couple of months ago, I thought I would come over from Germany to see her here in England, while she was visiting her family. It comes in handy that I like her family for real. They're all very welcoming and funny in their own idiosyncratic way. Despite having only met them relatively recently, it had been a good laugh hanging out with Uncle Joe and the rest of the gang. They may seem like the typical career-driven people and perhaps they are even, but at the same time, Emma's family, including Joe and George, are very open-minded and have their hearts in the right place. Unfortunately, my time here would be coming to an end soon.

"What would you guys like to drink for Sunday roast this evening?" Jay asked. Given that I'm doing my best to avoid more serious life questions at the minute, such as "What do I want to do?" or "Where do I want to live?," I've adopted the same behaviour when answering somewhat easier questions such as this one too.

"I am easy" is my way of saying "I don't know" and sometimes even "I don't care." Emma at least is able to answer Jay's very easy question in a more creative way.

"How about we get a nice bottle of wine and some beers for everyone," she said.

Maybe I should learn from her to stop procrastinating, at least regarding the simple everyday questions such as "What do I want to make for lunch?" or "What do I want to do in my spare time?" Such advice is especially apt for the present moment, where it can be difficult for me to find an answer to the most primitive of questions asked by people. I get so caught up thinking about my life that I somehow forget to think about what I want for lunch or which movie I'd like to watch.

We were waiting at the traffic lights. Jay turned her head around to the backseat.

"It's a shame what happened, Ben, and that you haven't heard anything from them yet," she said.

*Yes, it is indeed Jay. Thanks for reminding me*, I thought. "Yeah," was my answer, knowing that my reply hadn't had any value in it whatsoever. What else was I supposed to say in such a situation, in addition to the fact that she didn't even know the latest news yet?

Either way, her words felt like someone pressing the finger into an open wound. It created pressure in my stomach. It was a feeling that I was very familiar with, but which I haven't felt in more than three years.

I turned my head towards the window and started looking outside again. This unpleasant feeling in my stomach didn't want to go away and my thoughts started drifting off to that time when it had first started.

It was a normal morning for me back then. When I finished school, I had started an apprenticeship. Why? Because that is the way you go about it in Germany. You study or you do an apprenticeship, or even go on a working holiday trip before studying. I didn't know what to study, so I went for the apprenticeship. The only problem was that I didn't know what I wanted to do at all. I didn't know what I wanted to be or what job I'd like to do one day. Unfortunately for me, that day came regardless, and I had to select something. So, I started an apprenticeship in insurance and finances. Why? Because my parents had recommended it to me.

They had both been working in the industry for many years, and the day that I had to come to a decision inched closer and closer. So, I decided to ask them what I ought to do. It wasn't very hard to predict what they would advise me to do. It was very obvious that they would tell me to take the same path because I'm good at talking in front of people.

Today, almost nine years later, I wish that they would have seen the real guy I was back then—helpless and without any orientation in life. I could dream of having a happy life, but I had no clue how to achieve that. Bless my parents. They did the best they could and advised me to head in the only direction they probably knew. I remember the first day of my apprenticeship and my first thought when I entered the office.

"So, this is how my life is meant to look like for the next forty-two years?"

Why forty-two? Well, that was the exact time it would have taken me until I received my pension, based on the retirement laws in Germany back then. But don't worry—there were enough people frightening me, from my colleagues to my friends, that we'll have to work way longer than that because the whole pension system was going to collapse in the next few years anyway. This was also the first and best argument I got taught in my apprenticeship in order to successfully sell private pension insurance and life insurance to other people. *Great*, I thought. The second thought that popped into my head was why am I doing this? Well, I never thought that there could be another way of living. I always thought that this was it. My grandparents did it, my parents and all my friends were doing it too. This is the way it has to be regardless of how I felt. If my parents taught me one thing, it was to finish something once you started it. Luckily the apprenticeship had a deadline—in two and a half years.

I somehow managed to complete it, together with my colleagues, who have since become my friends. Some of them had similar feelings as me, and some of them would have already accepted that this would be their reality for the rest of their lives. To be honest, to me, a few of them genuinely seemed fulfilled and very happy with it.

However, despite a very successful apprenticeship, the company was going through a regression, which meant it would be a difficult period for young people like us. I got offered a limited contract for a single year; we would just have to see on an annual basis how I would perform and how the company would develop.

I started looking into other jobs and companies in the same department, but with a higher chance of a long-term contract to make me feel more secure. I mean, it was still thirty-nine years until my pension back then, but some might have worried already that it wouldn't even have been sufficient to live off, to enjoy a happy and fulfilling life when you are sixty-seven.

I was fortunate and received a job offer that sounded too good to be true. A higher salary, the latest iPhone, a new computer and a flashy car in a high performing new company on a long-term contract. I felt proud of myself, to have achieved something like this at such young age, but there were people who were even prouder than me, my parents.

Everything seemed like it would fall into place for that secure and happy life, without worrying about financial issues and being prepared for every worst-case scenario that could possibly and would probably happen in the future. But on the day I signed that contract, something happened that I hadn't taken into consideration before. I was sitting next to my new boss, reading the contract. The conditions were fine and couldn't have been any better. He was looking at me expecting my signature any second. I had the pen in my hand. I looked at him and a single thought popped into my head. *What the fuck am I doing here?* The next second, I signed the contract.

"We are home, guys," I heard Jay's voice saying. Emma looked at me.

"Are you okay?" she reached her hand towards my face and touched my cheek.

"I'm okay. Don't worry."

We jumped out of the car.

Jay opened the front door and shouted, "Remember, guys, to stay hungry. We've got our big Sunday roast tonight!"

I nodded my head like a five year old.

Emma replied in a seemingly sarcastic tone. "Sure, Mum. How could we forget a classic British Sunday roast?"

We went inside, and I didn't feel quite well. So many thoughts were running through my head, while at the same time I was still feeling this pressure in my belly.

"Sorry, guys, I think I will take a little nap," I said.

"Are you okay?" Jay asked.

Before I could answer that, Emma tried her best to protect me from having to reply to Jay.

"All good, Ben. Have a rest. Mum and I will relax in the living room for a bit," she said.

I went upstairs to Emma's bedroom, where I was staying at that time. I laid on my back and stared at the ceiling as my mind dozed off once again.

# 4.
# DIARRHOEA

It was my first day at the new job. Back then, I really thought I had it all sorted—everything under control. I'd soon find out that the very opposite was the case.

The first few days went fine. I got used to the new tasks and new people more and more, day by day, but every morning when I got up I could feel that something was missing. My motivation was lacking—a feeling that had not just coincided with starting the new job. I tried to convince myself that this was normal and expected when starting a new job, a new challenge. It really should feel different though, shouldn't it?

It was at that moment that I realised that this feeling had not come out of the blue. I had brought it along with me from my previous job. With each passing day, it just got worse and worse. On one hand, my performance reviews were positive and got even better as time went on. Everyone confirmed that I was doing well. My boss and other people in higher positions projected a great, bright future for me in the industry.

The more I worked, the harder it got for me to get up every morning. One morning I noticed something heavy in my stomach. It was not the usual missing motivation. This was something else. It was like an extremely heavy rock, situated right in my stomach. This rock got bigger and bigger every morning, making it harder and harder for me to get up when the alarm went off. At some stage, it almost made it impossible.

One morning, as I whipped up something quick for breakfast and began eating it, it started making me feel sick. I just wanted it to leave my body. I bent over the toilet and put my finger in my mouth, but nothing would come out. In the early stages of the job, one out of five mornings were like this—most Mondays, then Tuesdays as well. Later, it was also on Wednesdays and, after a while, I felt like this every single day from Monday to Friday. It was okay on a Saturday, but when the rock started to appear in my belly on a Sunday morning, it got to a point where I felt that I had reached my limit—I couldn't bear the situation anymore. I went to the doctor. I explained my physical symptoms to him, and he signed me out of work for a week. Diagnosed with "diarrhoea."

I didn't have the courage to tell him the truth about how I really felt. I felt ashamed about it myself. "Why do I feel like this?" I have everything I could possibly want. A nice big flat, a secure income, a flashy car, an iPhone, MacBook, literally everything. Yet when I wake up every morning, the first thing I could do is run to the bathroom and puke.

I enjoyed the week off work, but the day before I had to go back it started all over again. I thought it might be the job itself. Am I just not made for it? But it felt as though there was something that was slowly trying to tell me that something else was causing this. I started applying for other jobs, but it didn't work. Was it me? Was it the industry? What was wrong with me?

Things got worse and I fell deeper into this hole. This rock, representative of my state of mind, had begun eating me up from inside. It all came to a head on a sunny Monday afternoon; I had just come home from work and as I sat on my bed, suddenly a little tear trickled down my face. One by one, these little tears started to gush, turning into a sort of waterfall. It was as though my mind had left my body and I was watching myself from the outside. The tears kept running and I asked myself out loud "Why am I crying?" My body felt empty on the inside, no sensation at all. No hint of sadness. Just nothing.

This incident was sufficient for me to go to the doctor once again. As I sat there, I admitted that I had lied to him. "There was never diarrhoea. I'm upset for no reason," I confessed. I started to tell him about the past few months and years, all the way back to that very day when I first had entered the office. I will never forget his answer.

"Ben, you are twenty-five years old, a young, good-looking guy. Nice, friendly, and sincere. You deserve to be happy. You deserve to wake up on a Sunday morning feeling like life is flowing through your veins. If you want to go to the park to smoke a joint, go and smoke that joint. If you want to go and travel the world, go and travel the world. We only have this one life. Start making the most out of it and stop tying yourself to the expectations of other people."

My tears stopped. I tried to say something, but I couldn't. I just felt a big, uplifting feeling running through my whole body and I knew that I would never forget this moment. Yes, this was a doctor. Probably the best doctor in the world at any rate, because for once in my life I felt that someone actually had listened to what I had said and had given me genuine life advice that wasn't based on personal experience but was rooted in the wisdom of life, the ability to listen and the creativity to think outside of the box. An attempt to help others, rather than just passing on your own ideology. I was so overwhelmed by his words that I could only ask him one simple question. "Can I give you a hug?" I sputtered

"Of course," he said.

To get back to reality here. The next day I went to see a psychotherapist, as what I described above is in medical terms defined as depression. However, the day of this visit to the doctor will always remain in my memory as the day I decided to change my life.

# 5.
# DO IT, BRO!

I quit my job, which was the least I could have done, but I also started planning to leave my old life entirely behind me. The most liberating moment of my life took place when I handed in my leaving notice. I felt like someone took a hammer and smashed that rock I had inside me into a million pieces. That same evening, I sat back and stared at a world map for ages. I hadn't done much travelling at all; most of the world was unknown to me save for what I had seen in TV shows, magazines or on the internet.

There was one place that caught my attention right from the start. First of all, it was far away, probably the furthest away possible from where I lived. Second of all, I had plainly no idea what life was like over there. I had no real comparison, no inkling. I'd never seen it on TV or in a magazine. When I tried to envision it, there was just a big black spot in my brain. I put my finger on the map to gauge the distance to home and said to myself, "That's far enough, I guess."

It was pointing at New Zealand. The decision was made. New Zealand it is. It wasn't my psychotherapist or my doctor who told me to give up my entire life in Germany to go as far away as humanly possible. No. It was me. I felt like I had been living my life for far too long up to someone else's standards.

I don't want to judge my parents. In their eyes, I had a pretty good life. The only person I can judge here is myself. I just didn't know any better. I took the advice of my parents, friends, girlfriend at this time, or my family members.

Every time I thought about making a change, I got discouraged if the first little thing didn't quite go how I'd envisaged it to. So, I always ended up sticking to the plan, the safe route, where I thought nothing could hurt me. More and more, I came to the conclusion that it was the plan itself that was hurting me. New Zealand wasn't about the fulfilling life, and not necessarily about travelling either. It was more about the one thing I needed the most in this situation—the reset button.

# Boy Oh Boy, Nairobi D - Do it, Bro!

Emma abruptly interrupted my thoughts, "What are you thinking of?"

"How I ended up In New Zealand," I replied

"We all miss you over there. I do the most, obviously," she said on the verge of tears.

"I know. I know, Emma. But you know that there is absolutely nothing left that I could do now. For some reason, I am not supposed to be there anymore," I said desperately, searching for an answer.

"Do you regret what happened?" she asked. I wasn't quite sure what kind of answer she would expect from me, but at this moment I answered truthfully.

"I like to believe that things happen for a reason. I just haven't quite figured out that reason yet."

Emma looked at me and started laughing a little bit.

That was the first glimpse of humour, in spite of our current circumstances.

"Okay, if you don't know the reason yet, then at least tell me what is going on up there since last night, Ben?" tipping her finger onto my forehead.

I know it would be best to just talk about it honestly, but it was her first time addressing the topic herself after the devastating news. I almost expected her to know how I feel, but could she really? In order to make her understand, I actually needed to talk to her, but it didn't seem that simple anymore.

So I just opted for another generic response. "I was just thinking of how I ended up in this situation."

"And how did you, Ben?" she asked.

"Well, if anyone knows, then you would for sure." I don't know if I sounded snappy or not, but judging by her answer I felt like Emma took it like I slightly flipped on her.

"Well, I will leave you to it then, Ben."

She jumped off the bed and left the room rather hastily. I lifted my arm off the bed to reach for hers, but she was already gone with her back towards me. I didn't have the energy to speak up and get her to stay.

I needed to figure out whether or not I should try to escape my thoughts, follow her and attempt to discuss last night. Yet at the same time, I could already feel my attention dragging me back into my mind. I felt like, for some strange reason, I needed to run past those thoughts in order to cope when suddenly I found myself at the airport with family and friends.

The day had arrived. It was time for me to leave my old life behind me and set off on a new path. I hate goodbyes. Let's be honest, who really likes them? There was someone though for whom it was even harder, my mum. She struggled a lot with the fact of letting me go to a place that was just a black spot in her mind as well.

She pulled me in very close and whispered, "Please look after your-self, Ben."

My dad was rather cold. "Safe trip," was all I got from him.

I didn't want to overrate my life choice. I was just doing what every eighteen-year-old would do nowadays after finishing school. Have a look at Hobbiton, smoke some joints, have a good time and come back. Unexpectedly though, I already had a slight feeling that even though I had told my parents and friends that I would see them soon, deep down inside I already knew it would be some time until I would really be seeing all of them again.

One last fist bump with my best mate Paul, who came to give his goodbyes as well. One last hug from my mum and I was ready to turn around and stride into the unknown. Full of tears fresh from the "good-bye sadness," I walked towards the departure gates, turned around to everyone one last time, waved my hand, blew a few kisses and turned around the corner. As soon as everyone was out of sight, my heartbeat dropped immediately. I tried to calm myself down, went through the security checks and walked towards the boarding gate. When I arrived there, I looked at the screen, which had the stopover destination Dubai written on it. I stopped walking for a second and said to myself, "Are we really doing this, Ben?"

A random guy next to me witnessed me talking to myself and said, "Do it, bro!"

I couldn't hide my laugh. It must have looked hilarious with my face still full of tears.

"Nervous?" he followed up.

"Yeah, a little bit," I said.

"Why so?" He pointed to the seat next to him for me to sit down. He was waiting in front of the same gate I was supposed to be boarding the aircraft.

"Auckland?" I asked him.

"Nice try evading, my question, but yes, Auckland," he chuckled.

"Sorry, my mind is a bit all over the place—I'm Ben, by the way."

"Nice to meet you, Ben, I'm Francis. The guy you still owe an answer to the question about you being nervous or not," he pointed out.

*Alright Francis, just give me a second to process this*, I thought to myself. "Ehm, yes, kind of, I guess. I've never been to New Zealand. I don't know what to expect, so yeah, I think that's reason enough to be nervous, right?" I hoped I was satisfying him with my answer.

"Yes, it does, mate. I don't want to take your excitement away, but Auckland is nothing special!" he said.

"How do you know?" I asked him.

"Well, mate, I am from there," he said.

"What have you been doing here in Germany then?" I wondered curiously.

"Just visiting my girlfriend," he answered straightaway. "And where is she, if I may ask?" as if I would have never seen a guy without his girlfriend at the airport.

"She is still here in Frankfurt. She lives and works here. We met a few years ago in Queenstown, and since then we see each other once or twice a year either here in Germany or New Zealand," he said.

"Once or twice a year?" I blurted out.

Francis jumped like someone had frightened him.

*Maybe that was a little bit too loud*, I thought. *But how can you have a relationship where you only see each other once or twice a year?*

"I know, not the normal kind of relationship, right?" he confirmed my suspicions.

"Definitely not. What does she or you do that you can't live in the same place?" I continued my cross-examination.

"She is an amazing artist. She paints and runs big exhibitions here in Frankfurt, Berlin and pretty much all over Europe, and I just study in Auckland," Francis said.

*Wow, painting*, I thought. *That sounds amazing.*

"Okay, definitely not an easy situation for you two then. What kind of paintings does she do?" I asked, hoping that he wouldn't mind it if I just continued firing questions at him.

Francis pulled a magazine out of his bag next to him and skipped right away to the middle of it. "Here you go—there is a whole page about her and her art." He pointed at one reddish painting, which looked like a woman's head on a yellow background in a very abstract orientation. Straightaway I drifted into my thoughts and feelings just by looking at this piece of art.

I knew before that I always had a habit of staring at photography and paintings for ages, letting my thoughts drift off, but that mostly happened while I was trying to sell life insurance to the friendly neighbour next door. It was that time when I was waiting in the car for my next appointment and thinking about a better future, or on the weekends when friends would take me to some little hipster exhibitions. Back then, it was just a way for me of dreaming and drifting off or just escaping for a few moments in the depressive environment that I called life.

"Wow! Looks pretty good," I said to Francis.

"Yeah, she's amazing, mate. She inspires and affects so many people and that's what I like about her so much. I never met someone with so much drive, inspiration and love for something in particular. Did you know that starring at an abstract painting with multiple colours stimulates the brain the same way an orgasm does?"

I couldn't hold back my laughter. Not just did it make me forget all my nervousness from flying to the other side of the world with no plan, but it also did trigger something in me that I wasn't really aware of before. My interest in art and creation.

"How do you know?" I tried to ask with a straight face.

"I was joking, mate," he said with a grin, pointing his finger at the text next to the painting. It was an interview with Grace Bellingham. I assumed it was his girlfriend.

His finger was fixated on a paragraph of text. "Abstract art challenges our brains to create our own interpretation, thereby stimulating the higher-level areas of our brain, responsible for creativity and imagination. This specifically challenges and teaches us to look at art, and also in a sense, at the world, in a completely new way."

I couldn't believe he got me there with his stupid orgasm joke. "I have to admit that makes a little more sense, Francis," I said in embarrassment.

"Can I read it?" I asked him.

"Of course, I need to go and check the bathroom anyway before we start boarding. Here, take it."

He handed me the magazine and went off to the bathroom. I grabbed the magazine and the page about Grace was still open. My eyes were going straightaway back to her comment. I had to read it again, word by word.

"...responsible for creativity and imagination—look at art and the world in a new way."

I don't know why this part resonated with me so much. Maybe because it fit the situation I found myself in very astutely, but there was also much hope and optimism in these words. I kept on looking at all the other pictures of her art on the same page. It was more than just fascinating. The feeling of expressing yourself in creating something must be truly wonderful. That was something I had never dared to do. It's the complete opposite of my experiences in life so far. My life had been dictated by what was already there. It was a life that had nothing to do with new perspectives and especially not with creating anything. Right in this second, I had a really bad idea, but I couldn't help myself. I turned around again and looked at the bathroom door. I was waiting to see if Francis would come out or not. My heartbeat skipped ahead by thirty beats. I looked again and then I could hear a little *zshhhrrrrrip*.

"Oopsie," I said to myself.

I know I could have just asked him, but I know that he would have never given it to me anyway. Now I was holding the page with Grace's article and her quote in my hand. I folded it into a tiny square piece of paper that almost looked like a little envelope. I grabbed my wallet and put it inside there. I closed the magazine and put it back in his back. Then I turned my face towards the gate, pulled my legs across, and acted like nothing would have happened.

A couple of minutes later Francis came back to his place.

"Inspiring stuff, aye?" he pulled out a decent New Zealand accent.

"Yes, indeed," I said.

"Have you seen the article about Tom Baxter yet?" he asked.

"No, I haven't," I said and thought straightaway that I should have just said yes to not give him another reason for pulling the magazine again.

"Hang on let me show you."

As he was going to reach for it, the airport speakers blared, "Emirates Flight 5676 to Dubai is ready for boarding now. Please come to Gate 65."

The magazine was already in his hand when he decided to put it back. "Alright, maybe later then," he said.

# 6.
# THE JET LAG BEFORE THE JET LAG

Unfortunately, Francis and I ended up in two different parts of the plane on the first flight. After landing in Dubai, I only ended up seeing him again in the waiting area for our connecting flight to Auckland.

"Still nervous, mate?" was the first thing he asked me when we saw each other. I was totally and utterly exhausted. The airport felt like a massive labyrinth in the form of a palace. They have trains going from one terminal to the other. "Come on, please!"

"Not so nervous anymore to be honest, more exhausted and tired actually," I replied and sank into the seat right next to him.

"Good" was his short and sharp answer. I wasn't quite sure if he was trying to say something else, or if I missed the start to a proper conversation, but my brain was pretty fried. I felt like the jet lag had already kicked in, but so far I'd only skipped two time zones. That was nothing compared to what was ahead of me.

"What's your passion, Ben?" Francis asked out of the blue.

"My passion?" I retorted, irritated. Why did he not just ask me what my hobby was? Straightaway he needed to take it up a notch to ask me for what I'm passionate about.

"Yes, your passion—the thing that gets you going in life."

Neither I nor my brain was prepared for a deep talk. It was just too hard for me to find an adequate reply because I simply didn't know the answer to this question.

I was freaking out by the pressure of replying, so I panicked and answered with a question instead. "What's yours, Francis?"

Francis started laughing, which made me feel even more irritated. "You are the master of evading questions, aren't you, Ben?"

I looked at him and shrugged my shoulders. He could see I was helpless and unable to answer once again.

"Okay, I will do you the honour. My passion is surfing. I love being in the ocean and connecting with nature. After a stressful day at university, I like to grab my board, jump in the car, drive to the beach and paddle out into the ocean. It's almost like meditation for me."

I had no idea what he was talking about. I had never surfed in my entire life. I went swimming in the ocean on a couple of holidays, but I never surfed or did anything like that. I panicked again and replied hastily—"I can inline skate." By this point, I felt like I was just making the situation worse.

Francis took it in stride, laughed out loud and put his hand on my shoulder. "It's okay, mate. You don't need to force yourself to find an answer. It's not that easy. A lot of people tend to answer with their hobbies. Like football or inline skating." He looked at me and continued laughing. "I'm only joking. I mean your hobby can be your passion, but not necessarily," he said.

"Okay, what's the difference then?" I asked. I hadn't even arrived in New Zealand yet and was already receiving my first proper life lesson.

"You will feel the difference," he said and stopped.

I was waiting for a few seconds, expecting a proper explanation, but that didn't come. "That's all?" I tried to extract more out of him.

"Yes, that's it, trust me you will feel the difference. Let me say only one more thing, if you don't know your passion now, don't stop looking for it until you find it," he said while raising his finger.

"How do you mean?" I fired back right away.

"Ask yourself what gets you going every day, or in your case, what would get you going every day. What would make your life exciting to the point that it would be worth just spending time with yourself and your passion?"

"No other people involved?" I double-checked.

"No, not really, remove all external factors. Imagine a world where everything is possible. There is only you and no one else. Just you and all you could do would be the one thing that satisfies you, what would it be?"

He saw me thinking straightaway.

"Don't worry, we both know you don't know the answer yet, but do me a favour, mate, and don't stop asking yourself this question until you find it, okay?"

"Okay," I replied to his words of wisdom like a little child who'd just been told off.

"Alright, mate, let me grab a coffee and then hopefully we will board our plane soon. Want one as well?"

"A coffee? Dude, it's 10 p.m.!" I said very surprisedly.

"It's 6 a.m. in Auckland," he smirked, and he could tell by my face that I was denying his offer of having a coffee that late.

However, he was so kind to explain his late-night caffeine desire. "Mate, you really never have left Europe, aye? The first thing I did when we took off in Frankfurt is set my watch to Auckland time, and since then my body clock has been acting accordingly to it. This way I'll minimise my jet lag to almost nothing." I understood and had to admit that he was right. I had never left Europe and had no clue what I was doing out here.

"Want one now?" he smiled and kindly offered again. "Okay, yes please," I replied.

"Choice, mate," he said and went off to the café opposite of us.

I had no real clue what he was saying, but my eyes drifted towards his bag and I had to think about both of our conversations again, in Frankfurt and now here. I felt like I was still tied up and full of fear to let go of my old life.

What is my passion then? Did I ever have one? I mean I loved football, but I was never particularly good at it. That was surely just a hobby. Anything else? Before I could continue down that road, I began smelling the taste of fresh coffee. My new "best friend" Francis was holding it right under my nose.

"Here you go, mate."

I stopped counting how often he'd said the word "mate" and just reached for the coffee.

"Thanks," I said, stopped for a second and added a long, dragged out "maaaate."

He laughed again. "Do I say it that often?"

I didn't mean to offend his English upbringing. In fact, it was refreshing that someone I just met a few hours ago would consider you as his mate without knowing you at all.

"Can I ask you one question?" I looked at him.

"Shoot!" he fired back.

"How did Grace get into painting?" I asked.

"Very good thinking, mate. I like it," he said, shaking his index finger at me. "Well, she was very lucky."

"Why?" I asked.

"Because she knew it since a very early stage in her life. She was privileged in that her parents would let her do whatever she wanted. They actively encouraged her to discover new things, be creative and to be as childish as she could be—to have fun..."

"No rules?" I interrupted him.

"Of course, you have ground rules, like in every other type of relationship. You know, it's a given fact that you don't cheat on your partner when you are in a relationship, right?"

"Yeah, of course," I confirmed.

"See, so it was pretty clear for her parents that certain things weren't allowed, but within the framework of those ground rules, she was as free as a bird to receive the one thing that is, unfortunately, a little too rare in our world."

"What is it?" I gazed up at him like a little boy.

"Unconditional love, Ben. Something a lot of parents aren't aware of. They have no clue how important it is."

"And that made her an artist?" I asked, feeling naive and somewhat dumb at the same time.

"Yes," was his short and precise answer—one I honestly didn't expect.

"Really?" I needed to reassure myself.

"It was clearly a huge factor that helped Grace figure out what made her happy and what satisfied her from a young age."

"...and what her talent is," I added in an attempt to sound like someone who knew something about these matters. But even then, it only took a few seconds for Francis to destroy my little contribution of wisdom with one simple question.

"What is talent, Ben?" he asked in a very hypothetical way.

"Ehm...the ability to pick up new stuff very fast," I replied, sounding like a definition from Wikipedia.

"A very rational answer. Come on, mate, what does talent really mean? Could you not become an amazing painter over the next few years?"

"I don't think I have the talent for that, to be honest," I said.

"Do you actually listen to what I say?" Francis said half-seriously, half-jokingly.

"Mate, you can fly to the moon in five years, if you only put your mind to it."

*That sounds very out of proportion*, I thought. "You are exaggerating," I pointed out to him.

"...and that's where you run against the wall of your own limitations, my friend. If you tell yourself you are not talented enough for something I can guarantee you one thing—you will never be talented enough."

I slowly understood where he was coming from and what he was trying to say. I wish I could have woken up the next day and believed his words, but my fear of failure had full control over me. It was telling my mind "this is not possible."

"Sorry, I don't want to overwhelm you, Ben, but I don't like people who restrict themselves. You know, how can you ever be happy if you haven't at least once lived up to your full potential?"

"But what if I don't know my full potential, Francis?" I kept doubting his words.

He stopped there for a second and could see that my inner self was falling apart, or at least what was left of it after twenty-five years in Germany.

"Ben, I don't know you very well, but if I can tell you one thing, you are good the way you are. Just enjoy your life, find your passion and make the most out of it. Whatever it is. If it's collecting post stamps, it's collecting post stamps. It really doesn't matter, okay?"

"Okay," I said, before daring to ask one last question. "Maybe we can go surfing together one day?"

"Sure man, I can teach you how to surf, no problem."

I felt a little relieved, but the craziest thing was that I felt something that I can't remember ever feeling before. There was some movement in my body and my mind. It was a movement that hadn't been there before. All of a sudden, it didn't feel as stiff as it used to be. I still had no real clue what de facto he said nor an answer to all his questions, but at the very least he really got me thinking.

"I guess it's time to jump on the plane home," Francis said.

When he said the word "home," my heart resonated for a fleeting second. I had no clear vision of where I was heading and no idea what to expect, but the fact that Francis was calling it home gave me a slight feeling of security.

# 7.
# KIA ORA, BEN!

The door of the aircraft opened. I grabbed my belongings, passed the stewardess wishing me a "g'day" and left the plane. A little breeze of saltwater air was hitting my face. It smelt pure and clean, considering I was at the top of a staircase of an aircraft in the middle of an airport full of air pollution. I walked down the stairs and followed the sign towards the baggage claim. When I arrived there, I could already see Francis. Once again, we didn't have the fortune of sitting together. However, he noticed me straightaway and waved his hand so I could see him.

"Kia Ora, Ben," he said.

*Whatever Francis*, I thought. I was tired and could hardly keep my eyes open and this guy was as fresh as a cucumber.

"I told you, didn't I?" he said and raised his finger to point at his watch. I looked at mine and it said 1:12 am, which it clearly wasn't according to the bright light shining through the big wide airport windows.

"How long does this luggage thing take?" I said, tired and annoyed. Francis once again couldn't hold back his laughter. I was happy he didn't take my moody attitude personally.

"Well Ben, to say it in your language, welcome to New Zealand. What's your plan?" My plan was to get my brain working so that I could figure out the way to the hostel that I booked for the first few nights.

"I don't have a plan," I said, struggling to keep my eyes open.

"These are the best days," Francis said and was starring at the first few suitcases that entered the conveyor. "But seriously, where are you going to next?" he asked.

I figured out that, since the moment I met him, we had only been talking about deep topics and things that require a lot of thinking; we basically forgot to talk about the simple things. Like where I'm staying, for instance. I told him the name of my hostel. He was about to offer me a ride with his mum, who was about to pick him up, when in the next second he had to apologise because we figured out that my hostel was located on the exact opposite side of town.

"I am sorry mate, but my mum is in a bit of a rush. We won't have time to drop you off there, but surely there is a bus going into town from here."

"All good, I came here by myself, so I need to figure it out for myself. You have already done enough for me, Francis."

He smiled and asked, "What do you mean by that?"

"I don't really know, but it was very nice to meet you," I said as he grabbed his suitcase.

"Yes, it was indeed. Give me your phone, mate," he requested.

I picked up my phone out of my pocket and handed it to Francis. He started typing. "Here is my number, mate, hit me up any time you want and we'll go for a surf. I have to go now." He gave me my phone back, turned around and started walking towards the exit.

"But I don't know how to surf!" I shouted to him.

He stopped, turned around, and shouted back at me, "Don't worry, mate!" At that point, he must have noticed that he had forgotten something. He ran back towards me and said, "By the way, I know that you ripped out that page about Grace."

I was shocked for a second and didn't know how to react.

"Keep it! But only if you promise me that you'll get into abstract painting, okay?" He looked at me and winked his left eye.

I was absolutely busted and stuttered, "Ehm, sorry."

"No worries," he said, as he started running again towards the door that had Exit written on the sign above. Before the door opened, he shouted through the whole airport, "Just promise me, mate!"

I just stared at him and saw the automatic doors closing. He was gone. I touched my back pocket, where I had my wallet. I felt it pushing against my right butt cheek, looked at the exit again and heard myself shout, "I promise!"

# 8.
# WHAT TOOK YOU SO LONG?

It had been a busy morning. I got woken by my friendly roommate, who was sleeping above me in my cosy twelve-bed dormitory. Respectful as he was, he was kind enough to set an alarm for all eleven other people in the room.

This pretty much sums up my first few weeks here. I am not going to sugarcoat it, it was horrible. The hostel I initially booked for the first few nights had, unfortunately, become my residence for the past few weeks. It was located right on the main road in the centre of Auckland. So, I got out of bed and joined the queue for the bathroom to brush my teeth and wash my face as quickly as possible. Afterwards, I went back to my dorm, got dressed and headed straight to the exit. As soon as I walked through the front door, the sunlight hit my face and I was blinded by the light.

All I heard were random noises, voices and a lot of traffic. I tried to take a shortcut to the place that I had frequented for the past few days, the Auckland Harbour. Compared to the rest of the city, it was very calm over there. Some nice fresh air, seagulls and the odd boat passing by. It was the one place where I was able to gather all my thoughts.

The most frequent of these over the past few weeks had been "What the fuck am I doing here?" or "Did I just escape for the sake of escaping?" or "Do I just need a break from my old life for a few months before heading back, like all the other eighteen-year-olds here who'd just finished school?"

I'd been there for almost three weeks now. All I'd done thus far was try to figure out paperwork and what I actually want to do with my time here. I realised that I'd arrived without any plan in mind. Not a single clue. This was the first time it had ever happened to me, and I could see how helpless I was. My parents always made sure I had a plan, even if it were only to be the manager of AXA AG one day.

The feeling of having no idea of what to do was very intimidating and quite scary too. There was no new money coming in. I was just living off savings—which was also a very new experience for me.

"These are the best days" all of the sudden shot back into my mind like an arrow that had just hit its target. "Francis," I muttered out loud. The fisherman to my left turned around looked at me and said, "I'm not Francis, mate."

I apologised and explained that I didn't mean him. I grabbed my phone and couldn't believe that I hadn't texted him yet—the guy who'd made my flight into the unknown so enjoyable and exciting. I got completely caught up thinking about what I had done by coming here, that I had entirely forgotten that he had given me his number.

I didn't want to waste a second and texted him immediately.

"Hey, man, it's Ben from the airport. I am super sorry that I didn't text earlier. Hope you are doing well. I'd love to hang out again soon. Let me know if you are keen. Cheers, Ben."

I hit send, immediately feeling terrible for taking so long to reach out to him. I was just thinking about how I could kill the time until he replies when in the next second my phone rang. It was him. He had called right away. I picked up.

"Finally! What took you so long?" he shouted into the phone.

I definitely didn't have an answer to that question but based on what I knew about him, making any excuses would be pointless at this stage.

"I honestly just forgot about it," I admitted straightaway.

"I could tell!" he retorted and then asked, "How are you doing then?"

"Yeah, okay, I guess," I replied.

"Alright, that says it all. What have you been doing then this whole time?"

"Not a lot to be honest. Just paperwork and living the hostel life," I admitted.

"Oh man and I thought I had some sort of influence on you when I met you," he said, brutally honest.

I'm pretty sure he did have a big influence on me, but for some reason I was still scared of taking risks and doing something fundamentally new. It felt like my parents or my old boss were around the corner watching and waiting for me to fail. They'd come up to me and say, "I told you so. Very naive to think that travelling to the other side of the world at the age of twenty-five would change your life." They were like demons in my head. Without telling Francis about these demons, I came up with a more generic reply.

"Yeah, you kind of have for sure, but I feel like my past is still having hold onto me."

"I understand, Ben," he said and it actually sounded like he did. "What are you doing right now?" he asked.

"Just sitting at the waterfront and staring at Auckland's Harbour Bridge. Why?" I asked.

"I might know something that will help you," he said.

"Help with what?" I asked cluelessly.

He completed ignored that question and said, "Send me the address of your hostel. I'll pick you up there in an hour. You better be ready," he said.

"Hey, would you mind telling me—" Before I could finish my sentence he had already hung up.

I kept staring at the Harbour Bridge not knowing what to expect at all, but while the sun was shining on my face I could let go of my demons for a millisecond and said to myself "Fuck it, let's do it."

# 9.

# LET'S GO SURFING, MATE!

I was waiting on Queen Street in front of my hostel. I love how spontaneous Francis was, but the fact that he kept his plan a surprise was something that I didn't enjoy that much.

Suddenly, I heard a honk and saw a waving hand. I recognised that hand from the airport. I looked closer. It was Francis smiling through the front window, sitting in his dark green Peugeot 206. Since it was the only car on one of the busiest streets in Auckland with a massive surfboard on top, it quickly became apparent what his plan was all about.

I ran over to his vehicle, opened the door and jumped into the front seat.

"You alright, mate?" he greeted me.

"Yes, very good, thanks," I replied.

"Let's go surfing, mate," he said in one of the craziest Kiwi accents I've ever heard.

Francis had only said two sentences and used the word "mate" in both of them. I was worried how long it would carry on like this. He tried to manoeuvre from one side of the road into traffic, then back to the other.

"So what's been happening, mate?" he asked again.

*Three times*, I thought. My answer, compared to the one on the phone, wasn't much different, but this time I was a little bit more precise in letting him know how I truly felt about this situation. "Not a lot to be honest. I can't really figure out what I'm doing here," I admitted.

"Doing where?" he asked.

"Here, as in New Zealand," I said.

"Or here as in on this planet?" he replied out of the blue. "So deep once again," was my instant response.

"Well, judging from the brief spell of time that we've spent together, I reckon you have a massive problem knowing what you want from life. If you want to phrase it in a hippie way like my mum would do, what is your purpose? Why are you here? And by here I mean on this planet?" he elaborated a bit more.

We hadn't made it past the first traffic light on busy Queen Street and we were already knee-deep into heavy topics again. Francis noticed that this wasn't lifting my mood, so he decided to hit me on the forehead.

"Let's not worry about this now. Are you ready for your first surf ever?" he asked.

From one disaster to another. Surfing was something I had never done before. All I knew about it was that cool dudes with long hair, who were meant to be the most easy-going people in the world, go out into the wild ocean, catch waves and do crazy things with their boards to prove their masculinity.

"How much time do I have left to mentally prepare for this?" I asked him.

"Forty-five minutes," he smiled.

The time flew by; we soon left the stress and noise of Auckland behind us as we hit the rural roads. Life became rather quiet abruptly. I was staring out the window, astonished by the pure beauty of New

Zealand's landscape. The green looked greener and the blue seemed bluer compared to what I was used to. It sounds pretty cliché, but it was true.

"You look like you're seeing this for the first time," Francis laughed.

"I am," I said with an astonished look across my face. "What!"

Francis shouted and suddenly hit the brakes. My face hit the car's dashboard in front of me, I looked up and shouted. "What the fuck?" I touched my nose and looked at my hand to check if it was bleeding.

"How can you have been here for three weeks and have not left the city?" Francis said almost like my dad trying to tell me off but under different circumstances. My dad would have never told me off for avoiding nature and staying in the city. In fact, he would have encouraged me to focus on finding a job, working and following his narrow-minded way of living. Maybe that was a decent hint as to why I hadn't left the city on my own yet. Instead of fully admitting it and addressing my fears, I answered with a simple "I know."

"Oh, man, we need to get you out of there," Francis said as he began driving once again. At first I thought he hit the brakes because of the shock of me not leaving the city, but when I looked up, I could see a traffic light that had just turned from red to green.

After this little incident, Francis went quiet and didn't say much at all. I was kind of expecting some more life advice or encouraging words to leave my comfort zone and push myself, but this didn't happen. He looked very thoughtful as if he was trying to figure something out. I had no idea what to say either; I just kept quiet too until we arrived at the beach. We found a parking spot right away. Francis opened the door immediately and jumped out of the car, taking a deep breath.

Obviously, it was nice and refreshing to be outside and take in the fresh ocean air. As soon as we walked over the sand dunes, I saw crystal clear water with waves rolling into the distance and the sun shining over them. There wasn't a single cloud in the sky.

"Perfect day," Francis said. I nodded and could feel the tension rising in my body. Even though everything looked like it was meant to be, I still had a lot of apprehension about what I was about to do. "Let's get back to the car to get changed," he instructed after checking the waves. I nodded again and followed him back to the car.

He took a massive nine-foot-long surfboard off his roof, looking like a cruise ship.

"This is going to be yours for the day," Francis said and placed it on the ground. His board looked tiny compared to mine, but I guess that's just how it goes. He took notice of my look comparing both boards.

"We want to make it as easy as possible, right?" he said.

I totally understood where he was coming from, so I decided to start the struggle of putting on a wetsuit for the very first time in my life. It looked so easy when I watched Francis doing it. What felt like thirty minutes later ended up being just the halfway mark. I felt like a proper city boy.

"Come on!" Francis started to push me the last few steps.

He grabbed his shortboard, and I tried to grab my cruise ship. We started walking over the sand dunes again. Right at the top of the dunes, I saw someone taking off on a wave; just to watch that was an incredible feeling in itself.

Francis signalled for me to drop the boards in the sand. "Okay this is going to be fun, mate," he said as he smiled across both cheeks.

*Sure, it'll be fun for you. You've been doing this for years*, I thought. I didn't say anything. It was obvious enough that I was scared, trying to keep my thoughts together. He started explaining to me the core principles of surfing. Where to lay on the board, how to paddle, how to pop up et cetera. After his brief five-minute introduction to surfing, he exclaimed, "Alright, let's go!"

He started running towards the ocean before I even had the chance to say anything. My legs were frozen. I couldn't move. I watched Francis run into the ocean, jump on his board and start to paddle. I was amazed by the energy that he was spreading. He was from A to Z absorbed by his surroundings, seeming so fearless, yet so cool at the same time.

Still, I was attached to the sand like the Eiffel Tower to Paris. All of a sudden, a little grommet passed by me—probably about six years old, with his board running towards the ocean and shouting "Woah!" He turned around looked at me and said, "Let's go!"

I heard a voice rising inside me. "If he can do it, you can too." I don't know why it would motivate me to see a six-year-old unconditionally fearless, but it was just the perfect example of what my subconscious has done to me over the past twenty-five years. It was time to break the pattern of fear.

I could feel my feet slowly starting to move towards the water. My heart was palpitating. I could literally feel it pumping the blood through my veins and I wasn't sure whether that was because I was so scared or so excited.

After standing hip-deep in the water, several waves splashing on my face, I decided to jump on the board and start paddling. I somehow managed to fight the waves that were coming towards me, when suddenly I saw a big white wave appear out of nowhere. I could see Francis waving and shouting "Go, go, go."

I tried to do everything I could to move this big, massive piece of foam as quickly as possible from facing the wide-open ocean to pointing towards the beach. The second my nose was facing in the direction of the shore I took one and then two big paddle strokes. The rumble came closer and closer. Everything happened so quick that I just pushed myself up and tried to jump in the position Francis had shown me back at the beach. My two feet landed on the board, and my hands were in the air trying to keep balance and with the high speed of the white wave, I was being pushed towards the shore. It was this unreal feeling of an unpredictable energy that was catapulting me back to the beach—a feeling I will never forget and one I am still talking about today. Back at the shore, my body full of adrenalin, only one single thought came up. *Again!*

I didn't want to waste a second to experience this feeling once more, so I straightaway tried to paddle out a second time.

An hour and several nosedives, wipeouts and whitewashes later

I arrived back at the shore and laid on my back facing the sky. I was completely exhausted, happy and so proud of myself for overcoming my initial fear. I was trying to let it all sink in as a shadow covered my face. A few drops of saltwater were dripping down on my forehead. "That was pretty good, aye?"

It was Francis, standing right above me.

"Better than I expected," I admitted to myself.

"You might be a natural," he chuckled.

"I don't know why, but it felt really good nailing something on the first go. It's never happened before."

"I don't want to discourage you my friend, but these were baby waves and you were surfing a cruise ship," he said, laughing again.

I didn't want to hear that. I was so high on life and genuinely wanted to take this moment in.

"Are you coming?" he said.

"Give me a second. Just go back and get changed. I'll be coming soon," I replied. Francis went off, back to the car. I stared up at the sky, thinking about what had just happened when I heard a voice shouting my name.

"Ben!" Emma shouted "Let's go! We're late for dinner!"

When I heard Emma's voice, I woke up straightaway, jumped off the bed and tried to figure out why and how I had passed out again. "Oh my God, I must have been sound asleep."

I stumbled downstairs, rubbed my eyes and said, "Sorry, guys. Give me five minutes and I'll be ready."

Both Jay and Emma were already at the front door waiting for me. I felt terrible—first of all, I was late and second of all because the unpleasant feeling in my tummy was still very present.

I quickly brushed my teeth and put on a fresh t-shirt, ran downstairs, grabbed my coat, put on my shoes and jumped in the car where both of them were waiting impatiently.

"What is up today, babe? You seem so off," Emma said in front of Jay. She was completely right about that. I had been solidly caught up in my head since last night. It felt like I was processing something up in here while the real world kept spinning around without me.

"I'm sorry, Emma. I don't know what's up. A lot is going on," I said, knowing that this was a lie. In the end, I just assumed Emma knew what was up since she was there when it all happened. However, I tried to avoid any further conversations about this in front of Jay, since she still didn't know the full story yet.

"It's okay," Emma responded, but I wasn't sure if she just said it to avoid the same thing I was trying to avoid, or if she actually had some respect and empathy for me being caught up in my head.

# 10.
# YOU GOTTA START SOMEWHERE

Jay was driving towards her mum's house, Emma's Nan. This was the place where everyone would celebrate the end of the week over a nice roast dinner; Emma was staring out the window, and so was I.

I really wanted to just talk to her, tell her how I feel and what was going on in my head. I was hoping she would just understand and assure me that everything would be okay, but I was too afraid that she wouldn't be able to. In fact, I knew that realistically she couldn't. My mind made its own decision—to focus on the trees that were passing the backseat windows, morphing into vivid memories once again.

We had just arrived at Francis' place, following my first-ever surf. He lived just on the city border of Auckland. From his little terrace, you can make out Auckland's Sky Tower in the distance, but you don't feel the congestion and overstimulation that you get from being right in the city centre. After a few minutes at his place, it was pretty clear to me that I had to clarify my situation.

"Just drop the stuff here, mate. Do you want a beer?"

"Yes please!" I said as I placed the bag with the soaking wetsuit in the corner of his terrace.

The sun was still shining bright, but close to turning into a beautiful sunset.

Francis came back from the kitchen with two bottles of craft beer in his hand. He passed one bottle to me. "Cheers," he said.

"Cheers, and thanks a lot for taking me surfing today," I replied as our bottles clinked.

"No problem at all, mate, but you should do something about your situation," he pointed out once again.

"Yes, I know," and indeed I knew he was right, but most of the time it isn't that easy to admit that someone else is right.

"Have you found an answer to my question?" he continued as he took a seat in one of his terrace chairs. I sat down in the chair next to him while I was figuring out what he exactly meant by this. He could see the question marks in my eyes.

"Your passion, mate."

The second he said it, it clicked in and I felt embarrassed that I hadn't thought about it any further. "No, I haven't," I replied. In the very same moment that I'd admitted that, I felt my wallet in my back pocket pushing against my upper leg again. It's almost as if something was trying to remind me of Grace's article.

"Well..." Francis started to say when he realised that I was about to grab my wallet.

He stopped talking when I pulled out and unfolded the page I ripped out of his magazine after we first met. I was expecting him to make at least a little comment, but when I looked over to him, I surprisingly could see satisfaction in his face.

After a few seconds of me staring at Grace's pictures again, Francis said, "Remember, you promised me something?"

I had no idea that he actually heard me shout through the airport noise. The exit door was already closed, and I was pretty sure he didn't catch it, even though everyone else did. I started thinking about it again for the first time since my arrival. I realised how exhausted my brain was. I didn't have it in me to consider the promise that I had made to Francis back at Auckland Airport. It's so easy to make a promise, but what in actual fact it means to keep it is a whole different ball game. I was unable to give him an answer once again.

"Come on, mate, grab your beer. I want to show you something," Francis said.

Without saying a word, I followed his footsteps. We went through the living room into a little square room that was attached to it. At first, I thought that would be his bedroom, but when he opened the door, I was flabbergasted. In front of me I saw a tiny room, roughly ten square metres in size, full of paintings, brushes on the floor and a wooden easel in the middle with a blank canvas on it.

My brain immediately clicked in. "Grace's?"

"Definitely not mine, mate," he smirked as we both chuckled. Francis took a sip of his beer. "It's still her room, but unfortunately she only uses it once a year when she's here."

I could feel his heartache about the fact that she was hardly present, yet still very much there—her heart and soul on display. That was the first time I saw the ever-happy Francis a little bit more pensive.

"She used to spend hours and hours in here, which was so unbelievably inspiring to me. I would cook dinner and she would miss it almost every day. 'Just five more minutes,' she always used to say, when two hours later she had to heat up her dinner in the microwave. I'd never met someone who could get so caught up in their passion. She inspired me to push further in surfing and my studies. She gave me the motivation to make every day as good as it possibly can be, and she still does. Unfortunately, not so often in this room anymore, but when I go in here, it feels like she is present, right next to me."

I could feel how saddened he was by the situation, but at the same time, there was something positive. Something was moving; something that was way more tangible in comparison to the monotone stiffness I had experienced so far.

"Let's paint!" I shouted.

It looked like I frightened Francis with my determination—I surprised myself too.

"But I can't paint at all, mate," said Francis, utterly dejected.

"Nor could I surf, but it is just art, isn't it? There's no right or wrong," I said, even more shocked as to where all this wisdom had come from so suddenly. It felt like the tables had turned for the very first time in many years. I didn't want to think about if I could fuck up something or not. I just wanted to do it. So often this thought held me back from having fun, enjoying things and failing at the same time. I guess you have to take failure into consideration when you start something new, but if you've stopped before you've started, you've already failed.

"You are 100 percent right, mate. Let's do it," he said.

His little moment of sadness turned into a smile, and he started unpacking the box next to him, which was full of paints of different colours and random stuff, more brushes, cutlery, combs, even a fan was in there. I was amazed by the variety of stuff in the box, but the second I saw it, it all made sense to me.

"Do you want another beer?" Francis asked.

"For sure," I said.

He ran back into the kitchen and returned with two fresh bottles. We started pouring the paint into the cups.

"Any idea what we want to paint?" he asked.

"Abstract art, I guess." I added, "No rules whatsoever."

Francis nodded and we started creating our very first piece of art.

Many hours, a few beers and a lot of fun later, we were both staring at a canvas full of random colours, little textured elements and some undefined kind of randomness in the form of cryptic letters.

What looked like an anonymous blackmail letter was our very first piece of art.

"Pretty impressive," I laughed at the absurdity of it.

"That was all you, mate," Francis chuckled.

"No, that was us together," I responded straightaway.

"You did all the painting part, Ben. I was just here coming up with some random ideas and supplied some beers."

The more I thought about it, the more I thought he could be right, but I just didn't have the pride to admit it. "Teamwork!" I shouted and raised the brush.

We both took a big sip out of our beers and decided to call it a night. It'd been a long day, full of new stuff and leaving comfort zones. It was a day that I will probably never forget.

# 11.
# PICASSO

I opened my eyes and could feel my head aching. I wasn't quite sure if it was the beers or not. I found myself in the foetal position crawled up on Francis' couch in the living room, and I could already smell fresh coffee. I decided to get up and put my feet on the ground; when I did so, I saw next to me the painting we did last night wrapped up as if it was ready to be shipped somewhere. Next to it were three different sizes of brushes, a little cup and some paint.

I had no clue how this ended up there or what this was supposed to mean. I didn't think we were that drunk. I tried to rub the sleep out of my eyes, turned around and saw Francis in the kitchen preparing some breakfast.

"How did this end up here, Francis?" I shouted into the kitchen. He was busy frying eggs, but instantaneously aware of what I was talking about.

"It's all yours, mate!" he shouted back.

It still didn't click, so I decided to wait for my first morning coffee before investigating into this any further. I walked up to the table that divided the big room into the living room and kitchen. I loved the open space. Through the window, you could almost make out the entire city in the distance.

"Here is your coffee, mate," Francis said as he placed a cup of fresh coffee right in front of me. "Sugar or milk?"

"Black, thanks," I said.

He returned to the stove in the kitchen, prepared two plates and came back with some fried eggs and some fresh-smelling bread.

"Get that into your system and you'll feel better."

*Do I look like someone with a hangover*, I thought.

"You look like you have a little hangover," Francis said in the same split second.

I smiled and took a big sip of my black, bitter coffee. I felt like the caffeine was kicking in almost immediately.

"So, Francis, why is the painting and all that other stuff wrapped up next to the couch?" I asked again.

"Because it's all yours," he repeated.

"No, it's not. We did it together and all the other stuff belongs to Grace."

"It's your first-ever painting, Picasso. Keep it," Francis said, patting my shoulder.

"But we did it together!" I almost started an argument.

"Ben, listen. I might have had a couple of beers last night, but I saw you, painting this picture. You were the driving force. I know you think you surfed like Kelly Slater yesterday, but I am afraid I have to disappoint you with your little whitewash on your nine-foot water truck."

"Hey," I interrupted him. "It felt amazing."

"Of course, it did and we should still go surfing whenever, but I noticed a very clear difference between you surfing and you painting."

"What?" I asked confused.

"It came naturally," Francis pointed out.

"What do you mean by that?" I asked, sounding almost desperate in my tone.

"It is not just the fact that you actually made me a promise, Ben," he laughed, "but it's also the fact that I saw you and your mind fully get into it. At some point, you didn't even realise that I was there."

What was he talking about? I wasn't quite sure if I could follow him or if I really couldn't remember how this painting came together.

"The last time I saw someone getting so much into art was when I met Grace."

"What?" I shouted. I just couldn't believe what he had just said and my mind was trying everything to not listen to his words. I ran over to the couch, lifted the canvas and yelled, "Look at it, mate, it's crap."

"No, Ben, it's art," he quipped back at me.

"It's not! It was a couple of beers, some random colours and some stupid ideas," I almost shouted.

"You forgot one very important thing here, it's about the process not the outcome, mate," Francis stated.

"I don't understand," I said almost annoyed. The level of confusion was rising in my head.

"I only met you a couple of times Ben, and every time, I experienced a little, scared boy, who was always too afraid to try out new things and push limits. Even when we went surfing, you hesitated so much. Last night, it was you who had the idea of painting, and it was you who didn't doubt anything for a second. For the first time, I saw this little boy, but instead of fear of failure, I saw fun, enlightenment and passion!"

"Puhhhh," I articulated aloud, putting the painting back on the floor and striding back to the table. His words undeniably needed to sink in. Maybe he was right, maybe he wasn't. I had no idea how to take them. "Why did I not see it then?" I said to him in a very neutral tone to calm down the slightly heated atmosphere.

"Maybe you don't want to see it," Francis said straightaway and continued, "Ben, I am not trying to push this on to you. It is entirely up to you if you take it or not, but I know what I have seen previously, and compared to what I have seen from you so far, it was a whole different world."

"Too many beers I reckon," trying to laugh it off with a bit of charm.

"Okay, here's the deal mate. I drive you back to your place, you take

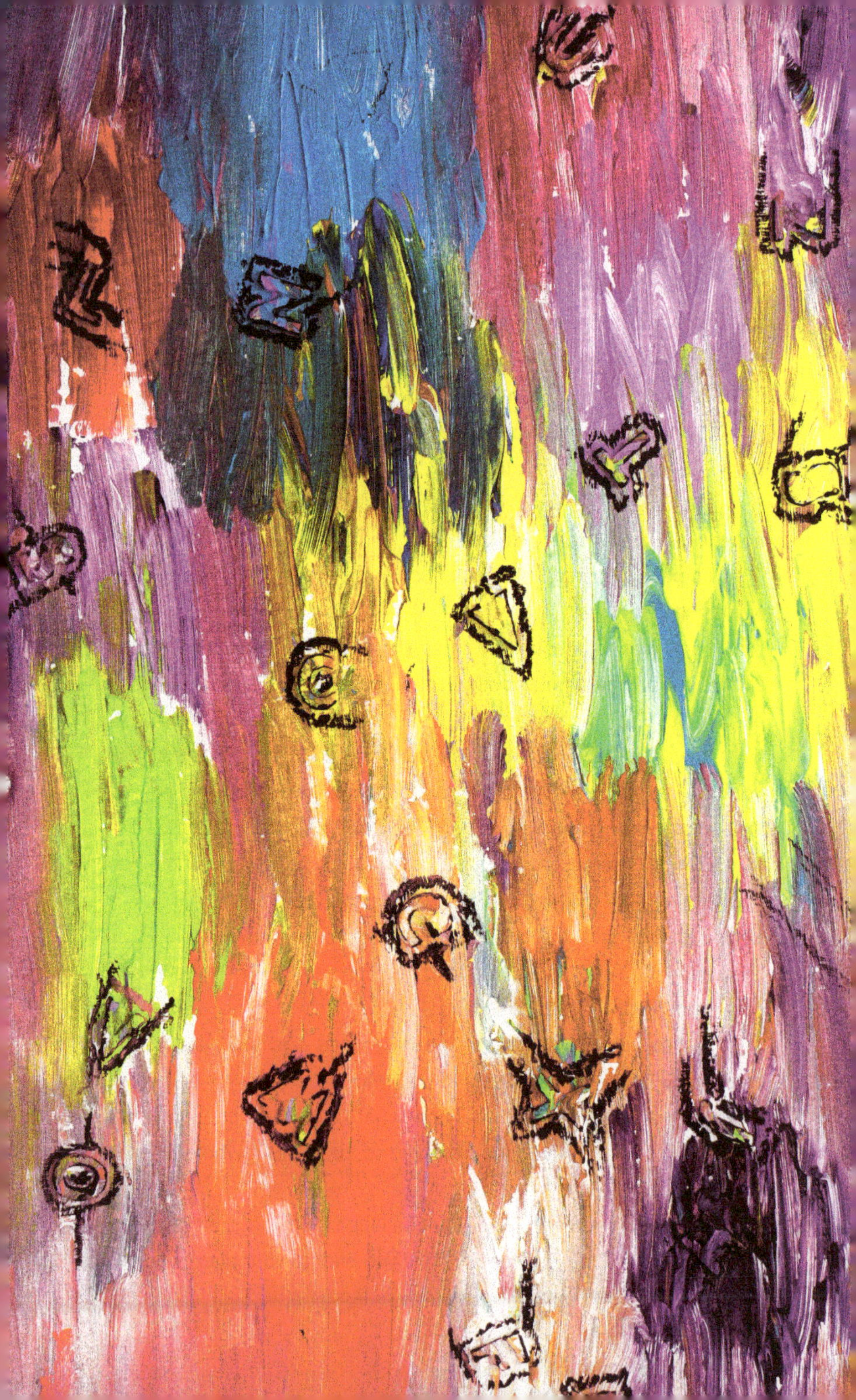

the painting, the brush, the paint and all the rest and keep it. If it ends up in the bin, then fine. If not, we might have a new Picasso, alright?"

I was thinking about his kind offer, but it was pretty clear that I couldn't take it. It wasn't even his stuff that he was giving away for free. "Man, I can't do that, it's Grace's stuff," I said to escape the situation.

"Mate, Grace is hardly here. The last time she used it was almost a year ago, and I know her. If she knew her stuff was going to be used by someone who is talented and passionate about art, she would be the first one to give it away."

Did he really just say talented? I had to defend myself.

"Man, we literally painted one piece of art that looks like a rip off of a newspaper headline after having a few too many beers. For me, it was nothing other than having fun. I didn't think about anything. Time was just flying by and I was happy."

"I think you just answered everything yourself," he huffed as he stood, proceeding to grab all the stuff and load it into the car. I didn't have the chance to say anything.

"Let's go!" he shouted through the open front door.

I hadn't even finished my breakfast. "Hang on, Francis!" I shouted back and went outside to him. "What do you mean I have answered it myself?"

He slammed the boot of his car and looked deep into my eyes and said, "Mate, when was the last time you thought about nothing, time was flying by and you felt happy?"

"Last night," I said and smiled.

"Jesus, before that?" he raised his voice.

"Ah okay, let me think," I said, digging deep into my mind.

After thirty seconds of silence, Francis said, "See, you don't even know because it's been such a long time, maybe you were a child and no one encouraged you to dig deeper into that feeling, but I see how broken you are Ben, and I saw how you were last night. You said it yourself. So just accept it. I'll drive you back into town now."

I had no chance to intervene. So I just accepted it, went back inside, quickly grabbed the rest of my stuff and jumped in the car, where Francis was already waiting for me.

"Off into your new future," Francis said, reversing into his driveway as he escorted me towards town.

His words somehow touched me, but I was still scared and reserved about the change that was most likely ahead of me. For now, I would go back into my twelve-bed dorm room with a blackmail letter, a brush, a cup and a random colour collection of paint. "Exciting times ahead," I whispered to myself.

# 12.
# CARIBOU

It took me a couple of weeks to get moving, but eventually, I was ready to leave the hostel and move into a proper flat. For some reason, I was sick of travelling before it had even started. I did a couple of trips with some people I met at the hostel, but it was all the same thing over and over. The stuff that really touched me, that lingered, happened with Francis.

Something in me told me that this could be my chance to actually change something. I mean, what would be the point of returning to Germany with a couple of work and travel memories like everyone else? The decision was made. Three weeks later I woke up in my new flat. The sun was shining through my window. The morning dust made the colours faded and grainy, giving them a lot of texture.

Francis helped me to find a flat. He was kind enough to connect me with a couple of his friends, who knew someone who knew someone, so in no time, I ended up in a flat with a French guy and an English guy. Both seemed super nice and chill.

After I opened my eyes, I looked around. Everything was still packed up. To be honest, I didn't have a lot of stuff anyway. Apart from my bed, the room was pretty much empty and my fully packed backpack was sitting in the corner. On top of it stood the painted canvas from that night at Francis' house.

His words appeared in my head again. "Enlightenment and passion." I always thought and was genuinely convinced that passion is something you either have or you don't. Once you try something, you know if you are passionate about it or not. I would never see passion as something that needs to develop with time.

Eventually, I managed to drag myself out of bed, went into the kitchen and poured myself a coffee.

Alexandre, my French flatmate passed by. "Good morning, Ben. How was your first night?" In his hands, he was holding a box full of cardboard and paper.

"Thanks, very good," I replied.

"That's nice. Any plans for the day?" he asked.

"Not so far. How about you? What are you doing with that box?" I asked him out of curiosity. By his reaction, I could tell he was very surprised by my question. To be fair, it came across as pretty random.

"Recycling, I guess," he said and shrugged his shoulders.

I laughed, embarrassed. "Obviously," I said, and to make it worse I added, "Would you mind if I have a look through it?"

Now it got awkward. I could tell that I may have made an absolutely weird first impression on him. We briefly met last night after I moved in, but we spoke only fleetingly as I was tired and went to bed early. To my surprise, he acted pretty cool.

"Go ahead. Never met someone interested in my recycling rubbish, but sure, why not," he said while putting the box on the table.

A white piece of paper rolled together like a papyrus roll, which was sticking out the box, caught my attention the moment he'd walked into the kitchen. Since then, I couldn't keep my eyes off it. So I took it out of the garbage box and rolled it out entirely. It was blank, and it almost covered the whole kitchen table.

"What is this?" I asked Alexandre.

"A big...piece...of...blank paper," he said bluntly.

I laughed, not because of his answer but more because of my silly question. "I think I got that. But what was it for?"

"I bought a big new world map for my wall and I guess it was wrapped up in it," he shrugged his shoulders, once again very irritated. "What are all these questions about, Ben?"

"Sorry to make it unnecessarily awkward, but can I have it?"

"Sure. You could have said that directly. It would have gone in the bin anyway," he said passing the roll. "Can I bring the rubbish out now?" Alexandre sarcastically checked in with me.

We both laughed and I tried to cover the embarrassment of how I tend to make simple social situations awkward. I took the paper roll and my coffee and went back into my room.

I don't know what had gotten into me. I didn't think about it too much. Something just took over and I felt like I was on autopilot. I opened my backpack, grabbed the cup, the brush and the paint and placed it all onto the floor in front of me. I unfolded the white roll on the ground and stabilised the edges with my shoes in two corners and the cup and the can of paint in the other two corners. The sunlight was flooding my room with light. I grabbed my speaker out of my backpack and put my personal playlist on shuffle. The last thing I remember listening to was "Caribou—Can't Do Without You." I was singing along before the algorithm decided to jump to the entire album and play it track by track.

# Caribou - Our Love (Expanded Edition)

Many hours later, I found myself dehydrated and with paint on my knees and hands in front of a collection of random colours. One might say that I got inspired subconsciously by the cover of the album that I was listening to, though someone else might say that it was a unique piece of art. Most likely, the first one was the case, if I had to guess. I needed to admit to myself, though, that I actually liked what I saw, but who wouldn't after spending two hours locked up in a room? It probably was a good start, but nothing outstanding.

Suddenly, I heard a knock at the door, and without any further thinking I said, "Come in."

Alexandre opened the door and was about to say something. He started his sentence with "Hey, Ben," and then interrupted himself. His eyes darted to the painting. "Oh wow, is that my recycling garbage?" he asked surprised.

"Yes, it is," I responded.

"Pretty good," he smiled.

Is that what I wanted to hear? This was my confirmation—yeah, it's good, but not good enough.

He continued, "Ehm…I was just wondering if you would like to have some dinner. My girlfriend and I cooked it and it'll be ready soon."

"Dinner?" I said pretty loudly. "What time is it?" I shouted.

"Eh, close to 6 p.m.?" he said, and it almost sounded like a question.

"What the heck? How did that happen?" I shouted again.

"How did what happen?" Alexandre asked not knowing what was going on once again. If he wasn't convinced by now that I was a weirdo, then I don't know what else I'd need to do.

"All good. Thanks for the offer, Alexandre. I'll be with you guys soon. I just quickly need to finish that," I said and just didn't want to make it more awkward than it already was.

So far he'd witnessed a German dude, who moved in the night before, asked to have a look through his garbage, then ended up eight hours later in his room full of paint, still nothing unpacked and who freaked out when he told him what the time was.

I mean, how did that happen? Losing track of time is one thing, but I just can't remember having ever spent so much time on one thing without a break. Or did I take a break?

In fact, I couldn't remember. I looked at the painting in front of me and discovered a couple of details that felt like they needed adjustments, which I quickly wanted to make before filling my stomach with some well-deserved dinner. "Just a few more touches," I said to myself. I dipped the brush back in the water cup, reached for the yellow colour and continued.

I touched up one thing and I saw another one. Every time I would discover another little thing that I wanted to touch up I said out loud to myself, "Okay, just this one and then I'll go eat dinner." My self-talk continued and continued until I shouted to myself, "Okay, stop now!"

I put the brush aside, stood up, had one last look, smiled and left my room to join the guys for dinner. I opened the door of my room and everything was dark. Awkwardly, I switched on the light and went into the kitchen. There was a plate covered with another plate, and on top, a little note, "For Ben." My first thought was, *Wow, the Frenchies eat dinner super quick!* Then I looked out the window and realised it was pitch black. I turned around to the microwave to heat up my dinner when I saw the digital clock showing 11:15 p.m.

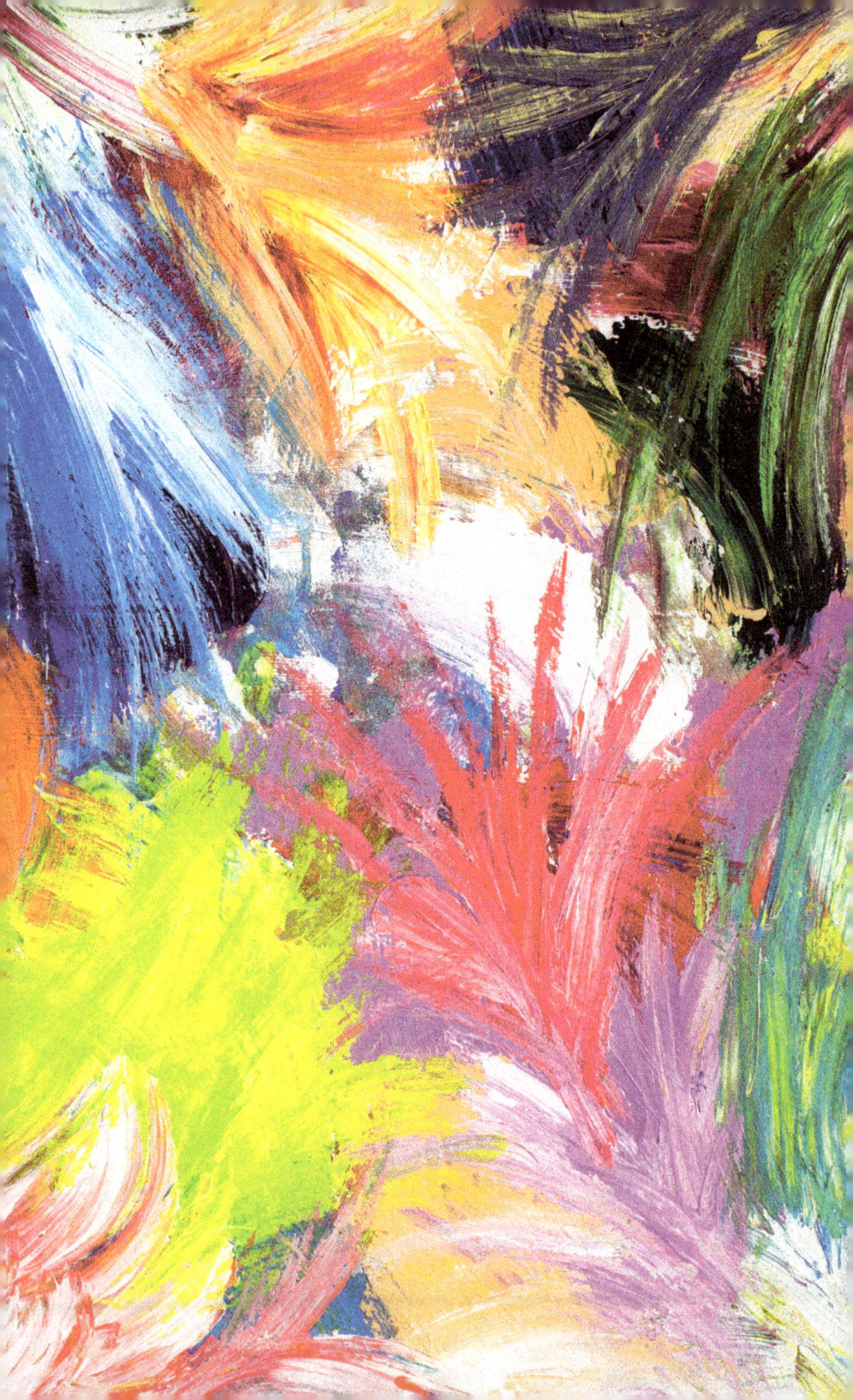

# 13.
# ARE YOU AN ARTIST?

The desire to be someone or something is pretty common nowadays in our society, and I can't deny that I felt the same desire myself. I woke up the next morning, and the first thing I saw was the colourful painting that I created the previous night. It was an odd feeling. I thought when I went to bed last night that I'd be so exhausted that I'd fall asleep right away, but the opposite was true. "Caribou" was on repeat in my head and vivid colours were shooting through it—it felt like I was painting the whole thing again. Looking at it now, I had no idea how I came up with it or what the thoughts behind it were.

"What am I going to do with it now?" I whispered to myself, thinking straightaway about just hanging it up the wall.

Before I could make a final decision, my phone interrupted me with a loud *bing*. I'd received a text message. "What are you up to tonight, mate?" Francis had texted. I hadn't heard from him in a little while, but I was super happy to receive a message from him again. "No plans, so far," I replied. It took less than thirty seconds for him to respond, "Keen to go to an exhibition downtown?"

I was kind of relieved he didn't ask me for another surf. I wasn't ready for it yet, but I told him I was down for the exhibition tonight, and we arranged that he would pick me up around six p.m. So, I still had a lot of time on my hands. I looked at the brush and the paint in the corner and said to myself, "Why not?"

I jumped out of bed, went into the kitchen and started to make coffee again. While the coffee was brewing, I thought—*What should I paint on today?* I decided to repeat the same approach from yesterday and went out through the front door and opened the recycling bin. It was kind of empty, but I could see some cardboard at the bottom of the bin. *That could be something*, was my immediate thought. In order to be able to reach it, I had to stick my head into the bin and lift my legs up. My entire upper body was actually inside the bin, and my hands were reaching for the desired piece of cardboard when I heard a voice shouting, "Seriously, dude? You are weird!"

I was super frightened not knowing who was talking to me. I tried to put my legs back on the ground, but I had too much swing with my body and the whole bin collapsed to the ground with me inside of it. All I heard was a big, loud laugh. I crawled backwards out of the bin, looked up and saw Alexandre again, laughing.

"You are so odd, man!" he managed to spurt out between fits of laughter. Once again, I tried to smile my embarrassment away. "Well, I was just thinking about doing another painting."

"All good. I'll slowly get my head around you and your weird behaviour. Next time, I will just pass by your room with my rubbish before I bring it outside," he said and continued laughing.

I was still laying on the ground, grabbed the piece of cardboard I was after and lifted it up in the air. "No need, man. Already got what I was looking for," I said.

Alexandre clocked on and said, "Oh, I see another piece of art in the making then?"

"Yeah maybe, let's see," I replied, second-guessing my decision.

"So, you are an artist then?" he asked just like that.

"Ehm...eh...no, no, no I am not," I said while trying to sound as normal as possible. I didn't expect that question and definitely didn't think of myself as an artist. Especially not after making one random painting with a bunch of arbitrarily selected colours.

"But you do paint, right?" Alexandre asked.

I wasn't quite sure if he just wanted to get to know me better, or if he was trying to figure out if I made art as a job.

"Oh, I have only done it once or twice."

"So more like a hobby?" he kept asking.

"Not really, I mean…I guess so," I stuttered.

"Lots of dedication for a hobby though," he said, laughing and pointing his finger at me, still sitting next to the collapsed bin. "Well, I'll leave you to it then, Ben. Good luck and have lots of fun," sounding like a parent.

"Thank you," I said, and Alexandre returned inside. I got off the ground, put the bin back up and grabbed the cardboard. Back in my room with my coffee and that special piece of cardboard, I thought, *alright let's do it all over again.* I put on the "Brainfood" playlist on my Spotify and started painting again.

# Spotify - Brain Food (Playlist)

As if everything would be on repeat, time passed by quickly and the next time I checked the clock, it was already close to six p.m. However, unlike the few times prior, I wasn't as relaxed. A lot of frustration had grown in me and instead of enjoying myself, I was confronted with a lot of thoughts such as "What am I doing here?"

I knew I needed to get changed, so I threw the brush in the corner, stood up and looked at what I had done over the whole day. "A five year old paints better than that!" I heard myself exclaiming. I was truly disappointed. Nothing turned out the way I had imagined it in my head. The painting felt and looked like a big mess. I know I have said similar things about the painting from yesterday, but at least it felt good and it did stand for something. This one here means nothing.

I guess it was all just beginner's luck. That was what was running through my mind while I was facing my wardrobe trying to find a clean shirt for tonight.

Before I could decide on my outfit, I heard someone knocking at the door. I was about to say, "One second please," but Francis had already entered my room and said, "Ready?"

"Do I look ready?" I snapped back. "And how did you get in?" I asked, almost angrily.

Francis took it well, but he obviously realised that I wasn't in the best mood. "Mate, I rang the doorbell three times. Your flatmate was kind enough to let me in."

I ignored the fact that I had overheard him ringing the doorbell and finally found a clean good-looking shirt. I put it on and saw that Francis was staring at the colourful painting from last night, which I had put up on the wall in the meantime. I was surprised that the mess on the floor didn't catch his attention first.

His mouth was wide open as he pointed his finger at the wall. "Who did this?" he asked slightly astonished.

I looked irritated and said almost insecurely, "I did."

"Are you serious?" he almost shouted.

I couldn't follow and asked, "What's wrong with it?"

"Mate, this is amazing. So beautiful!" he said.

I wasn't quite sure if we were talking about the same picture. Yes, I did like it, but in the end, it was still just some random colours put together in a somewhat nice context.

He came up to me, hugged me and patted me on my back. "I knew it! I just freaking knew it!" he shouted.

"Knew what, Francis?" I asked out loud.

"You are an artist!" he shouted.

"No, I'm not," I threw back at him immediately.

"Look at it. There's the proof!" he said and had his arms wide open facing the artwork on the wall.

"Yes, exactly look at it, there is the proof," and I pointed at my latest work on the floor.

"Oh," Francis said and stopped. His enthusiasm was gone from one second to the other. It was pretty clear he couldn't hide the fact that the painting on the floor was pretty shit.

"Ehm...yes," he said.

"It's okay, say it," I pushed him.

"Well, next one then." He smiled.

His reaction broke the last part in me. I felt like I almost wanted him to say that this one was amazing too (even though we both knew it wasn't).

"Come on, mate, the gallery won't stay open just for us," he said.

I tried to erase the disappointment from my mind. The next second I grabbed my jacket, shut the door behind me and we went off to the exhibition.

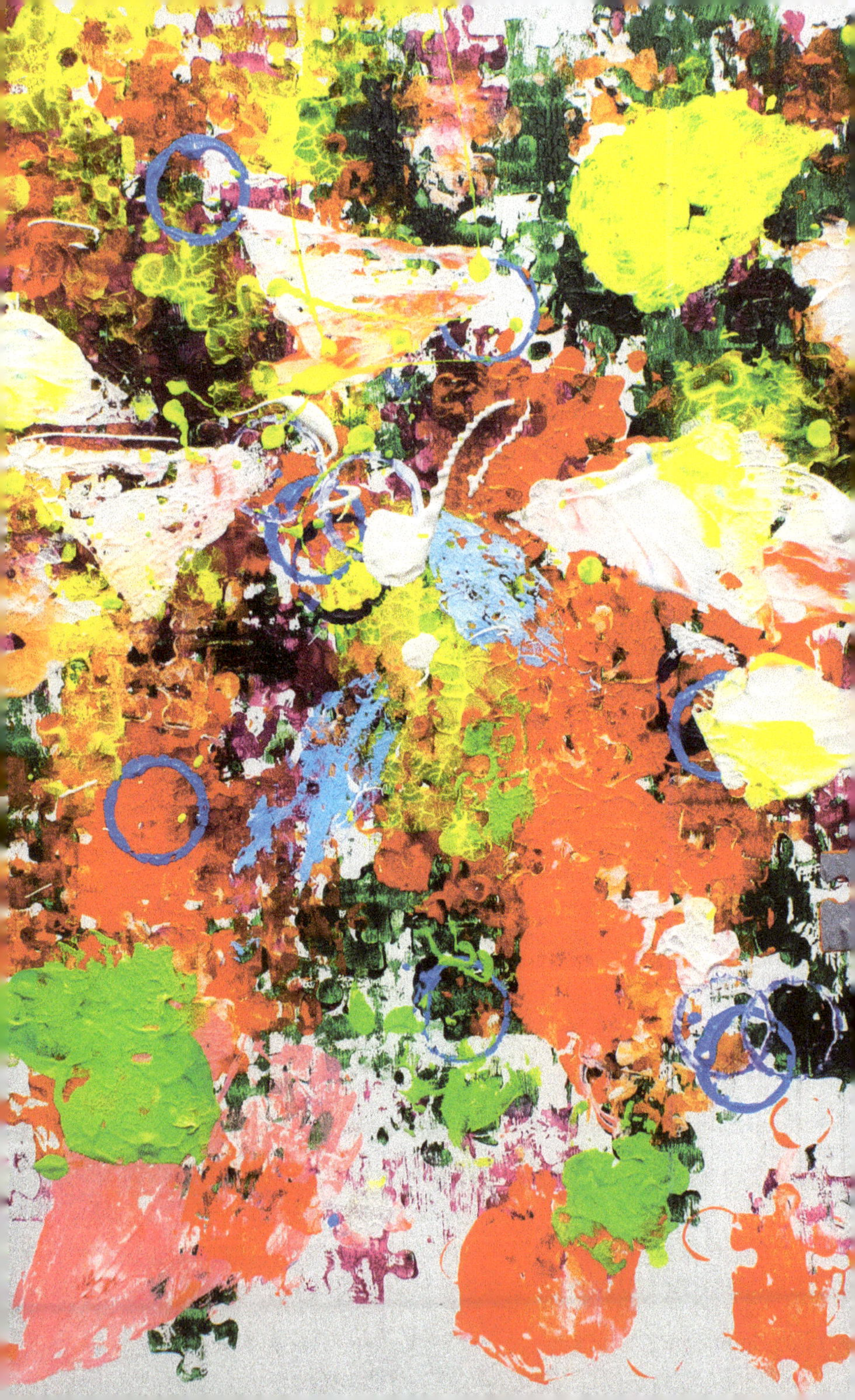

# 14.
# I AM NOT AN ARTIST

In the car, Francis could tell that I was trapped in my head, a skill that I developed in my early twenties to compensate for the fact that my feelings were taking over my mind. He realised and tried to intervene. "What's up, mate?" he asked kindly.

"Nothing, I've just been thinking a lot. Maybe a little too much," trying to explain myself.

"Thinking about what?" he followed up.

I tried to simplify the mess in my head and was surprised by my own answer. "How much I would like to be an artist," I said very honestly.

"What do you need to do in order to be one?" he asked immediately.

It was a very simple but effective question. I was so confused that I had to answer his question with my favourite question in return, "What do you mean?"

The second I noticed his smile, I knew his question was intentional. It almost felt like he knew straight from the moment he entered my room what was going on inside me.

"Who decides whether you are an artist or not? Think about it," he said and slowed down the car.

He started looking left and right, checking for a car park. So it was clear that we were close and we wouldn't have the time to continue this conversation. Maybe he just wanted to give me the time to think about it in more detail—I don't know.

As soon as Francis claimed a spot on the side of the road, we jumped out of the car, and he looked me in the eyes over the roof of his Peugeot, asking, "Why so nervous?"

I don't know how he sensed it. Maybe it was blindingly obvious, but the second we got out of that car, nervousness added itself to my already existing undefined mixture of feelings. I guess it was the fact that I was about to confront myself with a lot of people that called themselves what I wanted to call myself. Leaving his question unanswered Francis followed up with a "Come on, let's go!"

We crossed the road and walked about 200 metres towards a big window with sculptures behind it. Outside was a little sign saying Auckland Pop Art Exhibition. When I looked through the window and past the sculptures, I saw lots of people inside, chatting and drinking bubbles. I had never seen so many paintings and so much art in one room. This time my mouth fell wide open. Yes, I had been to a few exhibitions in Germany, but always as an inexperienced visitor, never with the desire of calling myself a creative—a painter. Francis grabbed my arm, dragged me towards the entry and we entered the room together. He pulled out two tickets and handed them to the woman next to me.

"I didn't know that you—"

Before I could finish my sentence, he shut me down by waving his hand, followed up by a little, "Don't worry."

I felt like a little child taken to a theme park for the very first time, my dad paying for the tickets.

It didn't even take a minute and a guy came up to Francis. "Hey, mate, how are you? Long time no see. How is Grace?"

I should have been aware of the fact that Francis would be kind of known around here, and especially his girlfriend.

"Very well, Henry, thanks. Grace too," he replied.

I was standing next to the two of them when Francis continued by introducing me.

"May I introduce Ben to you? He said.

"Of course," Henry replied and turned towards me.

"Nice to meet you, Ben. What brings you to us?" he asked.

I wondered whom he meant by us, but before I could ask that question, Francis suddenly assumed the role of my legal guardian for the night and proceeded to answer all questions on my behalf.

"He is an artist as well, and relatively new in Auckland."

"Well, not really," I tried to get in between before Francis was making up more bullshit.

"Not really what?" Henry followed up. "Not an artist or not new in Auckland?"

"The first one," I said.

"Well, aren't we all artists?" Henry said and added, "Artists of our own life."

*Very philosophical*, I thought.

"Sure, but you know what I mean," I answered.

"What do you mean?" he continued to dig deeper.

"I mean like painting art," I said and started to get slightly annoyed.

"But that's what I mean, Ben," Henry said.

Francis took a little step back, almost like he wanted Henry to take over the brainwashing. I couldn't get rid of the feeling that Francis may have planned all this through, from the very start.

"Who decides to call you an artist?" Henry asked.

*Here we go again*, I thought. Francis' cheeky smile was unavoidable. I could see it from the corner of my left eye.

"I don't know. People? Society? Man, I am just not an artist," I replied, feeling that my words were showing that I was becoming more and more annoyed.

"What makes you think that?" Henry continued. He wouldn't stop until I gave him a detailed explanation of why I didn't feel like an artist. So, I thought the only option was to tell him the truth.

"I was painting all day and it was just rubbish. My five-year-old cousin could have done it," I admitted.

"I have seen it. It was pretty bad," Francis laughed.

I wasn't quite sure if he wanted to be funny or to provoke me.

"Ben, have you ever created something that you are proud of?" Henry asked me.

"I guess one was okay," I said.

"The one hanging in your room is amazing," Francis interjected.

"Yeah, but it was just luck." I tried to defend myself.

Francis and Henry looked at each other, nodded and then looked at me.

"Come with us, mate," Henry said.

I felt as if I were in a cult, that they were guiding me to their next ritual as part of their tradition. The three of us went up to a woman who was standing only a couple of feet away from us in front of some very nice paintings. Her artworks were all mostly painted in black, but in a variety of shades and layers. I'd never seen anything so detailed and professional.

I was immediately drawn into her work and couldn't stop staring when Henry went straight up to her and said, "Hey, Cassy, this is Ben. He would like to know how many shit paintings you have done in your life?"

I couldn't believe his question and felt a little ashamed, also slightly embarrassed about his direct tone of voice towards her.

However, unexpectedly, Cassy seemed to enjoy it. She laughed, looked at him and said, "I stopped counting, Henry." Then she looked at me and said, "Nice to meet you, Ben."

I was still questioning what was going on when Francis pulled me over to the next guy and said, "Ben, this is Matt, one of the best artists you can find around Auckland." Then he turned to Matt and said, "Hey, Matt, this is Ben. He is wondering how many paintings in your life you've thrown away."

It was almost a similar reaction. He laughed and said something like, "About a hundred."

A question came through my head that I felt like voicing straightaway, so I did. "And how many have you kept?"

"Thirty-five, forty maybe." He said it so casually as if it were the most normal thing in the world.

Then he added, "I even chucked one artwork last night. Once in a while, I just come up with crap only. It's pretty normal and part of the creative process."

The spiel continued. We went over to the guy with the sculptures and to almost any other person that was a part of exhibiting their creations. The answers were so similar and so fascinating at the same time.

We ended up in the same spot where we started, close to the entrance. A waiter passed by and Henry grabbed three glasses of what looked to me like a nice white wine.

"Do I need to say anything else, Ben?" Henry looked at me, raising his eyebrow.

I was thinking about my response when I saw Francis taking a big sip out of his glass. Then he started what seemed like the beginning of a speech.

"Mate, just let go of the thought that people are born as those amazing creatures they present themselves as to the outside world. Some of them perhaps actually are that, but at least 95 percent of them just put in the hard work. They dedicated their lives to it, overcame their self-doubt and kept creating. Every failure, rejection or shit painting was just the experience they needed to go through in order to create that one amazing piece of art that someone will never forget. It's the same when I go surfing. Out of 100 times, the one manoeuvre works once or twice, but if I wouldn't have tried it those 100 times, I would have never felt that amazing feeling of achieving that radical turn on a big wave."

*It definitely is a little speech*, I thought. I looked at Henry and he just nodded, while Francis continued.

"So do me a favour, when I drop you off tonight, just go home, look in the mirror and call yourself, whatever you want, but it should include the word artist. I mean, at the end of the day, only you decide what you call yourself. Nobody else gets to make that decision for you. The colourful painting on the wall in your room is amazing, and many more will come, including lots of shit ones as well, but just admit to yourself that you might have found your passion in this. So just accept it and enjoy it," he tapered off.

I was slightly overwhelmed.

Henry put his arm around my shoulder. "Mate, I hardly know you, but I can only say that Francis is right."

I was unable to hide my smile and couldn't remember having ever received such support for something that I had so much self-doubt about, especially from people I hardly knew. At the same time, it was good to hear that many other people have faced or are facing the same problems, even after years of experience.

I raised my glass, toasted, "Cheers, guys," and took a big sip.

That was my very first exhibition here in New Zealand. After this, it was pretty clear to me that I want to be that guy, standing in front of his own art, explaining what feeling went through my body and mind while painting the picture, and how magical the night or day was when I created it.

# 15.
# BIG NAN

"Ben," I heard Emma's voice again. "Ben, Jesus. What is wrong with you?" she said in a very annoyed tone.

"What's up, babe?" I said innocently, just to cover the fact that I had gone off dreaming again on the way to the Sunday roast.

"Ben, we're at Nan's place now. Come on!"

I could feel that I was pushing her anger management a lot today. I jumped out of the car and she pulled me aside.

"Just tell me what's up, Ben?"

"It's all good." I pulled out my standard answer.

"We both know that's it not, so it would be very helpful for both of us if you would escape out of your head and let me know what's going on up there," she said, pointing her finger at my forehead.

I still struggled to understand why she kept asking me what was up since she'd been there from the beginning when the drama was running its course. As much as I was closed up, she didn't want to address the topic either, and now it felt like we had missed the cue to actually talk about it properly. Therefore, my mind had made the decision to process it all on its own.

"Let's go inside, babe. Everything is fine, really."

We both knew that that wasn't true, but it was also clear that her

Nan's driveway was not the right place to talk about it. She just accepted it without saying a word. At the same time, I should have been very thankful that Emma knew me so well, that she was familiar with my getting caught inside my head.

Jay was already inside and we followed. We hung up our coats, took our shoes off and went into the living room, where her Nan was resting in her armchair, patiently waiting to welcome us.

"Hey, Big Nan," Emma said, kissing her cheek and smiling like a little child. I knew that Big Nan meant a lot to her. Emma was a family person through and through. She would have done anything for her family. It was the complete opposite situation to my family. I was one hundred percent enjoying how thoughtful and lovely they were with each other. The rest of the crew weren't there yet. Jay was in the kitchen while Nan, Emma and I were in the living room, talking about the day. Nan didn't join the Sunday walk as she needed to rest.

"Big Nan, would you like a tea?" Emma said. *Could it get more British?* I thought.

"That would be lovely, honey," Nan replied, and Emma left the room to make a cup of tea in the kitchen.

It was just me and Big Nan left in the living room. Big, because she was taller than little Nan, who was the mother of Emma's father.

For a few seconds, we were left in silence, and I was transfixed on one thought in particular, *Find a topic to talk about, come on!*

While I was thinking about that, Big Nan said, "So how are you, Ben?"

"I am good, Nan. Thank you," I replied politely while thinking about how nice it was that it was completely normal for me to call her Nan as well.

"No, how are you really?" she insisted.

She could see the surprise in my eyes. I was wondering if Jay or Emma might have mentioned anything about the current situation or something like that. I needed to reassure myself.

"What do you mean exactly, Nan?" I asked her.

She reached for my hand, took it and said, "I can't even imagine what you must have been through, but one thing I can imagine and I can see, you are not okay and you know what? It's totally fine to not be okay after what happened."

It was pretty clear she was confronting me with the truth, and the moment she said that I was pretty close to shedding a tear, but I was able to hold it back. At the same time, I was overwhelmed by the fact that someone I had hardly spoken to seemed to understand how I felt at that moment.

"Thank you," was the only thing I was able to say.

She pushed my hand even harder, and her eyes were telling me that I didn't need to thank her for confronting me with the truth.

"I just don't know how to deal with it, Nan," I said and sank my head to the floor, trying to avoid crying by any means necessary. Without me saying anything further, she took over talking again.

"You know, Ben, not everything in life goes as planned, and that's totally fine and normal. All that matters is how we react to it and what we make out of the unplanned stuff that comes our way."

She was right, and her words were making me both sad and happy at the same time. Again, silence crept in and I wondered how long it would take Emma to make the tea. I turned around and saw her in the door frame, smiling nostalgically with a cup of tea in her hand.

The moment she realised I'd seen her, she jumped up and walked towards Nan. "Here is your tea, Nan," she said. Emma looked at me, smiled and stroked my cheek. "I love you, Ben," she said. It was pretty clear that she had heard our little conversation.

I smiled and grabbed her hand, then turned back to Nan.

Big Nan looked at both of us and said, "Look at you two. I've just realised that I never heard the story of how you both actually met each other, and I think it's time to finally find out, don't you think so?"

Emma laughed and pointed at me. "It's your turn, Ben."

I started laughing as well. "It's a long story, Nan."

"I love a long story," Nan said.

The three of us smiled, and I said, "Alright, Big Nan, here we go."

# 16.
# A TRIPLE SHOT FLAT WHITE

It had been a pretty hectic day. I had just wrapped up my last painting, the one I had just finished the night before. I was not even sure if it was ready. This would later become the story of my life—I would never be able to tell if my artwork was finally finished or not. It can always be that little bit better, but every single step can also be that one step too much—the step that ends up ruining it. This makes it tricky, especially with paintings. Once the paint is on it, there is no way back. You can't just try to remove it. You need a strong imagination, the courage to make decisions and to take the consequences despite the outcome. The more I thought about it, the more and more unsure I got about this last piece of art. I wanted it to be perfect.

I carefully loaded the last painting into the back of my car and made my way to my first-ever exhibition as an artist.

I couldn't believe that this was about to happen within just one year of living in New Zealand. I still remember that day I was standing in front of Henry and Francis like it was yesterday. Since then, I have been on an emotional rollercoaster with myself. I painted like a maniac almost

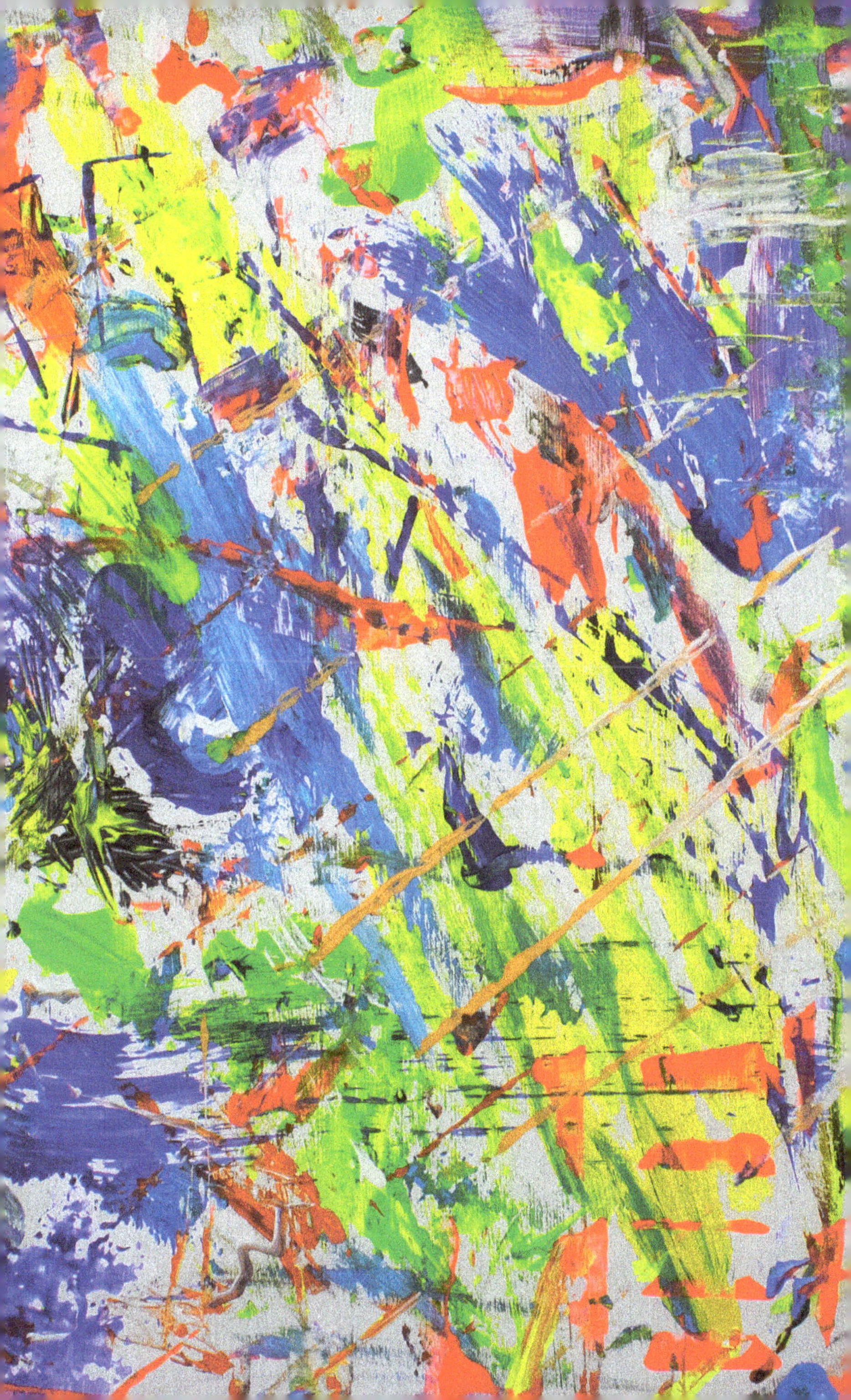

every day, not necessarily with less self-doubt, but I just kept on going and promised myself that I will stick to it no matter how often I'm going to fail. This unexpected journey had been crazy so far, and it was about to turn up another notch.

I met this guy, Sam, who wasn't a painter, but he loved art and had founded a collective for artists in New Zealand, to give them the opportunity to exhibit their pieces—something seemingly essential for an artist, in order to live from the activity they love to do. I met Sam in the café I was working in at the time. He stomped through the door one day, looked me straight in the eyes and ordered a triple shot flat white.

I said, "Seems like you had a proper bad night of sleep."

He smiled and said, "It's my usual, bro. Anything less than a triple shot wouldn't do the trick."

I laughed. "I would climb the walls after a triple, mate. How has your day been?"

By now, and thanks to Francis, "mate" had become a natural part of my English vocabulary.

"Very busy, man. Very busy. Got an exhibition on tonight and still behind schedule," he said.

"What kind of exhibition?" I wondered.

"I run an artist collective for abstract art."

"Oh, you're a painter?" I interrupted him.

"Nah, not really. I just like art. I draw like a ten year old, but I love to connect like-minded people and build a network for them, so they have the chance to exhibit their work," he explained.

"That's very kind of you." I turned around and started making his coffee. I filled the cup with three proper shots of fine, roasted coffee, frothed the milk and created a swan out of the foam. I pushed the lid on top of the cup, took a deep breath, turned around, passed him the cup and said in a very shy and quiet voice, "I'm a painter."

Sam grabbed the coffee while looking at me and said, "Cheers for the coffee, man."

My face froze for a second, and I didn't know what to do.

He faced the door as he was about to leave and turned around again. He grabbed something out of his pocket, then made a few steps back towards me and said, "This is my card. Send me an email with some of your work. I'll have a look at it. But next time stand up like a man, push out your chest, say it with pride and stop mumbling. I could hardly understand you, but I assumed you said that you're a painter."

I had a big smile on my face as I grabbed his card and said, "Says the mumbling Kiwi, but thanks. You'll have that mail in your inbox by tonight."

"Cheers, bro," he mumbled again in a very thick accent.

That same night following my shift, I took pictures of what I considered my best pieces and sent him a whole portfolio. The next day, I was pretty nervous at work and checked my phone, what felt like a million times. I refreshed my mail app four times an hour, and even before I went to bed, I checked it about six more times.

He probably had a busy day after the exhibition, I said to myself as I tried to fall asleep. The second night I told myself to stop being so impatient since it had only been forty-eight hours.

*I'll give him a week*, I thought after five nights.

I don't want him to see me as an annoying idiot, I told myself on the seventh night.

Hopefully, he comes back to the café so I can talk to him, the voice in my head said to me after ten days.

After two weeks, I had lost faith and pretty much told myself to forget it, it's not going to happen.

I slowly stopped checking my mail and almost ceased to think about it. It had been twenty days without a reply. I was cleaning the coffee machine and my shift was almost over. Everything was pretty much packed up until I heard a voice saying, "Do you still do coffees?"

"No, sorry, I am just packing up," I said without looking at who was speaking to me.

"Not even a triple shot?" I recognised that voice now, and of course

I remembered the only customer that I'd ever had who took three shots of coffee in a flat white.

"Ah hey, mate," I said in the most neutral way possible. I didn't know if I should be happy that he'd come back again or mad that he'd never replied to my mail. Then I remembered how he told me off last time, and with a very determined voice I decided to say, "You didn't reply to my mail."

He winked an eye and said, "You didn't follow it up, mate."

My face froze again and so many thoughts at the same time were running through my head. One question was on top of all these thoughts, though. "Did you do that on purpose?" I asked, almost angry.

"No, bro, I was busy and I get about twenty of those emails every week. I just can't reply to everyone and look at everything. Otherwise, I wouldn't get my own stuff done. The focus is the collective. I can only reply to those who are annoying the shit out of me every week, so they stop annoying me when I give them what they want."

I was confused. "So, if I was an annoying idiot with shit paintings but followed up with you every two days, then you would have replied?" I asked, and this time I actually was angry.

"No, mate, it's about balance. Of course, the focus is on the quality of your work, your talent and your skills, but those things just by themselves don't make you a good artist! It's also about your will. How much do you want to make this your living? How much do you want to inspire other people with the messages your art spreads? How much do you want to see your paintings in other people's living rooms?"

"Okay, okay, I get it," I said.

"But to answer your question truthfully, yes, actually the annoying jerk with the shitty artwork would at least get an email back from me," he admitted before apologising.

"Sorry, man, but I was super busy and forgot about it."

"All good. I could have followed up at least once," I replied.

"It's in your hands, even though it might not seem like it sometimes. It's all up to you. How much do you want it?" he asked.

"I don't know," I said.

"There we go. Maybe make your mind up before next Friday."

"Next Friday?" I wondered aloud.

"Yes, I have another exhibition on at the Auckland Art Gallery and one of my artists just jumped off, so there are a few free spaces on the wall that need filling. Are you in?"

I didn't need to think about it for a second. "Of course I am! Thank you, man! Thanks a lot!" I tried to stay calm, but inside I felt like I was bouncing up and down on a trampoline.

"Alright, I'll see you next Friday. Never forget you need to work hard for your dreams in order to achieve them. Assuming that this is your dream," he said.

I just nodded my head.

"Mhmm, there's just one condition," he followed up.

"Whatever you want!" I replied.

Sam smiled, "One triple shot flat white please."

# 17.
# MEETING EMMA

## Boy Oh Boy - Meeting Emma

I was still thinking about how I had met Sam when a loud honk startled me, ripping me from my thoughts. I looked up, refocused and noticed that there was no one in front of me. Fifty metres ahead there was a green traffic light.

"Ohhh shit," I muttered to myself. I accelerated and crossed the intersection just in time, right before the green light turned back to amber. I looked at the clock in the car and realised that I was running very late.

It had been exactly one week since Sam had invited me to that exhibition. I had my top five pieces of artwork in the trunk of my little wannabe Jeep—a Toyota RAV4. All I could think about was the exhibition and if someone would actually buy one of my pieces. After all, I had nothing to lose.

I would meet lots of new people who might struggle in the same way that I always do. We might even share some of the same thoughts. Either way, I knew this night should be a success and would be the first little milestone of a life without a proper plan. I could hear my mum's voice in my head. I hadn't told her what I was doing yet, but I would imagine she would have many questions. Can you live off it? How much money do you get? How does that contribute to your pension? Ben, you need to think about your future! What about when you get older?

Ever since I set forth on this adventure, she had been worried about me and my future. It's not like she wanted to stop me or convince me not to do it. It was just her way of projecting her concerns onto my life. In her ideal world, I'd be back in Germany already continuing my sales career, but this thought never ever crossed my mind again since Francis took me to the pop art exhibition. That day, I entered a different path, one that was about to turn my life upside down, in the most exciting way possible.

One last left turn and I arrived at the Auckland Art Gallery. Lucky for me, I found a parking space just around the corner. I grabbed my paintings one by one and entered the art gallery two hours prior to opening. The first person I spotted was Sam, who welcomed me.

"Hey, mate, I see you've found your way just in time."

"Yes, I did. Thanks for the opportunity, man," I replied gratefully.

"No worries. Come with me and I'll show you where you can put up your artwork."

It was a single, large room with nice, wide windows. In the middle was a three-sided wall, in the shape of a triangle if viewed from above. One of the three sides was still blank.

"There it is. That free space is for you. Hang your paintings up in the dedicated area, and then join us for a welcome drink. I will introduce you to the others and at eight p.m. we'll open the doors," he explained.

I responded to him with a quick "Cheers, mate," and immediately started putting up my work. After hanging up the last painting on the wall, I took a step back and glanced up at it. Overall, I was pretty satisfied with it. On the other side of the room, I saw a group of people gathering together, and in the middle of it was Sam with his big head. He waved me over. I followed his wave through the crowd, and he reached over to hand me a fresh glass of bubbly.

"Are you happy with how it looks?" he asked me.

"Yes, I am, mate. I think it's okay."

"Just, okay? What did I tell you about presenting yourself with pride, my friend," Sam retorted.

"Yes, I know mate," and I corrected my initial answer to an "It's great."

With a shake of his head, Sam changed the subject. "Anyways, let me introduce you to the others." There were six other artists present, three women and three men. He introduced me to every single one of them. There was one guy who caught my attention straightaway.

"Hey, I am Matt. How are you?" I could tell by his accent that he was European as well, and his face looked pretty familiar.

"I'm fine, thanks. How are you?" I replied in a very polite manner.

"That's Matt, he's Dutch and one of our most talented abstract painters. These are some of his paintings." Sam gestured and pointed at the wall behind us. Indeed, they looked very intimidating, like everything else present in that room. There was one painting in Matt's area that I definitely had seen before.

"Do I know you?" I asked him curiously.

Matt looked a bit surprised, but then he started thinking and said, "I actually think we might have met before."

"Henry?" I said.

"Yes! Now I remember!" Matt shouted. "And how many paintings have you thrown away in the meantime?" he asked amusingly.

We both had to laugh, while Sam looked rather confused. We told him about our first meeting at the pop-up art exhibition, and Sam beamed—I already had made a connection to someone in the collective.

I kept looking around at every other piece of art. All of them looked so much better and more professional in my eyes. More details, better colours, more advanced techniques, just better. I am my biggest critic just as everyone else probably is, but sometimes it gets to the point where I start to dislike myself and start dismissing my work in front of other people.

The clock was showing 7:55 p.m., and Sam made his final announcement. He wished for nothing but fun and good sales for everyone tonight. I grabbed another glass of bubbly and placed myself next to my wall of art. My paintings were hanging right opposite to Matt's. I could tell by his look that he was searching for the words to start a conversation with me about my work.

"So, when did you start painting then?" he asked.

"Just about a year ago. Literally, a couple of days before I went to that pop-up art event with my mate Francis."

"For real? Wow, that makes your work even more impressive," he said, almost slightly overwhelmed.

I didn't know how to react. It's hard to take compliments from others because I don't consider myself to be any good. "Thanks, Matt, to be honest, your work is really amazing. How did you get those colour shades in the top right one?"

I sincerely meant it. I truly thought of him as an amazing artist, and I wasn't even sure if I would sell anything tonight. I tried to reduce the pressure I'd put on myself. I told myself to just relax and enjoy having the opportunity to be here tonight.

Matt looked at the painting I had just pointed at. He was about to delve into properly explaining the technical aspects of his shading skills when right at that very moment someone tapped me on the shoulder.

"Excuse me," a female voice said.

I turned around and in front of me was an overwhelmingly beautiful girl. My breathing turned into irregular short gasps. "Ye-Yes, please," I managed to say.

She had slightly curly blond hair, rose-tinged lips, shiny white teeth, little freckles on her cheeks and round eyes.

"Who is the artist behind these two paintings?" she asked in a very charming but also peculiar British accent.

"Ehm, th-those two were actually painted by me, why?" I realised in that very same second that the "why" was quite unnecessary.

"I'm just curious. I really like those two, and I was just wondering what the thoughts and the message behind them were. I thought the artist might be able to help me out with that," she queried in the most heavenly tone.

Her conclusion made total sense, apart from the fact that I had never painted with a proper message or thought in mind. I simply paint, and when I think it looks good, I am done—the work is complete. There's nothing more to it.

I didn't want to look like a total fool, and I glanced at the two paintings she pointed at. One of them was completely in black and white; you could see the outline and shades of a human being in a very sad and abstract environment.

The other, however, was quite special. It was very colourful, looking like a cluster of palm leaves divided into the entire colour spectrum. It was the first artwork I had ever done. Technically the second, but I still don't consider the blackmail letter as art—the one that Francis and I had painted. At this moment, I realised that I did at least have a story behind this one.

"On my first night in my flat here in New Zealand, I locked myself in my room, listened to the entire Caribou album 'Our Love' on repeat and came up with this to cheer myself up and show myself how colourful and full of joy this place actually is. It was the first-ever real painting I created," I heard myself explaining.

"And the other one?" she asked right away.

I laughed, and told her, "I have no idea." She smiled back at me, making me smile even more.

"Why do you ask?" I wondered.

"I don't know—it's very interesting that one artist has such a contrast in his work. I was wondering what might go on in his head, that he

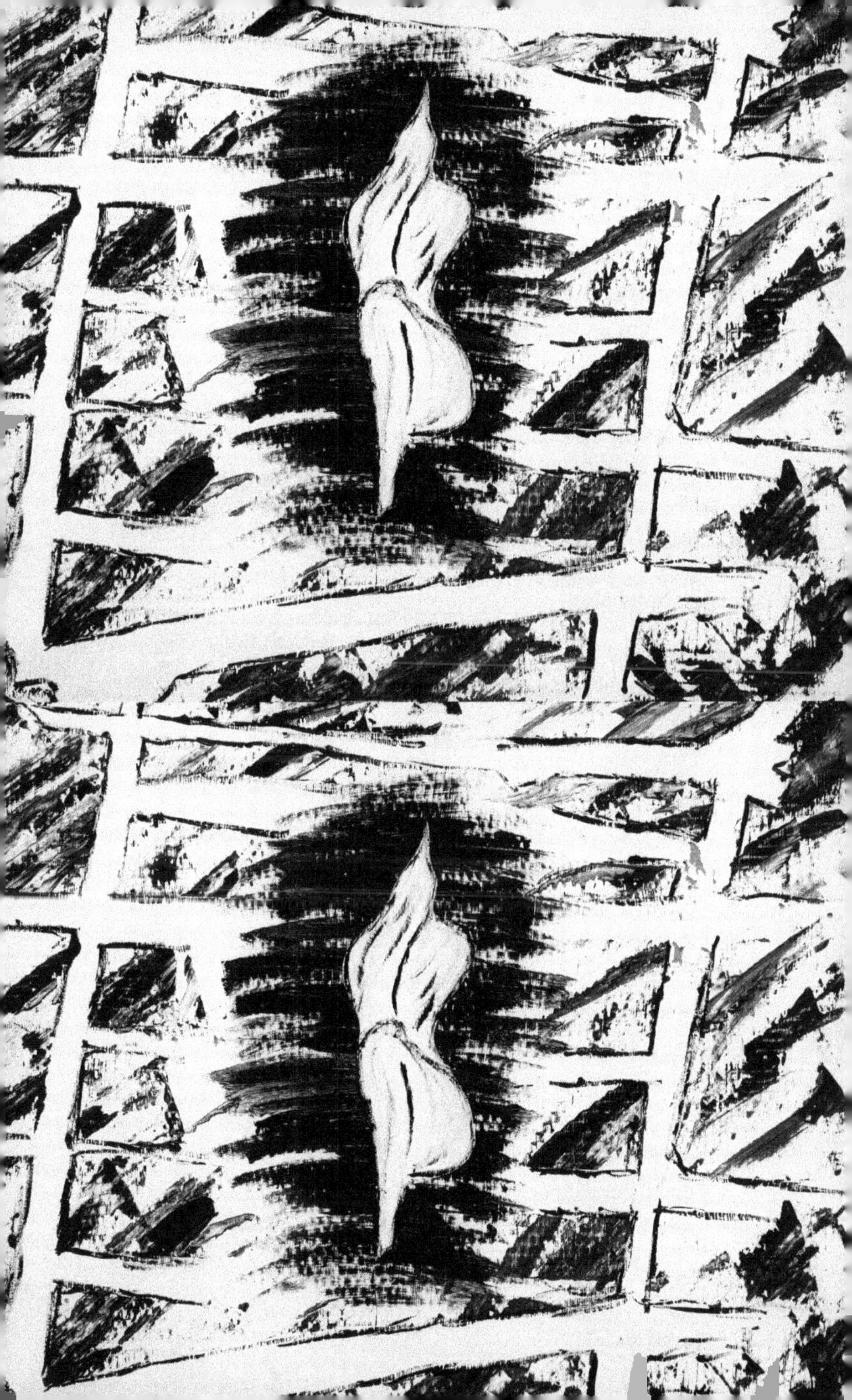

can create such a dark atmosphere in one painting and such a bright, colourful landscape in the other," she said, with a lot of curiosity in her voice.

"That is a very good question," I responded, amused.

Her head started to gravitate towards Matt's paintings. She was about to turn around and leave when I was able to come up with a follow-up question.

"Where does this deep interest in art come from?" I asked, hoping that she would linger for a while longer.

"I just like it. It takes my mind off the typical day-to-day business. It makes me wonder and inspires me to aspire to new adventures in life, ones that I probably will never go on anyway."

"Well, you made it halfway around the world for some reason. I consider that an adventure in itself." You could see the surprise on her face.

"How?" she asked, looking confused.

"Your accent is pretty obvious," I laughed.

"Okay, smart arse, you can't hide your German accent either," she retorted.

*Fair point*, I thought, but would never admit that out loud. "I'm Ben, by the way," I spurted out, summoning the courage to introduce myself.

"Hi, I'm Emma."

"Nice to meet you, Emma. I hope you're enjoying the exhibition so far," sounding as though I'd been doing this for years.

"Yeah, I actually have, up to the point where I met a weird German who likes Caribou," she said in a slightly provocative way.

*Challenge accepted*, I thought to myself.

"Fair enough, my evening has gotten weird as well. I met a very confused British woman who asked some very strange questions."

I don't know if our little conversation could be considered flirting, but there was something about Emma that caught my attention from the very first second of our encounter.

"I understand. I might see you later. I have to go and ask a few more strange questions," she said, as she walked away.

I laughed and wished her a lovely evening, and I could see her wandering off towards Matt. I felt somewhat paralysed and kept thinking about that big smile of hers. The night went on, and apart from Emma, I had several more interesting conversations, but nothing as promising as selling any of my paintings. After a while, I looked around the room and tried to find her again. It was a pretty large room filled to the brim with people. I convinced myself that she was gone, and I could sense some sadness and regret welling up inside of me. I would have loved to be able to spend a bit more time talking to her. I figured that I could use a top-up of my now empty glass and strolled over, only for a melodic British voice to chime from behind my back.

"Are you looking for one of these?"

I turned around—there she was again. "Actually yes, I wouldn't mind another," I responded, flabbergasted.

I cannot truly describe my elated feelings at that moment but, to say it in a simple way, I was happy to see that Emma was back. We started chatting about art, music, her reasons for coming to New Zealand and all those sorts of things. After some time had elapsed, I looked up and noticed that almost everyone had gone. Matt came up to us and said,

"You guys look like you're getting along really well."

I was overwhelmed and didn't know what to say, so I said something stupid like,

"Yeah, similar interests."

Emma looked at her watch and realised what time it was.

"Ahh, man, it's already past eleven p.m. I gotta work tomorrow. Where is my friend?" she asked.

"She said goodbye about an hour ago, Emma," I laughed.

"Oh really? Shit. I really need to go. It was super nice to meet you, Ben."

"Yes, it was," I spurted out, not knowing what else to do.

Emma gave me a short hug and turned towards the door.

I looked somewhat helplessly at Matt.

He figured what was going on and uttered something very quietly but clearly. "Come on, man." Then he gestured towards Emma.

I wasn't quite sure if I would be brave enough to tell her what was on my mind, but as she grabbed the door, I shouted out to her, "Emma, wait!"

She stopped, turned around and I ran after her.

"I'm—I was wondering if...you'd like...ehm...to meet up sometime?" I managed to construct a full sentence.

She smiled, looked at me and said, "I *would* like to, if I am honest. I enjoyed tonight, but I can't. I have a boyfriend. Sorry!" She turned back towards the door and left.

I was standing at the entrance, a little shocked. I looked at Matt and shrugged my shoulders.

Yes, that was the night I met Emma.

# 18.
# PENGUINS MATE FOR LIFE

I was laying on the bed in my room, watching YouTube videos on my phone about how male penguins impress females. *Yes, I should be painting*, I was thinking, and *Yes, I am procrastinating*. In the same second, while thinking about how I could waste more time and distract myself from what I would rather be doing, a notification popped up on the top part of my phone screen and a loud *bing* interrupted the voice of the YouTube narrator. It was right in the second where he was talking about the "X factor" a male penguin could utilise as a game-changer in finding a mate.

"Emma W. sent you a friend request," I read in the Facebook notification box that popped up on my phone. It took me about two seconds to realise what had just happened. My breath stopped and I dropped my phone. *Luckily my phone screen has never ever cracked in my whole life*, I thought, leaving it on the floor upside down. *Maybe it's someone else and not the person I was thinking about*, was the thought that followed immediately. *Do I know another Emma?* was my third thought.

"Sam!" I shouted through the whole house.

"What's up, mate?" I heard him say with a slight echo.

A while ago I had to leave my old flat because Alexandre and the English dude had to give up the place and after my second exhibition, Sam told me that he had a big spare room in his loft I could use as a bedroom and even for painting if I'd like. We'd been flatmates for over a month at this point.

"Do you know a girl named Emma?" I shouted again.

Sam's head popped around the door frame. "Why are you shouting, bro? I'm right here. And no, I don't know a girl called Emma," he said. "Ahhh wait." It looked as though he remembered something. "Apart from the girl you kept talking about for weeks after your first exhibition. The one with the boyfriend. Her name was Emma, wasn't it?" He looked a bit unsure.

I don't know why I even asked him. Perhaps I just wanted this friend request to be from someone else.

"Ahhh yeah, maybe, yeah. I think her name was Emma," I played along.

"All good, don't worry," I said, wanting to escape the situation. I bent over to pick up my phone.

"Fuck!" I screamed.

Sam, who had already left the room, turned around, ran back towards the door, popped his head around the frame again and asked, "What's up?"

"My phone screen just cracked! Shit!" I said.

I opened my Facebook app, looked up my notifications and saw it again. Emma W. sent you a friend request. I clicked on her profile, but already the little picture in the notification timeline gave it away. Just to be 100 percent sure that it was her, I loaded her profile page, opened her profile picture and dropped my phone again.

Sam was still in the door frame.

"What's up, mate?" he asked the third time within the last two minutes.

"It's her!" I said.

"Who?" he asked.

"The girl from the exhibition, you idiot."

"Ahhh, the girl with the boyfriend." Sam clocked on and asked, "What's up with her?"

"She sent me a friend request on Facebook," I said.

"Okay, I still can't figure out the reason why that's worth a new phone screen," he said with a big smile.

"I don't know, I was just shocked for a second."

"Why though?" he wondered.

"I don't know. I enjoyed meeting her at the exhibition and I've been thinking about that night a lot, but then I forgot about her. I mean she has a boyfriend anyway."

"Exactly, so where is the problem?" Sam said.

"There isn't one, it's all good," I agreed.

I just wanted to get rid of him. He wasn't much help, to be honest. Or maybe he was, by just taking it easy and not overthinking the whole situation like I was doing. Just because I am accepting her friend request doesn't mean I have to marry her. But then the truth passed through my mind. What if I like her for real? If we were Facebook friends, I could stalk her and virtually fall in love with her, but she wouldn't fall for me because she had a boyfriend. The whole thinking process made total sense to me. I would just probably get hurt.

"And now you are officially friends on Facebook," Sam said with the biggest smile ever.

"What the hell did you do?" I was raging. I was so caught up in my thoughts that I didn't realise he'd grabbed my phone and accepted her friend request on my behalf.

"Calm down. You are completely overthinking it. You just have to stay in control," he said.

I laughed and asked, "In control? Do you think I have lost control?"

"Ben, I've known you for a while now. Not saying that you have lost control, but I know that you are the master of overthinking things and, in my opinion, life is a lot easier than you think. Just stop searching for the meaning in everything, and stop being afraid of the consequences. Just go with it. Yes, you might get hurt if she still has a boyfriend, but at least you'll have had the experience. Isn't that better than always protecting yourself from your fears and not really living, because in the end you always hold back?"

I felt like I'd heard similar stuff before from a different guy with the same accent. Maybe he'd hit the nail on the head though, just maybe. It's still very hard for me to admit that someone else might be right, but in this particular case, I think he was right.

"Give me my phone back, you cheeky idiot," I smiled wryly.

Sam passed me the phone and said, "I'll leave you to it," as he left my room.

"All good," I mumbled to myself sarcastically. "You've already done enough damage."

I let myself fall back onto my bed and stared at the ceiling, pensively. "Okay, just relax and stop overthinking. It was just a friend request."

Anyway, I just preferred to get on with my penguin mating studies, to keep procrastinating and distract myself from the painting I'd initially wanted to paint. At least, that was the plan, until another loud "bing" interrupted my penguin documentary for a second time. Once again, a little window on my phone popped up—

Emma W.: Hey! How are you?

# 19.
# COLD SHOWER

"**C**ome on, let's go, I want a beer!" Sam shouted down the hallway. We were meant to catch up for a few Friday drinks with some folks from the collective. We did this once a month to talk about upcoming exhibitions or work in progress, but honestly, mainly to drink. I was late as per usual—I was still painting. After I finished my one-hour documentary on penguins, it left me with just a little time to paint before I had to get ready. It felt like a vicious circle. I can't be creative unless I watch stupid stuff to distract myself from actually picking up the brush. I waste so much time that I usually end up with just twenty to thirty minutes until my next appointment. So, I finally start to paint, get a little creative and then get so pissed off with myself and everyone else, that I have to stop again after only a short amount of time. At this point, I usually say to myself, "If I didn't have that stupid appointment, I would have accomplished so much more."

"No, you wouldn't!" Sam said.

"Oh, man, did I say that loud?" I asked while I could answer that question myself as well.

"Okay, two minutes and I'm ready," I said to Sam.

I put on a sweater, jumped into my sneakers, grabbed my jacket and ran downstairs after Sam. It took me ten minutes (not two), so he was already out waiting in the taxi.

"You pay for the waiting time," he said.

I just smiled and hoped he wouldn't make me as I jumped into the car.

"How is it going with Emma?" He asked with his big cheeky smile again.

*What a dumb question*, I thought

"What do you mean? How is it going?" I replied defiantly.

"Are you texting?" he asked.

"No, we aren't," I raised my voice.

"Why not?" he kept asking.

"Well, she texted me and I didn't reply. End of the story."

"Why?"

"Because I didn't want to," raising my voice even more.

"You're scared," he smiled.

"No—I'm—not!" I stated out loud and clear.

"Yes, you are. Scared you could hurt yourself. I told you." His sarcasm and ironic tone of voice got me thinking again.

"Just stop it, mate, and tell me when the next exhibition is happening," I demanded.

"Why? You haven't even finished a single new piece of art since the last one, Mr. Procrastinator," putting on his cheeky ironic smile again.

"Is that my new nickname?" I asked, simultaneously thinking that it was pretty accurate.

Sam confirmed that I was procrastinating too much when, in the same second, the taxi stopped. I looked outside the car and a few drops were trickling down the backseat window. It was a rather fresh, wet evening, but through the raindrops, you could see some lights and a few people with cigarettes outside, in front of something that looked like our usual go-to bar.

"Here we are, guys," the taxi driver said and turned around.

"Let's go, Ben," Sam said, putting a twenty dollar note in the taxi driver's outstretched hand.

We jumped out of the car, ran towards the door to avoid the rain, pushed it open and stumbled into the bar like two big, clumsy elephants. Everyone turned their heads towards us, and a small group of people in the left-hand corner shouted "Hey!"

Matt and a few others from the collective had been waiting for us. We joined them around the table, ordered some drinks and started to talk about the upcoming exhibition. Sam was presenting some facts about the next dates, location and time.

During this, Matt leaned over to me and asked, "So, how's it going?"

"Yeah, it's alright. How are you?" I asked back to be polite.

"I'm fine, thanks, mate. Any new work done?" Matt asked me in a somewhat judgemental tone.

I never really talked to him apart from a few of the previous exhibitions when our art was hanging opposite or next to each other. "To be honest, I'm procrastinating a lot lately," I admitted.

"Are you?" he shook his head.

"Yes, I am, and I'm certainly not proud of it," I winced meekly.

"The question is why are you procrastinating?" he asked.

*What an interesting question*, I thought.

"Let me guess. You think you aren't good enough," he said, winking an eye.

"That is probably a good point," I replied.

"Most common thing, my friend. You keep holding yourself back from reaching your full potential," he said.

"But it sounds so arrogant when I tell myself that I am really good at painting," I said, trying to sound as objective as possible.

"It's not arrogant to wake up in the morning and tell yourself you're great," he said.

"Yeah, I know," I answered, but did I truly know?

"And you probably tell yourself, don't even start—it's not worth it," he kept hitting the spot.

I felt like Matt was reading my mind. "How do you know? Have you been there?" I asked him.

His answer didn't even take a second. "Of course! Everyone has been there, in a way. The most arrogant thought you can have is that you think you are the only one feeling like that. The main thing is that you need to know is how to get yourself out of it."

"Yeah, and that is probably where I struggle," I admitted.

"You know what, Ben? You already took the biggest step in your life anyway."

"I don't understand. What do you mean by that?" I looked at him like a penguin trying to figure out how to jump from one iceberg to another, without falling into the ice-cold water.

"Well, most people don't even make it to the point you're at. Most people have a plan."

"What plan?" I asked.

"Well, a life plan, I guess, to make them feel safe. They have a job and a stable income that will guarantee them some sort of protection from harder times, when something unexpected happens that wasn't part of their plan. Then they can react accordingly and do everything they can to return to the initial coordinates as quickly as possible. It also protects them from procrastinating, because their path is already laid out."

"That doesn't sound too bad," I said.

"Yeah, it's okay. But do you just want to live 'okay' or 'not too bad'?" he asked.

"I don't know. I would like every day to be awesome, but sometimes I feel like it's impossible," I replied.

"Yeah, it is hard to guarantee that, but what I meant is, with your paintings, you follow something that fulfils you on a different level. Who knows if you're ever going to live off it. Only God knows. But the question is what do you do after finishing your shift in the café?" Matt asked.

"I go home and watch documentaries about the most stupid stuff in the world. Did you know that penguins mate for life?" I said and started laughing out loud.

Sam looked at me like my dad used to, his eyes trying to say something like shut up! He had noticed a long time ago that Matt and I were drifting off topic, but he didn't make any attempt to interrupt us—that's Sam. He saw that this wasn't just a conversation about football, women or beer. Sam was into deep chats as well, and he supported them throughout the collective, even if that meant that you wouldn't pay attention to his presentation.

"Yes, but you just do that to distract yourself from what you actually wanted to do, right?" Matt picked up on my last words again.

"I would love to go home and paint like Leonardo da Vinci, and sometimes I feel like I can and paint for hours. I forget about the time and I am just happy, but recently, most days, I end up watching videos on YouTube," I explained.

"Maybe you think I'm dumb, but there's a difference between coming home from work and watching something because you don't have anything else to do with yourself, or coming home and watching something because you think you aren't good enough for the actual thing you wanted to do. You are already one step closer. A massive step closer," Matt tried making a point without interrupting Sam's speech.

"It feels like an inner fight sometimes," I tried to whisper.

"I feel you, my friend. For a long time, I felt the same until one day, the morning was unusual. I got up and felt devastated and caught up in my head for no reason, until the moment I jumped in the shower. It changed my day and later on my life. It was just a cold shower. I am saying this because it can be that simple. It's a trick in your mind. If you tell yourself you aren't good enough and you don't stop comparing yourself with other people, it's nearly impossible to find your inner peace and wake up your creative flow. You have to go easy on yourself. You have to see the whole process. Without knowing you that well, I guess your paintings today have improved massively compared to the artworks you did one year ago, two years ago or three years ago."

*Two or three years ago I wasn't even painting*, I thought. Matt noticed that I was thinking deeply. He was right though—I hadn't seen things that way.

He continued, "This is about personal progress and not you comparing yourself to the rest of the world. It is not a race. It is about you doing what you love to do. The act of painting and being creative makes you happy, not the acknowledgement you might get from the outside world."

He totally got into his flow and every sentence hit like an arrow, into the middle of the target.

I didn't even dare to interrupt him, so I just said, "I think you are right."

"One last thing, before Sam comes and gets between us anyway. In my opinion, having a plan in your life doesn't mean you have a happy life. Yes, it might give you some sort of security, but to me, having a plan mostly means a life full of missed opportunities, because you didn't have the courage to let your plan go and take the risk."

That last one hit me deep inside, like a lightning bolt. I think he was fully right, but I was brought up to believe that it is important to have a plan, a career, a steady income and goals to constantly improve your financial situation.

"There is one thing I didn't quite understand," I said to Matt.

"What is it, my friend?" he asked curiously awaiting my reply.

"What has the cold shower got to do with all that?" He started laughing, and right in that second, Sam appeared behind us.

"I see you guys enjoyed my speech. I hope you got all the information for the next exhibition," he said. Even though I said Sam would enjoy and support deep talks, I supposed we may have pushed the boundaries in terms of interruptions a bit too far.

"Of course, man, we got it," I pretended.

"Do you guys want another beer?" he asked us.

"Yes, please!" I said, speaking for both myself and Matt.

Sam turned around and went towards the bar.

"Just one thing about the shower," Matt started. "If you get stuck in the morning, evening or anytime during the day while you trying to be creative or productive or just not feeling it, take your pants off and have a nice cold shower," he smiled. "Trust me, it will change your day immediately," he followed up.

I didn't have anything to add to this and just thought that this was a nice way to finish that life-advice session with Matt.

# 20

# LAST ROUND

"You won't believe who I just saw, guys!" Sam said, excited like a little child as he plopped three full pints of beer on the table. "No, we probably won't," I replied in a bored tone.

"You can guess—I'll give you a hint!" he said.

"Stop playing those stupid games, mate," I groaned.

"Long—blond—hair…"

Right in that second, something clicked in my head and immediately my facial expression changed from very bored to super scared.

"No, no, no," I said.

"Yes, yes, yes, bro," Sam said.

I looked at Matt and could see that he hadn't clocked on yet. I almost started to panic, not knowing what to do.

"Just relax and drink your beer, mate. It's all good." Sam tried to calm me down. He could tell by my reaction that his attempt at a joke didn't really make anyone laugh apart from him.

"I should go home now," I moaned.

"Don't be stupid," Sam said.

I didn't even dare to look around, because I was actually afraid to bump into her. I grabbed my jacket from the chair underneath me, looked at Sam and Matt and said, "Sorry guys, but I need to leave." Sam was shaking his head and Matt's eyes were full of question marks. I slammed my beer and hammered the empty pint on the table. "Bye."

But as I turned around, I bumped into a big bunch of hair. I stepped back a bit, hit the table behind me, scooped the hair out of my mouth and eyes, then looked up and heard,

"Hey, Ben."

I was speechless. There she was again. A few months after the exhibition, where she told me that she had a boyfriend, Emma was literally standing right in front of me.

"Hey," was all I managed to squeak out.

"Well, since you haven't replied to my message, I thought I should ask you in person. How are you?"

*Well, since you started flirting with me just to tell me, the moment I had all my courage together, that you have a boyfriend, is reason enough not to answer your stupid Facebook message*, I thought.

"I'm fine, thanks," I replied. "What are you doing here?" I followed up after a few seconds of silence because I didn't know what else to say. I just wanted to run out of the bar but thought I would look like a fool, so I decided not to.

"Just having a few drinks with some friends," she said with her British accent. I could have answered that myself. What else is anyone doing on a Friday night in a bar?

"Actually, I've been stalking you," she added.

I wanted to reassure myself that I got it right, but she noticed my surprised face and followed it up with a short "just kidding." I wasn't in the best mood for jokes even though it was the weekend and I already had a couple of beers.

"Well, I was just about to leave," I decided to say.

"Oh really, that's a shame. I was just about to ask you about the artist's meaning behind this beautiful piece of art?" she said, and pointed at a painting hanging behind the bar—mine again. The owner of the bar is a sucker for art and came to almost every exhibition. That's why we do our monthly meetings here. Last time, to my own surprise, he bought one of my paintings and hung it up in the bar. I was wondering if she knew that it was mine, or if she just wanted to refer back to the conversation we'd had when we met for the first time.

"Ehm...it's mine," I said.

"I know," Emma replied.

"How?" I wanted to know.

"Saw it on your Facebook."

"So, you *are* stalking me?" I asked.

"Only a little bit," she admitted.

I was trying to figure out what was going on with this girl and, at the same time, I noticed the same sensations as last time. Again, as a reaction to self-protection, I wanted to run away.

"Can I buy you a drink?" she asked.

I was holding back and didn't know what to say.

"Yes, you can!" Sam shouted from behind me.

I forgot both of them were still standing right behind me, watching this freak show.

"Don't run away please. I'll be right back in a second," Emma teased as she ventured to the bar. I wondered whether I had a choice. I didn't even dare to look at Sam, I could easily predict his face telling me to wait. I was surprised he didn't tie me to the table so I couldn't run away.

It's easy for me to run away. I do that a lot. When I just procrastinate, I run away from my actual fear of not being good enough to create a painting worthy of my own expectations. I don't know why or how, but a voice in my head told me to stay.

Emma came back with a pint of lager and a glass of what looked like purply red juice.

"I hope you like lager," she smiled.

"Yes, I do. Thank you. But it looks like you don't."

"No, I can't drink beer. I don't really like it," she said.

"So, you don't drink?" I asked, thinking she would want to toast with a glass of freshly pressed juice.

"I do. Vodka cranberry," she said short and sharp, just so she could get straight to the point in the next second.

"So why didn't you answer me?"

Emma didn't even waste a second trying to make small talk. However, I wanted to accept the challenge of her being so direct. Therefore, I thought it would be a good idea to go with the truth.

"Isn't that obvious? You have a boyfriend."

"Had," she interrupted me.

I guzzled my beer and then spurted half of it onto the floor.

"Ah, okay," I said and looked to the side, very shyly.

"You like me, don't you?" she confronted me.

Now I was a little bit overwhelmed by her brutally direct way of addressing feelings and thoughts. I'm used to people making up excuses or stories, just so they can avoid saying what they really think and feel. For some reason though, I slowly started to enjoy her honesty. I decided to brave up a bit and play along.

"Maybe that's why I didn't reply," I pondered.

"I thought so."

"Well, I don't like girls flirting behind their boyfriend's back."

"I understand that. That's one reason why I left."

"I don't get it," I said.

"I left because I felt like we had a little connection and I couldn't handle it. My relationship had run its course a long time ago and I had reached my breaking point, but I hadn't ended it yet when I met you, and I didn't want you to think exactly what you thought in the end, you know?" she said abjectly.

"I kind of do," I replied.

She lifted her glass to toast.

"Cheers to what?" I asked, rather confused.

"Cheers for being honest and a very interesting artist. I very much like your stuff, especially the *Caribou* painting," she said.

"*Caribou* painting! That's an interesting name for it. Let's call it that. Thank you," I replied.

"Yes, it's my absolute favourite," she said almost a little shyly.

We kept on talking and talking and I totally forgot about Sam and Matt. At some point, I turned around and couldn't see them anywhere.

"Have you seen my friends?" I asked Emma.

"No, I haven't, but have you seen mine?" she asked.

We both turned around peeking through the bar, a bit lost. Lots of people have already left. Oliver the barkeeper noticed our desperate and timeless looks.

"Sam and Matt left about an hour ago, mate," he shouted across the bar. "And the rest as well..." he continued just to finish with a classic "...last round by the way."

I absolutely lost all sense of time and space, almost like the first time I met Emma, and almost like that time I'd painted the Caribou artwork.

We both already had a few drinks, and you could see in our eyes that we both were thinking the same thing.

"What's the plan?" she asked.

# 21.
# THE NEXT MORNING

## BAILE, Haulm - Knows No End

I opened my eyes and saw a bunch of long blond hair. Some of it had found its way into my mouth again. I wondered how can someone have so much hair, and why it always ends up in my face.

What perhaps everyone else would have predicted had happened. I didn't know what to do. Emma was still asleep. I was overwhelmed by my own feelings and had a bit of a headache. I tried to reach the water glass next to the bed. I took a sip and tried to rearrange last night in my head. Still overwhelmed by the situation, I was thinking about grabbing my clothes and just leaving. If I did that, then we would both classify this as a one-night stand. If I stayed, we might as well have breakfast together and it could grow into something serious, but does she want that? I mean, she just came out of a relationship.

*Last night was so amazing*, I thought, even though I was afraid once again. I don't know what she thinks. I turned to the side, put my feet on the ground and reached for my pants.

"You are not trying to sneak out, are you?" I heard Emma saying.

*Busted*, I thought. "To be honest I don't know what I am trying to do here. Maybe you can tell me."

"Hmm, how about you leave your pants on the floor and relax. I can get up and make us some breakfast," she offered.

"So, this is not a one-night stand then?" I asked.

"Do you want it to be one?"

"Not really, Emma, I hate one-night stands. I'm just really unsure since the last time I was in this situation was years ago. But back then, I at least knew that I wasn't into her. It's a bit different now," I said completely honestly.

"Well, if it were a one-night stand, I wouldn't offer you breakfast. That's for sure," she said.

Emma got up, put her pyjamas on and left the room. I had a look around her room and was wholly surprised about what I discovered there. I saw a lot of very interesting photographs hanging on the wall and from the ceiling. I didn't quite understand. Both times we'd met, we talked and talked for ages, but she never mentioned anything about photography. When I had asked her about her hobbies, she said sports, partying and catching up with friends. Her room clearly didn't confirm that. It more looked like the bedroom of Paul Ripke.

I took a closer look at some of the pictures. There were photographs of stars, portraits and nature. I was amazed by how stunning they were—purely inspiring. One, in particular, caught my attention; it was this beautiful breaking wave at a beach, probably somewhere in New Zealand. I took it off the wall to hold it in my hand and take a closer look when the door opened again.

"Hey, what are you doing there mister?" Emma almost shouted.

"Sorry, I was just having a look," I said.

"Put them away," she said determinedly.

"They are amazing, Emma."

"Put them away," she repeated. "Breakfast is ready."

I was a bit confused and didn't know why she'd reacted this way, but I was also starving and looking forward to something to eat. I hung the picture back onto the wall and followed her into the kitchen.

When I entered the kitchen there was this big table set up with a five-star breakfast. Any Mercure hotel couldn't have done it better.

"There you go Picasso, enjoy your breakfast."

Did she just call me Picasso? I decided not to comment and sat down at the table, with a wry smile across my face.

"So, Emma, what are all those photographs about?" I had to ask.

"Nothing Ben. None of your business," she said.

"Uh, very sensitive topic?" I retorted.

"Not really," she said and followed up, "It is just not a big deal. Just a hobby."

"A hobby that you haven't mentioned once yet. I'm just wondering," I said.

"Well, we've met twice Ben. Sorry that you don't know my whole life story yet," she said, starting to sound a tad pissed off.

I could feel the tension building. The mood slowly started to change, moving in a weird direction.

"All good Emma. Just thought your pictures were amazing."

"Thank you," she said as she stared at her plate.

I started munching on my scrambled eggs. Breakfast was delicious. Is there anything this woman couldn't do? However, I wasn't able to entirely let her photography skills go. The more I thought about it, the more excited I got.

"You ought to publish those pictures. They're so good. The world needs to see them!"

"Ben!" she exclaimed. I felt like I was missing the cue to stop here.

"I mean, why not? You have nothing to lose?" I said.

"Jesus Ben, it's none of your business!"

I jumped for a second, wondering what was going on, and kept munching. The attempt to talk about her photography had totally discouraged me from also talking about us and last night, but I definitely didn't want to leave without knowing what this was all about. So, I decided to stick to the plan from yesterday, which got me here in the first place.

"Okay, but maybe you can tell me, what this is about then?"

"What is what about?" she replied.

Something fundamentally changed from the moment she rolled out of bed.

"I mean us, last night, this whole thing," I wondered. It took her a few seconds. Then she put her avocado toast down.

"Ben, this might sound harsh, but I'd like you to leave now."

The piece of bread in my mouth got stuck in my throat and I tried to catch my breath. I grabbed my glass of orange juice, swallowed the piece that got stuck and gazed at her. I didn't know what to say. I got up, went back to her room to grab my things and left the house, without even saying goodbye.

# 22.
# WHERE AM I?

W hat just happened?

Probably one of the most amazing nights I'd had in ages had turned into a throw-out within just a few minutes. I shut the door behind me, stepped onto the footpath and looked left and then right.

"Where the hell am I?" I said out loud.

Maybe I had a few too many lagers last night. Without any inkling of what direction to take, I turned right and started walking. My head was banging, not from the hangover but from what had just happened. Did I do anything wrong? I literally had no idea what to think. I just felt that my fears, which were holding me back from getting in touch with this woman again in the first place, had been confirmed.

I decided to pull my phone out to call Sam.

"Whaaaaaat's up, mate? Wake up next to your princess?" he asked and started laughing loudly. It was silent for a few seconds after he stopped laughing. Sam realised that something was wrong. "Are you okay, Ben?"

"Not really, man. I basically got kicked out and have no clue where I am?" I said, very desperate.

"Well, as long as you are still in New Zealand I'm not concerned," he said and started laughing again after he stopped himself. "Sorry, bro. It's just like, you know…"

"It's okay, bro. I would be laughing as well if I were you. I will tell you exactly what happened later, but right now I am just trying to figure out where I am," I explained.

I tried to describe what I saw to him, but he didn't recognise any of it either.

"Sorry, bro, I don't have any idea where you are. How about you start telling me what happened last night or this morning and keep walking until you start recognising something?"

"Okay, well, long story short, bro. You guys left at some point last night without saying goodbye."

"Hang on," he interrupted me. "We said goodbye about three times, but you guys just wouldn't react at all. Ask Oliver."

I smiled for a second. "It doesn't really matter. Emma and I had an amazing night. We went back to her place where it got even more beautiful. Then I woke up this morning and she wanted me to stay for breakfast, which I did. While she prepared breakfast in the kitchen, I figured out that she must be a photographer or something, because she had all these amazing shots in her room. I had a closer look at some of them. Then she came back into the room, saw me and the mood changed immediately. I told her at breakfast what an amazing photographer she is, and she didn't really react until the point where she asked me to leave halfway through breakfast. I have no idea what happened, man," I elaborated. Sam didn't take a second to reply.

"Bro, there are only two options. Either she is back with her ex-boyfriend or she is a better-developed version of you."

"What?" I was speechless.

Neither did I know what he meant by a better-developed version of me, nor did I even want to think about the first option. "What does a better-developed version of me even mean?" I asked him.

"Look, do you remember how I first met you at the café?"

"Yes, of course!" I said.

"I think I can be honest here—we've known each other long enough by now," he said, took a little breath and continued. "To be honest mate, you were an overly self-conscious sack of potatoes," he exclaimed and started laughing once again. "Sorry, I hope you know that I mean well, but you were the worst artist I have ever met in terms of self-presentation and having self-esteem. My grandma's cat had more self-esteem than you." I interrupted him, "Ehm Sam, I think I got it."

"Anyway, you were full of self-doubt, and you probably still are if we were to talk about your career as an artist. Maybe it's the same for Emma with her photography, but even worse?"

I wasn't quite sure if I could follow him.

"What do you mean?" I asked.

"Well, maybe she is embarrassed by her work and doesn't want anyone to see it or know about it."

"But why would you put it up in your room then?" I interrupted.

"I don't know man. This was just my impression. I think she just didn't know how to handle your enthusiasm for her photography, and that's why she shut down and kicked you out."

He got me thinking now. "Hmm, do you think so?" I asked, to reassure myself.

"Or she is back with her ex-boyfriend," and his dirty, loud laugh rattled through the phone again. I just let him laugh and didn't even try to say anything until a few seconds later when something caught my eye.

"Wait, mate!" I shouted.

"What's up?" he asked.

"I think I know where I am."

"Great, where?"

"Do you remember the vegan café outside town?"

"Yeah."

"I think I am there."

"That's thirty minutes away, bro."

"I know," I replied, now able to take the situation with a sense of humour as well.

"I'll come and get you, my man," Sam offered.

"Thank you, bro. I'll see you soon."

# 23.
# OUT OF THE WAY FELLAS

I heard his car what seemed like five miles away since it was as loud as a helicopter. I could see his big smile straightaway, and he was trying everything possible to not break out into loud laughter. On the other hand, the legend that is Sam brought two flat whites that saved my suboptimal morning. Due to the emotional rollercoaster, I'd somehow entirely forgotten about the hangover.

Sam stopped almost in the middle of the road next to me, opened the door, looked at me with big eyes and said, "I want details now. All of them."

"Trust me you don't. I still have no idea what happened," I said desperately.

"Looked like a fun night though!" Sam riposted.

"Why didn't you say goodbye, or take me home?"

"Dude, I already told you. I said goodbye about a million times, but you guys were just deeply in love."

"Ahh stop it, Sam," attempting to shrug him off.

"No seriously, you should have seen you two love birds. At some point, I just gave up. You were deep in conversation, wouldn't pay attention to Matt and me at all...and you were a little drunk as well," he laughed and continued, "but honestly mate, give me the detailed story now."

I gave him another rundown of what had just happened and how I made it from amazing avocado toast with scrambled eggs, to being in front of the door without a goodbye, within a few minutes.

"Trust me, she was just embarrassed, man," he said straightaway.

"You think so?" I asked.

"Ben, are you still drunk? It's obvious."

Right at this moment a big "fuck off" and long loud honk interrupted us. A guy pulled up next to us, "Move your arses out of the way fellas!" he shouted.

That was the moment we realised that Sam's car was still half on the road, and he was leaning over the passenger seat while I was holding the open door in one hand and the flat white in the other hand. We hadn't even realised that I hadn't jumped into the car yet.

"I hate to say it," Sam started, "but this guy is right. Jump in and we'll keep going."

I was just so confused now. I jumped into the car and Sam started driving towards home.

"You get what I mean, though?" he asked in order to pick up on where we got interrupted.

"Okay, let me try to understand. You are actually trying to tell me that she didn't let me finish my scrambled eggs and kicked me out of the house after the most romantic night ever because I said I liked her pictures?"

Sam broke into a grin spanning cheek to cheek. "When you say it like that, it sounds ridiculous, but you told me that you called them amazing multiple times and basically told her to put them out. That sounds a bit pushy. Don't you reckon?"

"Yeah okay, maybe, but I still can't see any reason why she would kick me out, just like that?" I answered still slightly confused.

"Dude, call it a lack of self-confidence that we all have, or whatever you want, but it seems like you stepped way too far into her comfort zone. You of all people, the wannabe da Vinci, should know that. She was embarrassed in front of you and instead of taking your compliments, she pushed you away. I know that might not sound very logical, but that's how it is sometimes, and I actually do understand her," ending his point.

I nodded my head and let his words sink in. I supposed he might be right, but what I didn't want to enter my head was how something so beautiful could turn upside down so quickly when I never had any bad intentions. The opposite was the case—I just wanted to tell her how amazing she was.

# 24.
# FALLING IN LOVE

I thought about Sam's words a lot and came to the conclusion that he most likely had a point—maybe she was just embarrassed. I sincerely hoped that she was. I couldn't stop thinking about that night. It was stuck in my head...her soft skin, her blue eyes, her freckles, her big smile and her laugh—a bit dirty, but soft at the same time (so infectious though). Should I text her? Seriously, why haven't I heard from her yet?

Everything had felt so perfectly meant to be, and then because of such a tiny, stupid thing, it was already over before it had even begun.

How many times have you seriously got that feeling that something is special? How many times in your life have you felt a deep connection to someone? I don't think it happens very often, but when it does, you ought to make sure you let them know how you feel. Maybe this is already the answer. I was so scared to reach out to her again, but I simply had nothing to lose. It'd been three days since that night and I hadn't heard anything.

I had two options. I could either tell her how I felt, have the chance to explain myself and maybe see her again or, everything would stay as it is. I shouldn't expect anything to change or that she would take the next step just like that.

I decided to text her but was very unsure of what to say. Maybe call her? Let's do it, my inner voice said. I reached for my phone and typed in *"Em"* when I realised that nothing would show up since I didn't even have her number. Alright, do I know where she lives? Not exactly. Sam! He would know. He picked me up somewhere close. I grabbed my phone again and rang Sam.

"Yepah, boy! What's happening?" he answered the phone.

He always made me laugh when he picked up the phone, but this time I had no time for it—I was on a mission.

"Yes, Sam! Do you remember where exactly you picked me up after the night with Emma?"

"Sure bro!" he confirmed.

"Can you take me there again, please?" I asked nicely and slightly hectically.

"Now?"

"Yes!" I said loud and clear.

"Alright!"

"Thanks!"

"Oh, where actually are you?" he asked.

"Home, where are you?" I asked him.

"I'm home as well, you idiot!"

We both started laughing out loud when one second later I stopped myself and shouted, "Let's go!" through the whole house.

I grabbed my jacket, knocked at Sam's door, told him to hurry up and waited outside like a little child waiting for Christmas.

We jumped in his car and he could tell that I was deep in thought. He then interrupted me.

"So, what exactly are we going to do here?" he asked.

*Fair question*, I thought.

"Actually, I don't know Sam. Let's just go and see what happens. I've been thinking about her a lot the last few days, and I feel that there was something between us. She needs to know that. No matter what."

"Your call, my man! I'm just your Uber driver."

"Cheers," I said.

Thirty minutes later we arrived at the place where he picked me up last time. By now he was so intrigued about how it would go that he decided to recreate the route from here back to her house together with me. The question was just how? Yes, we had an amazing night, and I was fully conscious the next morning, but we also had a lot of drinks and it wasn't that easy for me to figure out what way I'd walked just a few days ago.

I tried to focus as much as I could to recreate my route from the vegan café back to her house in my head. After asking a few random people, fifteen minutes later we turned into the street that I believed was hers. A few seconds later, I realised that it was her street. I saw a yellow wooden house just a few metres in front of me to the right. I remembered the palm tree in front of the house, where I'd cut myself when walking through the door. I looked at the little wound, it was already crusty. I touched it and thought about the feeling I had when I left this place the last time.

Sam noticed how doubtful I'd become all of a sudden and encouraged me with a simple, "Nothing to lose."

I pointed at her house, and he stopped right in front of it. I jumped out of the car with no idea what to say or plan in my head. Sam said something like "Good luck," but by then, I already had tunnel vision and was focusing on her front door like a creep. With no idea how to start or what to say, I walked up to her door. I was just lifting up my fist to go for a knock when the door suddenly opened. It was her. You could see the shock in her eyes, but I must have had a similar look myself. I think we both were mumbling and stuttering at the same time

"You-yo," she tried to say.

"Hi, hey, hmmmm," I tried to start.

It took a few seconds until one of us was able to formulate a whole sentence. It ended up being her, and it wasn't a nice one. "What are you doing here?" was the first straight sentence she shot out.

I still didn't know what to say. She was right, what am I doing here?

"Are you stalking me?" she asked. Luckily, I at least had an answer prepared for that.

"Do I look like a stalker?" I said. I could see a teeny-tiny smile coming over her lips.

"No, but seriously Ben, what are you doing here and how did you find me?" she asked, looking a little helpless.

"Well, I suppose I spent a night here, and I still remembered the way. I'm here to have another avocado toast and an orange juice because the last one was quite nice, but things didn't end up as I'd hoped."

I don't know where this confidence had sprung up from, but just seeing her gave me a slight feeling of comfort, as our little argument had never happened. Emma started slowly picking up on it

"I am out of avocados, unfortunately, but I was just on the way to get some more. Do you want to join me for a walk?" she asked.

Sam was still in the car behind me, leaning over the passenger seat. He acted innocent and asked, "You all good, mate?" I just put my thumb up, turned back around to Emma and said, "Yeah, why not."

# 25.
# AVOCADO ON TOAST

"**W**hy did you come back?" Emma asked, not wasting a second to get straight to the point again as we started walking towards the supermarket. *There she was once again*, I thought, *straight up and direct, exactly the way I got to know her.*

"I want another avocado on toast with scrambled eggs," I declared, hoping that she would laugh. Luckily for me, she did.

"I never thought Germans could be funny, but you've started to prove me wrong, Ben," she chuckled, bemused. "But seriously, why did you come back?" she asked again.

For a second, I was thinking of cracking another joke, but then I thought it was time to get my courage together and tell her how I truly felt about the situation. I reminded myself of Sam's words and went for it.

"I'm sorry, Emma," I started.

"Sorry for what, Ben?" she asked.

"I guess, I was a bit pushy and didn't think it all through, looking at your personal stuff," I said. I mean at the end of the day, that's what it was—her personal stuff.

"Look Emma, I don't want to confuse you, I might even be a little confused myself. I don't know how you feel about this, but to me, it doesn't happen very often, that I feel so strongly connected to someone."

"So connected that you wanted to leave straightaway in the morning?" she interjected. Damn, she had a good memory.

"No, no, look, Emma, I was super overwhelmed by the entire situation, and the last thing I wanted to do was mess this up. The opposite is actually the case. You're smart and funny and we had such a great time together. For the past three days, I've been thinking about you nonstop and how I might have messed this up before it had started."

"You didn't mess it up, Ben. I did!" she said all of a sudden.

"What do you mean?" I asked.

"I wanted to reach out to you straight after you left and apologise, but I wasn't quite sure what to say and didn't know how," she laughed. "I didn't even have your number, and the past has shown that you don't reply to Facebook messages either," we both started laughing.

*Oh my God*, I thought right in this second. I totally forgot that we were friends on Facebook, and I couldn't believe the effort Sam and I had put in to find her house again. It could have been that simple. Before I could tell her about my now silly-looking mission to find her again, she continued explaining herself. "My reaction was over the top and selfish."

"May I ask, why?" I interrupted her.

"I just can't handle it, Ben. I'm not a photographer or anything like this. I don't know what I am, or who I am, but definitely not the amazing photographer you were talking about. I just wanted you to stop saying this because that's not who I am."

For a second, I just wanted to say, "Yes you are, but I didn't think that would make it any better, so I tried to be a little bit more considerate. I wanted to figure out what was going on in her head, so I went for it.

"But do you want to be?" I asked.

"I don't know Ben, to be honest. I obviously like and enjoy it, but I couldn't deal with the pressure you are living with," she said.

"What pressure are you talking about?" I asked.

"Come on. I mean, it's pretty obvious—you are juggling between your badly paid job in the café, hours in your room painting and then exhibitions. Everything that's driving you is that dream of becoming a famous artist one day," she said. Not sure if I agreed with the word famous, but everything else she said was pretty spot on.

"I understand," I conceded.

"I don't like pressure. I don't like if people compliment me or try to push me to do something I am not comfortable with, you know?"

"Yes, I actually do. I didn't quite understand so much before, but I get a better picture of it now with every word you say."

It felt like a weight started to lift from her. A stupid question came into my mind, that I felt the need to ask. It felt like my old German subconscious wanted to ask her.

"But, what is your plan, then?"

"Do I need one, Ben?" was her immediate reaction. "I have a lot of other stuff to figure out at the moment, so I don't need any of this," she said honestly.

I didn't know what she meant by her last sentence, (unsuspecting that I would find out soon), but I thought that her question was pretty interesting.

Do I seriously need a plan? Do I need a goal? I think she was making a fair point there. I'd never really thought about it, but I know that I always was told how important it is to have a plan and a goal to aim for. Otherwise, what else would your life revolve around? Her question triggered all those memories from the times before I had even gotten to New Zealand. I could hear my dad saying, "Be prepared when you start your first job. Think about what you want to achieve in your career." I couldn't make a single decision without my parents permanently questioning me and asking what my plan is. My mum would then probably say something like, "Okay, but what's next? If you are about to quit your job, you need to have the next one lined up."

Everything always needed to be planned out, but what if things didn't go as planned? Until now, I pretty much didn't have to think about it. When I arrived in New Zealand, I didn't have a plan for the first time ever, but I also remember how much that freaked me out. Thanks to Francis, I discovered a very valuable treasure—my passion for painting. Through that, I found a little bit of security by defining a goal that could easily be misunderstood as a plan. "I want to be an artist one day who lives off selling his paintings." This was a goal so grand that it would take a tremendous amount of time to even get halfway there.

"No, you don't need a plan," I retorted, surprising myself. "Don't think I have a plan just because I have a dream. Just for the record, I don't want to be famous. I just want to be able to live off it one day."

"Of course, no one wants to be famous," she responded with a sense of sarcasm, and I could see how the left side of her mouth would form a cheeky but very endearing smile.

"Okay, I give up," I said. I could already see the supermarket sign in front of us. I wasn't quite sure what to do, or what was about to happen. All I knew was that I didn't want to wait another three days to hear from her.

"Here we are, I guess," she started, leaving a lot of room for interpretation.

Quite often, I'm stuck in my head, and I'm never sure whether to say out loud what's running through my mind, or to just judge my thoughts as idiotic and remain silent. This time I decided to go for it and went all in.

"Emma!" I almost shouted, and I could tell that she didn't expect such a blast in her ears. We both looked at each other and started laughing, then I started again, "I'm sorry, that came out wrong. I don't want to make a speech out of it. I actually would like to ask you for your number so that I can text you someday."

"No," she said.

Here we go again, was the first thing that came into my mind, but this time she didn't manage to stay serious for very long and gave in pretty quickly. "I have a better idea—how about you join me? We buy some avocados, you finish your toast that you were meant to finish a few days ago and maybe after that, I will give you my number. How does that sound?"

It feels crazy to be so sure about something. There was not a single shred of doubt running through my head, and everything felt like it was meant to be just the way it had turned out.

"Let's do it, Emma," I said.

# 26.
# LOVE IS NOT ABOUT THE GOOD TIMES

"What a lovely story," Nan smiled. The three of us were staring at each other, almost nostalgically. Nan continued, "Feels like you two were meant to be."

It was very nice to hear someone like Nan say something like that, but what looked like the almost perfect love story wasn't exactly how it appeared. It was without a doubt one hell of a rollercoaster, but it was nice to see that the deep connection we'd both experienced right from the very start had led us somewhere. I thought Nan noticed that a few little doubts were starting to run through my head.

"You know what I've learned in my life?" Big Nan started.

We both looked at her, intrigued to find out what she was about to say.

"Love is actually not about the good times at all. A lot of people think love is a straightforward path and always great times. It might even be the other way around. Sometimes the bad times seem like they're dominating. It is proven that negative stuff tends to stay longer in our brains. It's much more difficult to convert the negative into positive, but it's so easy to convert the positive into negative."

"As a matter of fact, the bad times aren't the actual problem, because sometimes we can hardly prevent them from transpiring. The most important thing in a functional relationship is how you go about those bad times. If you deal with them in a respectful manner, and you don't lose the connection you have with that person, then the opposite will be the case, and you will come out of it even stronger. Too many people give up too early in life and in a relationship. You two have this bond, I can see it and feel it. Make sure you take good care of it," she said, gazing into the distance.

I almost felt like this was indirectly addressed to me because I was the one who had completely shut down, not talking to Emma about what was going on in my head.

Emma took my hand and held it really tightly. We both looked into each other's eyes. We knew that we had that connection that Big Nan was talking about.

Nan smiled, closing her eyes at the same time, and it became apparent that she needed to rest again. She confirmed our suspicions, falling fast asleep within seconds, leaving Emma and me to stare at each other for a little longer.

"She is right, I guess," I said.

"Right about, what?" Emma asked.

"About us and the bad times. I mean we both know that all the glitter wasn't gold. You remember?"

It was silent for a moment. Emma knew exactly what I was referring to. I could feel myself opening up. Unfortunately, just about the past and not about my current state.

"Yes, I do. Do you want to talk about it?" Emma said.

I thought this could be a good time to open up some more.

"Yes," I replied simply, and we started talking about when it was not entirely clear if we would actually end up being together. I mean the times when Emma had to face herself and her reality.

# 27.
# SOMETHING IS NOT RIGHT HERE

Since Emma and I had been seeing each other for quite a while now, I'd spent so much time with her and less with painting and creating. However, my time was more than well spent.

"I love Emma," that was pretty clear to me just after a few months with her. This connection and the accompanied feeling she gave me was so strong—stronger than everything I'd ever experienced. I was waiting for the right moment to tell her, but I didn't quite know when. This sounds like the perfect love story, but it wasn't. There was one thing Emma was dealing with that I didn't handle really well at all.

I learned that Emma was traversing through life without a plan. Her free spirit was exactly what inspired me so much. She was living the freedom that I couldn't live—two ultimately different lifestyles. However, very often she would take her liberties too far and would take substances that I wouldn't consider taking, in order to feel happy and free. Yes, we are talking about drugs. What looks pretty harmless to one can look pretty harmful to the other. Emma was open to it, and furthermore was consuming them in a rather consistent manner. I was always wondering where this woman got her energy from. She was never in a bad mood unless we'd talk about her amazing self and who she'd like or wouldn't like to be.

She'd bring joy to everyone around her. Friends, family, me, literally anyone, but she couldn't bring true joy to herself. She'd use the weekends to escape, running away from her shitty job, running away from the problems that life threw at her and running away from the most important question, Who do you want to be? The side of her that made life look so carefree and fun was chock-a-block with illicit substances.

I am not saying that Emma was an addict. She definitely wasn't, but almost every weekend I'd see her gravitate towards places I wouldn't want to go to. Some might call me old fashioned or narrow-minded, but from my perspective, I didn't see any point in creating my happiness artificially. For me, it just didn't make sense. My life might be full of pressure and goals, but the one thing that brought me joy was painting. Just locking myself in a room for hours painting nonstop would naturally bring me satisfaction. I do have to face my self-doubt, but at least I am facing them—something that Emma hadn't done up to now.

I was extremely overwhelmed by the situation. Meanwhile, Emma and I had spent another amazing week together. After work we'd sit on her porch, drink red wine, smoke cigarettes and talk gibberish about outer space, living in a hut by the beach and natural catastrophes such as tsunamis and earthquakes. We would drift off into super irrational stuff, where people listening might have asked themselves what the hell was wrong with those two?

Nevertheless, these things changed at the beginning of almost every weekend. It was Friday evening again. Emma, once more, had an evening with friends lined up. An evening with friends in this case could have had many meanings, but we both knew that this meant that I wouldn't see or hear from her until at least the next day, maybe the afternoon or sometimes even longer.

She was totally easy about it and would say, "Come on there's nothing wrong with it," after I had asked her again why she would need that in her life.

"Emma, I like you, and I hope you don't think that I'm the kind of guy who doesn't enjoy a good party. You should know that by now, but I can see that something is not right here," I pointed out.

"What do you mean?" she replied while we were sitting on her bed. She was all ready to go, but I had finally aired my thoughts to her. We'd been dating for exactly twelve weeks now, and this was the third weekend in a row where she would go to what she called "an evening with friends."

"It's okay, just go." I had already given up before the conversation even started. It felt pointless to me. She wouldn't get it anyway. Not in this situation, not right now.

"Ben, you really are overreacting. I need to go now. You know you can always join," she said.

Yes, I could Emma, but that is not my world. I enjoy the company of people who don't need to think about their next high, to escape from reality, while talking to them, was the honest opinion in my head.

"I'll see you when I see you," I heard myself saying instead. I grabbed my stuff and left, knowing I wouldn't see her for a while, or if I'm lucky I'd pick up what would be left of her on Sunday.

"Have a good night," I finished off, closing the door behind me. I exited through the front door, and instead of taking an Uber, I decided to walk for a little while to process my thoughts and understand how to deal with this situation. I chucked on my headphones, hit play on the Discover Weekly playlist and tried to comprehend this dilemma.

## Bonobo - Breaking Apart

For some strange reason, I was hoping she would run after me. I looked back a couple of times, but obviously she didn't. There are not many things about which we disagree in life, but this is a major one. When I think about Emma, I feel safe and understood, I don't feel the need to be different around her. As a matter of fact, the opposite is the case, I can be purely me. If only she would stop escaping from her problems and start facing them. The challenge, making it so hard for me to accept her lifestyle, is that I can truly see that she is running away from something, and that her weekends are just a reflection of her unknown identity—a way to avoid the question of what her purpose is on this planet, to say it in Francis's mum's words.

Halfway home, I realised that it was far too long to realistically walk all the way, and I ordered a ride for the second half of the trip back to my place. When I opened the front door, Sam was already awaiting me with a bottle of beer. "It's party time," he said.

My first thought was, *Where is the difference between this guy having beers on a Friday night getting drunk, and the woman I like so much getting high on drugs and partying for twenty-four hours? Am I the one not open-minded enough, or am I the one who's actually figured out that such a lifestyle can fuck you up?* It seemed pretty obvious to me.

Sam was still holding the bottle of beer in his hand with the expectation of me being excited about a good old drink on a Friday night. I felt bad that I had to disappoint him.

"I'm sorry, mate. I'm not really feeling it tonight."

"Uhh, what happened, bro?" he asked.

"It's Emma," I said straightaway.

"Of course it is. Is she out again?" he asked, raising his eyebrow.

I just nodded.

Sam already had all the background information about it and understood my opinion. Therefore, he made a very valuable point. "Man, I know it's hard for you to understand, but you only have one chance. She needs to figure it out herself."

Well, I don't need to mention that he was right. At the same time, it sounded like a sentence a wise old woman would say.

"Of course. I know, Sam, but I just think that this woman could be the one and seeing her like this tears me apart. This isn't her," I said before emphasising it again, "It's not her, Sam!"

"It might be her, it might not be. You don't know yet, and maybe that is what you need to determine now."

I guess deep inside I just hoped that I would be her escape, her go-to, and not some chemical substances.

Sam and I had talked about this already many times, and he knew exactly what was going on. He taught me the most important thing—you can't change people, they have to change themselves. He believes me that Emma is generally a great person, but he also knows that she has found a different way to deal with the problems that she is facing in her life. I guess this discussion about drugs will always be a controversial one—to use them or not, or why is a drug such as alcohol so socially accepted while others aren't? I have been there. I've heard all the stories from her and her friends, and I am seriously fed up with it. The difference was obvious. I wouldn't enjoy a drunk, annoying person either who would get on the piss every weekend, but the other stuff is even worse. It's about the new standards that you set yourself. Here, we're talking about another magnitude that you don't reach on a natural level. The next sober party, the next event or the next get-together will not be as happy and not as much fun as the one when you took drugs. People start to struggle to enjoy themselves. The lows start to get as present and as strong as the highs. Your life turns into an extreme spectrum, and the most important thing, where you will have to pay the price one day, is that you are pushing your real problems away. That day when you inevitably have to face them, it'll be even more overwhelming. That's where a lot of people fall apart.

I got so caught up in this that I almost forgot about the fact that I had an exhibition the next day. I was struggling. Everything, literally everything, was telling me that Emma was the one. The feeling she gave me was indescribable. I knew for myself that I loved her, but her weekends were freaking me out and were holding me back from telling her how I truly felt. My mind kept on spinning and spinning until I somehow managed to fall asleep without hearing a thing from her.

# 28.
# THE ONE

The next morning, I checked my phone—there was no message as per usual. I was upset, but I knew that I had to focus on my exhibition today. I already didn't feel so good about it. I'd spent a lot of time with Emma over the past three months, which had been amazing, but it also meant less time for painting and creativity. I didn't manage to come up with a lot of new art. So, over the past few events, I'd been exhibiting more or less the same pieces. That wasn't necessarily bad but also didn't give me much confidence for today. On top of that, all I could think of was what went down the night before. It'd been the same thing once again, and I couldn't handle it. It was tricky because, on one hand, it was pretty clear to me how I felt about this woman and that I wanted to be with her, but on the other hand, I couldn't cope with her escaping from reality, including me, so often. I took it personally and that was the issue.

I spent the day trying to hold it together, awaiting some sort of sign of life from her. It was already late afternoon and still nothing yet. Filled with insecurity, I arrived early at today's location for the exhibition. Within a few hours, everything was set up. Matt, Sam and the others were excited because it had been a couple of weeks since the last one, and Matt hadn't been part of Sam's exhibitions in a long time.

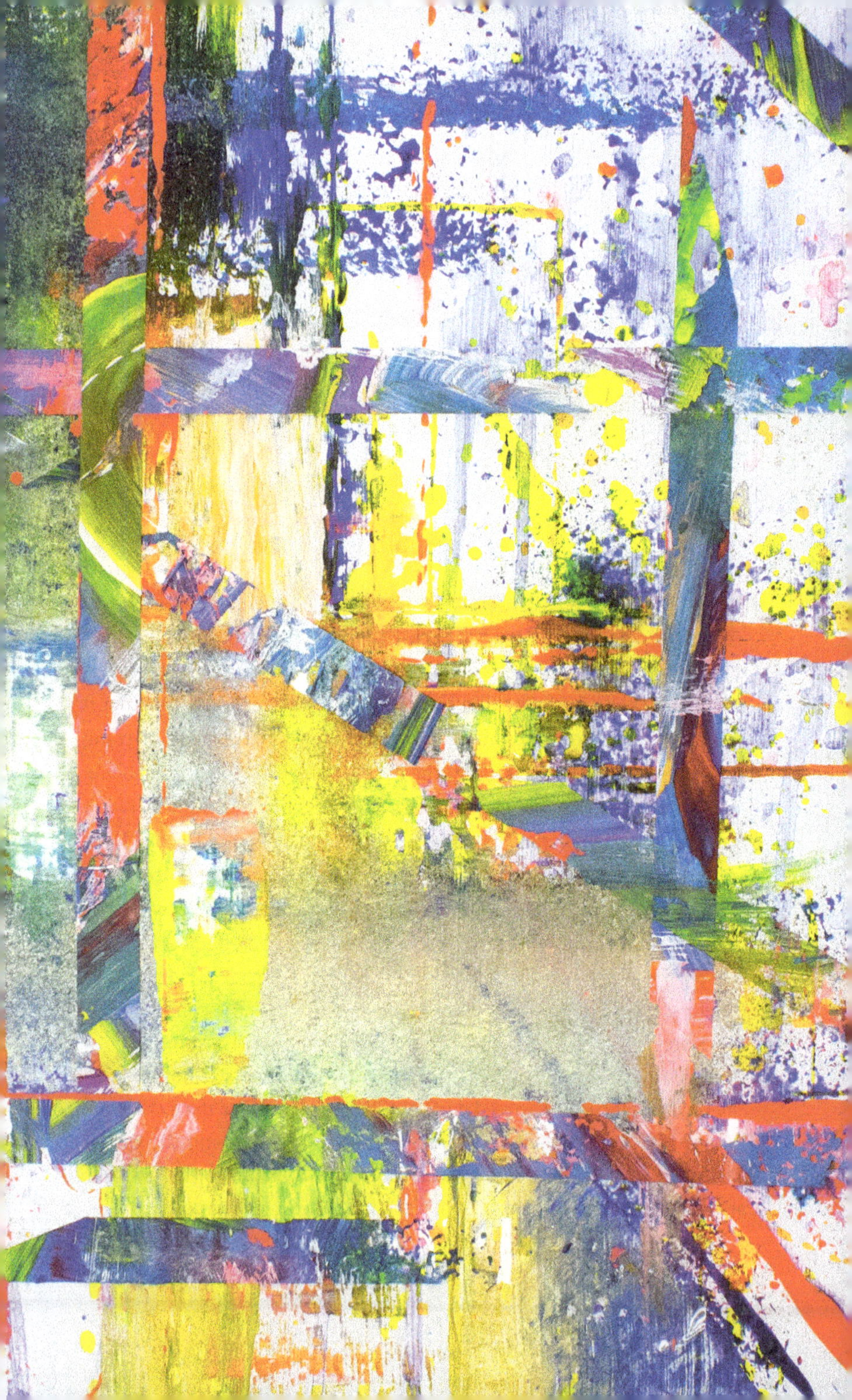

I should have felt the same, but I neither felt excited nor confident, not just because I had only been part of a dozen of exhibitions ever, but I was also somewhere else in my mind.

I had planned to tell Emma how I felt about her and about us last night, but despite my good intentions, it had ended up in a big fall-out. She'd gone out with her friends, and I hadn't heard from her since. Twenty-four hours later, here I was in some gallery in front of my paintings and all I could think of was her. I tried texting her, but there was still no reply.

It was such a mess in my head. Since the day we officially started dating, Emma came to every exhibition. It was only a handful, but she was there—always the first one to arrive and the last one to leave. She helped me organise, carry and sell my art. Even so early on in our 'getting to know each other' phase, she was always holding back her own needs. Yes, she loved art, but not so much that she would need it almost every week for four hours or more after work. Same pictures, same people, same small talks over and over. She did all that for me. She was the greatest and most supportive person I'd met and still, here I am now doubting whether we'll have a future together or not.

I think Matt could tell that something was going on with me because he came over and asked, "Are you okay, mate?"

Should I lie or just tell him the truth? "Not really, to be honest."

"What happened?" he wanted to know.

"Sorry, I don't want to bother you with my problems, man. This is supposed to be a fun night, right?" I said.

"Yeah sure, but it obviously isn't for you, so just let it out and we might be able to turn this night around," he said with a little smile, then paused intentionally because he wasn't finished yet. He looked at me and added an almost sarcastic sounding, "Or not?"

His refreshing mood made me laugh a little. To be clear, I'd had many talks already with Sam and even Francis about the topic, and both of them were giving me good advice already. However, I thought it couldn't harm to get another point of view on it. So, I decided to tell Matt about the current situation when a voice interrupted us. "Hey, guys!"

I turned around and saw a very familiar face that made me smile. Unfortunately, it wasn't Emma, but the face I saw belonged to another very special person. It was Francis.

"Hey, mate," I said, elated to see him. "What are you doing here?" I asked, a tad surprised.

"Well, you invited me, and I really wanted to see if my good old friend Ben had kept his promise. I'm super sorry that I missed your first exhibition and all the others so far," he said while opening his arms to dive in for a big hug.

I hadn't seen him in ages. Regardless of my joy caused by his presence, he sensed straightaway that the atmosphere wasn't as euphoric as expected.

"Everything okay?" he asked after he and Matt had shaken hands. They knew each other as well. Matt had collaborated with Grace—it felt like if you wanted to be an artist in Auckland you needed to know Grace Bellingham.

"I was just about to tell Matt about Emma," I said.

As I mentioned before, Francis already knew about it a little bit. Therefore, he said, "I see, continue and I will just listen in silence."

I looked back at Matt. "You remember the girl from the bar?"

"Of course, I remember, dude," Matt said with his continuous smile.

I was surprised by the determination in his answer. I wondered where this was coming from. "Do you?"

He continued, sounding as determined as before. "Dude, you guys were deeply in love already back then. Even a blind guy would have been able to tell. She was the one with the boyfriend at your very first exhibition, right?"

"Yes she was, Matt," I retorted, wondering why this story seemed to stick in everyone's minds.

"Have things not been going as expected?" he asked.

The answer to that was pretty clear. "Oh, definitely not," I admitted.

"How do you mean?" Matt asked slightly confused.

"Never mind," I said.

I didn't feel like getting too much into detail about our past, but one thing for sure. So far, it surely wasn't the most ordinary falling-in-love story.

"Where is she today?" he asked, proving that he was able to sense the situation very well, "Or is that the reason for your long face?"

The three of us turned silent. Francis looked down to the floor. Matt looked at me, expecting an answer. I decided to answer his question with another question in return.

"How do you know someone is right for you? You want everything to be perfect, but there is something in the way that you can't tag along with. Could she not be the right person, even though everything else feels in place?" I asked Matt and Francis.

Francis took the lead. "Dude, I think once again you've answered it yourself. You said, 'everything else feels in place.' You told me and Sam many times that you know it's not her. You know it's not the life she wants for herself, but so far she doesn't know any other way to escape. I understand you want to be her escape, but not everything works like in the movies. You'd no doubt be delighted to earn her trust one day and be able to convince her that you can be her happy place when she feels pressure. If you want to create this environment for you two, you have to create that safe place. It doesn't just come from nowhere."

I was astounded. Sometimes I ask myself whether I deserve to be surrounded by such amazing people.

"What if she doesn't feel the same though?" I asked. By now, Matt had a better inkling regarding the situation and took over.

"Don't be a fool, Ben. I don't know much about your time together so far, but I saw you together, and you clearly couldn't keep your eyes off each other! I bet you have a deep connection, but it's up to you if you want to be the first one to give her your trust, without expecting anything in return."

I was amazed at how much both of them were aligned, even though Matt wasn't fully aware of the main issue.

However, it seemed like both were trying to persuade me to take the risk, without expecting anything in return. Such a thing is easier said than done, because if I leave my comfort zone, expecting something in return is usually my way of going about it.

When I'd put myself out there and texted Sam to get a place in his collective, I was expecting something in return. When I'd asked Emma on a date, I was expecting something in return. So, if I asked her to be with me, I would, in return, expect her to stop escaping, but what if she wouldn't and I couldn't cope. I guess the wires in my brain were just connected that way.

"Time to break old habits," Matt said as if reading my mind.

"How do you know?" I wondered.

"You're just very easy to read," Matt laughed.

As per usual at Sam's exhibitions, we had some wines. While Matt was getting a second round for us, I kept thinking about his words. What if he was right? I pulled out my phone to see if Emma had texted me. I was hoping she would come, as she knew how much this meant to me. Had I offended her that badly last night? My phone battery was about to die. Should I call her or not?

I had the phone in my hand and was standing in front of my paintings. I was staring at one particular artwork. It was the colourful *Caribou* painting—Emma's favourite. Since the night at the bar, when she'd given it its name, it reminded me of her and our amazing, real first encounter.

"Call her!" I heard Francis say.

*This guy!* I thought. He was always there, and his words always felt so right to me! Even though his request seemed to be the best to do, I was still craving some reassurance.

"You think so?"

"What happened, Ben? Why isn't she here?" he asked.

"We got into a fight last night and I haven't heard from her since," I told him.

"What did you say to her?" Francis asked.

"What do you mean?" I said.

"I mean you must have said something, right?" he said.

"Man, she's just out partying, not giving a fuck." I raised my voice.

"Is that what you said?" he asked rather calm.

Jesus, was this guy just mirroring me? I could feel some anger building up inside of me. At the same time, I could feel how he was provoking me in order to get me out of this state of unresponsiveness.

"No," I said with a slightly raised voice. Francis nodded. Simultaneously, Matt arrived back, handing us glasses of wine.

I continued, "She wanted to go out anyway, and it was just a situation that I didn't handle really well. It's her losing control to forget, to feel free and not face reality."

"You don't like to let go, right?" Francis smiled.

"This is not about letting go guys. Yes, I like to let go, but I don't do it every weekend, and I face the challenges life throws at me. I'm pretty sure I'm not doing everything right here, but seeing someone you care about and you think you have a connection to wasting her life over something like this and cutting you out for long periods of time, is something I can't cope with. If you think that means I can't let go, then I can't let go, congratulations! At least I can face myself and my problems and work through them!" I shouted.

It looked like Francis almost regretted what he'd said, but he was also aware that he'd trigged something in me, likely on purpose once again.

"I'm sorry, mate. I didn't mean to offend you, but at least you're here now," he apologised.

"What do you mean 'I'm here now?' " I asked.

"You are taking action," he said.

"I haven't done anything yet, guys."

"Yet!" Matt said as if he wanted to say that I should go and do something about it.

"Give her a chance," he continued.

"Yes, I agree. Give her a chance!" Francis confirmed, just to follow up, "You know it's not her and from the rest, all we heard was, 'She's the one!' "

"Did I say that she's the one?" I asked.

"It's pretty obvious," Matt pointed out, and they both nodded their heads unanimously.

# 29.
# CLIMBING THROUGH THE WINDOW

Matt and Francis were right. What was I waiting for? I had nothing to lose. In fact, I had a lot to gain, if I could only overcome the fear of giving Emma my trust. I had to take the risk. In the end, it was a chance for both of us, and one thing had become pretty clear to me over the past few months—I was in love with this woman. Despite the way that she dealt with her own problems, she made me a far better person. All our random conversations about space and time, carrots, chia seeds, music, art and the future had made me realise how much I wanted this girl to be my partner for life.

"Excuse me, how much is this artwork?" I heard a random male voice say.

I got totally carried away, standing next to my wall of paintings. Matt and Francis had already left wandering around and the voice repeated, "Excuse me." I turned around staring at the ceiling for a second, then looked at the person who was about to buy my most beautiful piece of art. He was pointing at the *Caribou* painting. I had no choice; I had to do what you have to do when you know that the time is right, and you are a 100 percent sure about how you feel for someone.

"I am super sorry sir, but this piece is not for sale, and I really need to go."

You could see the confusion in his eyes.

I started running towards the door of the gallery. I had the door handle in my hand when realised I should at least say something to the guys. I turned around and just shouted, "Francis! Would you mind looking after my paintings? And the *Caribou* painting is not for sale!"

Everyone turned around, looking at me, including Sam. He had no clue what was going on. The last things I saw from the corner of my eye was Matt going over to Sam gesticulating that everything was alright and Francis moving over to my paintings to tell the guy it was definitely not for sale. I ran out the door and reached for the phone in my pocket when I figured out that my battery had died. Uber wasn't an option. I ran out onto the street, waving both hands, hoping that some kind of vehicle would stop and pick me up. It was already pretty late at night and Auckland's sky was pitch black. I wasn't even sure if the passing cars could see my little hands waving in the dark from the side of the road. After a couple of minutes though (which felt more like ages), a taxi pulled over. I opened the door.

"I need to get to Vermont Street, ASAP."

"Alright, thirty dollars, jump in," the driver replied instantaneously.

"Thirty bucks? Are you serious? It's not even a ten-minute drive!"

"Do you want a ride or not?" the taxi driver retorted.

I checked my wallet and I only had twenty bucks left.

"I only have twenty, bro," I said.

"I am not a freaking Uber. Shut the door and get away!" he shouted.

Alright, I didn't have the time to freak out about that guy. I was on a mission. "Fuck it," I said out loud and started running down the street faster than Usain Bolt. I thought if I ran as fast as possible, I might be able to be there in thirty minutes. It was already past bedtime, and I hadn't heard from her at all. She might have texted me, she might have not. She also might already be asleep, but I just couldn't wait. I loved Emma, I wanted to be with her and she needed to know that. Now!

So many thoughts were running through my head while I was giving it all I had.

What do I do if she doesn't feel the same? What if she isn't home? At some point, I decided to stop this unnecessary train of thoughts, when Vermont Street peaked around the next corner. Fully out of breath and drenched in sweat, I arrived at her house. Everything was dark. It looked like either no one was home, or her flatmates were all asleep. I was trying to get around the corner where her bedroom window was when I noticed a little light through her window. Emma likes to sleep with her little bedside lamp on.

*Jackpot*, I thought and whispered to myself, "She's home."

There was a high chance now that the rest of the house was already asleep, so knocking at the front door and waking everyone up wasn't an option. Her window was quite high up, so I couldn't easily reach it. I was scouring the ground for stones to throw at her window to wake her up.

I felt like a fourteen-year-old again. I started throwing the stones against her window, one by one. "Come on," I said to myself. "Wake up!" Nothing happened. I guess, it was pretty obvious that she was fast asleep. Her window was closed, and it was impossible to reach it without a hand. I needed to come up with a different plan.

I was already so deep in this teenage love story that It was too late to stop now. I then remembered that nine out of ten times she forgot to lock her window properly. There was a slight chance that I could just push it open (if I could only get to it). Slowly, my master plan was coming together. I would climb up the house to her window, open it, wake her up and tell her how I felt. "Sounds like a plan, aye?" I said to myself, sounding like a full-on Kiwi.

I was looking for something to jump onto, in order to reach that window. I went around the corner to the garden and found a little box that looked stable enough to give me the necessary boost I needed.

I put the box right under her window and started climbing. I pulled myself up to peek through and could see her, nice and cosy, wrapped up in her blanket, quietly sleeping.

I reached for her window and tried to push it up. "Bingo! It's un-locked!" I said almost too loudly. I pushed it up all the way to the top and tried to climb in, headfirst, my hands on the frame. I was halfway through when I noticed that I hadn't latched the window properly at the top. By then, it was already too late to stop the catastrophe. The window dropped down right on my back. I tried to somehow keep the scream of pain to myself, but the bang of the window crushing against my body was already loud enough to wake Emma up. She jumped up, looked at me and started screaming out loud. I was trying to calm her down. She was reaching for her lamp when I shouted "Stop! It's me, Emma, it's me!"

"Holy shit Ben! What the fuck are you doing?" she howled, slightly shocked.

Well, I guess it must have looked rather awkward, and I wasn't quite sure how to explain myself. In my head, this was going to pan out slightly differently.

"Hmm, what can I say Emma? I need to talk to you," I said as I tried to calm her down.

"Are you not supposed to be at your exhibition?" she said.

"Well, I am obviously not!" I answered.

She was still sitting on her bed with one arm attached to the lamb, ready to throw.

"So, what do you want to talk about then, Ben?" she asked a little exasperated.

"Hmm, would you mind helping me out of this slightly uncomfort-able position?" I asked back kindly.

I could see her confusion about the whole thing slowly turn into a tired, little smile.

While she lifted the window up and helped me enter her room, I thought about how we hadn't exactly left on the best terms the previous night. Luckily, this thought disappeared in the next second. She got straight back into bed and covered herself with the blanket.

I placed myself next to her.

"So Ben, are you going to tell me what all this is about?"

"Yes, sorry for the trouble Emma, but I couldn't wait any longer. I know not everything is perfect yet. I mean when is it ever perfect? Anyway, that isn't the point. Since the very first time I saw you at the exhibition, I haven't been able to get you out of my head, and the past few months have been the best of my life. Including the whole rollercoaster ride that we've been on. We're two people with very different lifestyles, but we have a really strong connection. Long story short, I don't want to have a single day without you anymore. Emma Anne Wilson, I love you!" I said, stopping myself to reflect on how cheesy the last few sentences must have sounded. Her facial expression confirmed it, so I felt the need to say it in a clearer way.

"Jesus Emma, I want to be your boyfriend!" I laughed. I could see a little blush, which turned into a shy smile. I was expecting some words or some sort of reply, but she just looked into my eyes, placed her hand on my cheek, came closer and gave me a soft kiss.

# 30.
# LAVENDER

It was still hard to believe what had happened in the last few hours. It felt like a dream when I opened my eyes and saw a familiar face, her eyes still closed.

The pillow I was lying on smelled of lavender. It was Emma's favourite scent, so much so that she put it everywhere, even on her pillows, to fall asleep better. I loved it, and at the same time it calmed me down as well.

Once again, I got caught up in watching her sleep. I couldn't quite believe that this woman next to me wanted to share her life with me. I was smiling, full of true happiness when Emma opened her eyes.

She opened them just a tiny bit, took her hands, rubbed her eyes and mumbled "Good morning," half asleep. She reached for my hand and said, "I'm happy you're here, Ben."

"Me too." I replied, stroking her hair.

You could tell she was still very tired and probably planned on sleeping some more.

"Sorry, Ben, don't get me wrong. I'm still overwhelmed by this whole thing, and I haven't had much sleep last night."

Suddenly, I could feel that this perfect moment was about to shift. I tried not to let my emotions get the best of me. "It's okay, I understand," I said.

At the same time, I could feel my enthusiasm and happiness turning into insecurity. The same insecurity that got me into a fight with her two nights prior. Emma could feel it too and tried to intervene straightaway.

"Everything is fine Ben, but I guess we still have to talk a bit because a lot of stuff has happened since we saw each other last."

"What do you mean?" I asked anxiously.

By now, Emma had realised that she wouldn't be able to drift back to sleep anyway—at least, not before we had talked this through. She could see the fear in my eyes.

"Ben, look at me!" she insisted.

I turned my face back to her and she continued.

"I love you and I am done running away from things. That became pretty clear last night when you got stuck in my window frame!" She had to stop herself because she couldn't suppress her giggling.

"I don't know if anyone has ever broken into my house before, and especially not to tell me that they love me! Let's face it, I've always tried to take the easy way out when problems occurred. I've pushed them away instead of dealing with them. I do understand that this might have hurt you, because disappearing for most of every weekend is not a good solution either, but it never had anything to do with you. It felt good in the moment, but I have to accept that this isn't the real world, and If I want the real world to make me happy, then I need to accept the challenges and problems of it and work through them. Otherwise, I will keep running away forever. I want to enjoy every moment of this, with you."

Her words healed all my doubts, within seconds. It felt like a massive weight had been lifted off my shoulders.

"Same," was all I needed and wanted to say while grabbing her hand. What looked and felt like two teenagers freshly in love is exactly what it was. It's very hard to describe the feeling of fully being into someone. So many times, we meet people who are nice and who may have a certain influence on our life, but out of the on average estimated eighty thousand human beings we meet in our lifetime, there are just a few who really strike us, who fully get us and are on the same page as us.

That feeling of vibrating on the same frequencies at the same time is so particular and impossible to explain. When you aren't in this position, it can easily appear somewhat cheesy, overrated and overdone. I can confirm, though, that this is one of the most beautiful feelings in the world, by far. Everything that was important to me beforehand—painting, a job, enough money, et cetera had become so minuscule within such a short space of time. Someone getting your feelings moving by just looking into your eyes is such a fleeting moment that, when it surfaces, you ought to do everything humanly possible to maintain it. I must have been the happiest guy to ever climb through a window in the middle of the night.

"Avocado on toast?" Emma said, starting to laugh in the same second.

I couldn't hold back. "Of course, Paul Ripke!"

For a tiny millisecond, I was afraid of scaring her off again, but she continued laughing and it was clearly obvious that the ice between us had finally and entirely broken.

We both got out of bed, went into the kitchen and started preparing breakfast together.

"So how does it feel?" Emma asked.

"How does what feel?" I probed.

"Being in a relationship with a famous and successful photographer," she smirked.

My smile beamed from cheek to cheek. Whether she meant it or not, it was very attractive hearing her talk about herself like this, without sounding arrogant. I decided to go for the counterattack.

"Well, how does it feel to be in a relationship with one of the best painters in New Zealand," I said full of feigned self-confidence.

"Uhhh, someone is full of himself," she replied.

We were just joking around, but the initial question still stood—

how did we both seriously feel about being in a relationship with one another?

At the same time, I think it felt liberating for both of us, to call ourselves good, famous, best or amazing—something probably neither of us had done before, especially not when it came to our passions.

"I think we should do this more often," I said.

"What? Avocado on toast?" Emma replied. We both laughed again.

"That too," I said, "...and also thinking of ourselves as amazing artists."

"That's true. That's something I've learned from you Ben," she said.

"From me?" I asked, shocked. I definitely did not consider myself to be an amazing artist, nor would I ever say any such thing about myself, so I had no idea how Emma could have learned that from me.

"Yes, you might not practice what you preach, but you're the one who kept pointing out my talent and passion for photography. You wouldn't shut up about me following my passion and standing up for it."

I blushed like a scolded toddler.

"You might not be aware of it, but you did, so it's about time that you start following your own words of wisdom on a daily basis."

"How do you mean?" I asked slightly confused.

"Ben, you live and breath art. Watching you at an exhibition, explaining your paintings to others, makes me smile. I love it. I could watch you for ages. You commit to putting your emotions into your creativity, creating something out of them. You send messages. You make other people feel something, and you let yourself be vulnerable by expressing all these emotions that you're carrying inside. That in itself is a gift that not a lot of people have. You take the risk of getting hurt by putting something out there, which is something really unique about you, that has an effect on others. You are a true artist and you are enough," she finished.

Her words were like a blessing to my soul, and it felt amazing to receive them. I felt like I had been fully understood by someone—something that doesn't happen very often.

"Thanks, Emma," was all I could croak. For the first time in my life, I had received a compliment and didn't feel like putting myself down. Usually, my natural reflex was to look for facts or arguments that would go against what Emma had just said, but not this time. This time, someone had just made their way straight into my heart.

"I am good enough," I silently whispered to myself while cutting the avocado.

"What did you just say?" Emma asked curiously.

"Nothing," I said, and reached for the pan to make the poached eggs.

# 31.
# SUNDAY ROAST PREPARATION

Big Nan was still fast asleep in her chair. Emma and I continued to talk about how we fell in love, our rocky start and the challenges that we had faced thus far. It was incredible to think about just how far we both had come.

"See what we've accomplished?" said Emma. "We'll be able to get through the rest of it as well. What are six to twelve months apart compared to the rest of our lives together?" sounding almost hypothetically.

That was exactly the point at which I broke apart.

How can you not mind being apart for such a long time? How can you not be afraid that something might happen? It all felt out of my control. It just felt as if someone had taken over, and that whatever would happen would happen without me being able to influence it. Emma would go back to her paradise, and I'd be stuck here.

These are all things I should have said to her face, but they ended up just being thoughts that I considered too risky to say out loud. I was too timid. Instead, I decided to keep it all bottled up and only acknowledge to myself how long we might have to be apart.

"Six to twelve months can be a very long time. A lot can happen," I said and knew straightaway that such a stupid sentence wouldn't make it any better.

So far Emma still seemed pretty sure about it all and was playing the "Everything will be alright" part.

"You said it yourself—we have a strong connection, so what could possibly go wrong?" she asked.

I could already see that this conversation would either end up nowhere or in a fight. I felt so misunderstood, and so did she probably, but I selfishly thought that since I was the one who lost everything, everyone should understand me and throw me a lifeline to which I could attach myself to. "Hey, you haven't lost everything! You have me," is what I would have liked her to say, but her going back to New Zealand on Tuesday was the sign that told me that I had lost everything, including Emma.

"A lot can happen, Emma," was the meaningless phrase that I repeated.

"Ben, this isn't going anywhere. I know you're hurt, and I totally understand, but we need to look into the future. Everything will be alright," she repeated, exactly what I didn't want to hear at this moment.

"That doesn't help, Emma!" I quipped back.

You could tell by the look on her face that she had decided to give it a rest for now.

"Alright, Ben. I think Mum could use some help in the kitchen. I'll go and help her prepare the food," Emma said as she stood up, striding into the kitchen.

I looked at Big Nan, resting peacefully. Then I checked the clock on her wall that was ticking away and noticed that there was still some time before the rest of the family would arrive at Nan's place for dinner. I let myself fall back into the couch, looked at the ceiling and remembered the time when Emma and I were fully on the same page, living and enjoying our lives together in New Zealand.

"It was such a great time," I whispered to myself and closed my eyes.

# 32.
# SHANTI SHANTI

It's been almost twelve months since I'd climbed through Emma's window and asked her to share my life with me. It's not a secret that we'd been through some up and downs. Not escaping and actually facing her problems didn't feel that easy for her, but what made me confident was that I could see who she truly was and why she really wanted to change her life.

Emma was a fragile diamond that you needed to take good care of. She was shiny and full of smiles all day. She tried to be there for everyone no matter how close she was to that person. She brightened the day of everyone in her life. The only thing she forgot sometimes was to take good care of herself, but especially, because of the first part, I loved her so much and could call myself very lucky to have her in my life.

"Nice picture, isn't it?" Emma said.

I was staring at this picture in front of me for what felt like an eternity. The picture was capturing an old man, sitting on the step outside his door in front of what looked like a house in a little fishing village, assuming somewhere in Portugal or Spain. In the background, you could make out a fishing boat and the sun setting over the ocean. It felt like the dream to me. Living by the ocean looking back on your life and truly being able to say, "You have given it all, and this life was more than totally worth it." I needed to stop myself from not drifting off too far into endless spheres of nostalgia.

"Very nice, it has some great cinematography to it and really gets me thinking. I absolutely like it."

Emma smiled across both sides, holding a little plastic cup filled with dry white wine.

"It's Beth's shot," she said.

Emma and I were at a photography gallery attending an exhibition organised by her friend Beth. It was very inspiring for me to see all these photographs. They were the kind of pictures that capture reality rather than drift off into some abstract world, but still, the creativity in those photos was far beyond me. I was amazed by how capturing reality can be so simple yet complex all at once.

"You must be Ben, right?" I heard a high-pitched voice saying. I turned around and saw a woman with brown hair wrapped up in a turban, wearing a flowing brown dress. My first thought was "that must be Beth."

"Yes, I am," I replied.

"Hey, I am Beth. I've heard a lot about you, my friend. Not just good stuff. I can tell you that," she said without any facial expression.

For a second, I was trying to figure out if that's the kind of humour she wanted to go for, or if Emma might have told her some insights about our rocky little start. Beth sensed the confusion and resolved it straightaway with a very loud laugh, "I'm only joking, Ben!"

Emma started laughing as well. I tried to put my fake smile on and not give away how annoyed I was about her tone of laughter.

"Emma is only telling me good things about you. In her eyes, you are the little brother of Picasso. I'm glad to finally be able to meet you," she said.

This time I started to smile and blush a little bit, but not because of what Beth had said. It was more because of Emma who had just grabbed my hand, right in the second that Beth had opened her mouth. The feeling of someone believing in you and supporting you unconditionally is definitely a unique one. It sets a kind of energy free that I'd not experienced before. What amazes me about it is that there is only little need in order to give someone that feeling of unlimited support.

The most important thing is—be there and don't question it. Emma was always there for me and she never questioned my dream.

I answered with a timid, "Thank you."

However, that wouldn't hold Beth back from asking more questions.

"Anything here inspiring for you then? I see you've been staring at my granddad for a while," she pointed out. Her direct way of talking and analysing me had developed into a challenge for me.

"This, I mean, is this your granddad?" I pointed at the picture I had been staring at for the last twenty minutes.

"Yes, he is indeed," Beth said and started to tell us the story with no need to ask.

"He was a happy man and didn't need a lot in his life. Lived by the ocean in Portugal for almost his whole life. He loved the simplicity of life."

"The simplicity of life?" I asked, confused since life was feeling like everything but simple to me.

"Yes, tell me what is there that you really need in life in order to have a nice and happy life?" she asked.

Now the conversation started to evolve, and Emma and I got intrigued.

"Money, a job, a house, some goals, maybe?" I offered.

Emma nodded, "I agree. So many challenges as well."

"Guys, for real? Come on. Where does your happiness come from?" Beth asked provocatively.

"What do you mean by that?" I asked.

"Okay, listen, I'll only say it once. So pay attention or write it down. True happiness comes from the inside," she said, making a rhetorical pause.

"That sounds very shanti shanti to me," slipped out of my mouth.

Fearing their reaction, I heard that big laughter once again and was relieved that she took it the right way.

"I totally get it, Ben. It does sound like that a little bit, but I have proof," Beth said.

"Show us!" Emma requested.

Beth pointed again at the shot of her grandad.

"This guy. He's the reason I got into photography. Back in the day, I spent a lot of time with him in Portugal. My parents were living in London back then, but whenever I could, I'd escape to go see him. He was living the opposite life of what his daughter, my mum, was living in London. Once I asked him if he could ever get bored here."

Now Emma and I were fully listening and drawn into her story.

"He said, 'I have more than your mum will ever have, Beth.' At first, I was shocked when he said that. I was only twelve at that time. I loved my mum, so I asked him why he would think that. He said that he had been there—having everything and nothing at the same time."

The confusion in our minds was bottling up. Emma and I looked at each other, very irritated. We didn't know what to believe, or where this story was going to take us.

Beth noticed that our cups were empty and turned around. She grabbed two fresh plastic cups of white wine from the table behind her and pushed them into our hands.

"Ready to hear more?" Beth asked.

I don't know if she was trying to get us drunk, but either way, we were absolutely ready to fully dive into her story.

" 'There's a reason why I'm where I am today, Beth,' granddad said to me back then. 'I really hope you'll understand that one day as well,' he continued.

" 'Understand what?' I had asked him.

" 'What life and happiness really mean,' he said.

" 'What does it mean?' I queried.

" 'Just think about where the word life is coming from. It comes from living. Do you think your mum or all these other people are living their lives?' he tossed at me.

" 'I don't know granddad,' I said in awe of his audacity. I was still so young at the time, how could I know?

" 'The key in all of this lies in simplicity,' he continued. 'The more simple your life is, the more beautiful it is. The more creative you are, the more living you get out of life.'

"Makes sense to me, but what about the feeling of achieving something in life? I even asked him that back then, because I could see that my mum was chasing something.

" 'Beth,' he said soothingly. 'Achieving what? For whom? There is no one in this world out there to whom I need to prove something. If I'm old and senile one day, sitting in front of my house, watching the ocean, looking back on all these beautiful memories and happy moments that I've had, then I'll be able to say that I've achieved the biggest goal of my life.'

" 'But you are such a good photographer,' I said to him.

" 'I know, but only because I don't have to prove it to anyone. The only person I have to convince is myself. I need to feel it. Art and creativity mean nothing else than letting your emotions lead you and confronting your true self. Art without emotions is not art. I know I'm a good photographer and that's what makes me happy. I don't need this proven by any magazine, exhibition or anything or anyone else. I'm going to be the one sitting in front of my house one day, smelling the salty air, looking back at those pictures and feeling the emotions that those moments have captured. If that's the case, I don't have to worry about it at all. Art is not about exposure. Art is about the simple fact of doing what makes you dance alone, makes you cry, makes you laugh, jump, be thoughtful, reflective. It simply touches you. Just you and yourself, no one else needed.' "

Emma and I were speechless. Her story totally got us, but one question was bugging me. I couldn't help myself.

"Why are we here then, at the exhibition, Beth?" You could feel that Emma felt my question was inappropriate. She squished my hand. I didn't have a choice, I needed to ask that question. Beth could feel it and nodded towards Emma, telling her indirectly that it was okay to ask.

"That's a very astute question. There's a simple answer to it. I'm just like my mum and didn't listen to him," she admitted.

"But why?" I felt like I was pushing my limits here, but I really wanted to know.

"This is the question I have to ask myself every single time I tell this story. Maybe it's time to revisit it again. You know, sometimes the right things take time, but in the end, you'll get there."

"Very shanti shanti," I said once more. I took a big sip from my plastic cup, and the first thing I heard was her annoying laugh yet again.

# 33.
# SHE'LL BE ALRIGHT

"Let's not keep talking about me and my problems, Picasso."

"Oi, the only person who is actually allowed to call me that is her," I snapped and pointed towards Emma. I hadn't told her yet that, in the early days, Francis used to call me this as well.

Beth laughed and said, "I didn't mean to offend you Ben, but tell me, where do you get your creative inspiration from?"

*Good question*, I thought. I had never really considered it.

"Maybe I need another cup of wine to answer that question," I smiled. Without wasting a second, Beth grabbed my empty plastic cup and exchanged it for a full one.

"There you go," she said, and handed me that fresh cup of white wine, curiously awaiting my answer.

To be honest, that was just my strategy to get a little more time, but I still had no idea how to answer her. I decided to just repeat my thoughts out loud.

"This is a good question, Beth," and I stopped. After a few seconds of awkward silence, Beth asked, "And?"

I guess a lot of people expect an answer that kind of goes something like, I go into nature, I go to exhibitions, listen to music, et cetera. Then you take a picture of yourself doing exactly this, post it on social media and everyone thinks you need to hear the birds singing in order to be creative. In my opinion, creativity is something else—a lot more complex than just staring at the ocean. Don't get me wrong. You free your brain from all the stuff that is going on in there, and you confront yourself with all the issues you are having. By doing this, you start to feel something, and maybe you can turn those feelings into art one day. So, on one hand, I guess for some people it kind of can be very simple, but on the other hand, it mainly appears to me as such a difficult thing to explain and understand. I guess, the truth is that I don't really know where I get my inspiration from. I just work through the stuff that happens to me in life—positive or negative. Those experiences I turn into art (almost like Beth's grandad had suggested). I wasn't quite sure if I wanted to start this topic again, and I was also doubting that she would agree with my point of view. Therefore, I went for almost the opposite answer, which was also true, in a way.

"Look, I don't really have an answer to this, I guess. Some days I paint, some days I don't feel like it and I still paint. Sometimes I start feeling something and it turns out to be a keeper, and sometimes it's just crap," I said.

"Interesting, at least not the standard nature blah-blah-blah-bullshit," she said.

For the first time, she actually made me laugh, and I was very surprised by her answer. Maybe I'd judged her completely wrong and she would actually understand. The only way to find out would be to ask her.

"How about you then, Beth?"

"Well, I don't want to talk about my granddad again, but he definitely mastered the creative process in my eyes."

"I totally agree from what I heard about him so far," Emma said, who was silently paying attention the whole time.

"Not sure Emma if I'd ever told you this story though," Beth said, raising her index finger. Without Emma and I saying another word, Beth decided to share another anecdote about her grandad.

"At the very beginning, when I started to capture life in a photograph, I was often dismayed—the classic sentiment of not being good enough. I compared my pictures with other photographers on Instagram, and the more I scrolled, the more discouraged I became."

"What did you do?" I interrupted her.

"The worst thing you can do. I bought more gear."

Emma and I couldn't hide our smiles, and Beth noticed.

"It's okay, I guess. All the shame is well deserved here. To be honest, it happens so often to so many of us. It took me a while to understand it all, until one day I arrived at my granddad's place again to take photos. I was in my early twenties, and with grandparents you never know how much time you have left, so I decided to visit him. I admired him for so many things and he knew all about my struggles as an artist. That day, I wanted to take pictures of him. I arrived at his place and started setting up all my different lenses, tripods, cameras and all sorts of equipment. Straightaway I could see the shock in his eyes. He came up to me, took my hand, looked at me and asked if I was ready to be a photographer?"

"I didn't need to think about it at all. 'Of course,' I had said to him. He then grabbed all my stuff and put it into the boot of my car. 'Now pick your favourite camera,' he said. I was confused but decided to go for the very first camera I ever owned, as it was the one I was most familiar with."

"What happened then?" I interrupted again.

"I wanted to reach for the appropriate lens and once again he intervened, grabbed my hand and said, 'No. This is all you need today. Let's go,' and off we went walking towards the beach. 'Look around you, Beth. What do you see?' he asked me. I saw plenty of beautiful old houses white and blue, the sun shining on tiles with incredible artwork on them. 'What are you waiting for? Take some pictures,' he insisted."

"I followed his request and tried to find a good frame, but the sun was shining right into the lens and I couldn't see shit. The picture was way too bright. I tried another angle, but from the other side, the entire texture of the picture was gone. 'I need my lens,' I had said to him. 'Why?' 'Because of the sunlight,' I answered, frustrated."

"What did he say?" my curiosity interrupted her a third time.

"He simply told me to 'figure it out,' and I was utterly confused.

'Figure out how to make this look good with just the camera you have in your hand and the stuff you can see around you,' he explained further.

"He could see my frustration levels rising. While I was playing around with the functions of my camera, without a single clue, he walked a few metres away, picked something off the ground and came back.

" 'Take this,' he said and passed me a big leaf that came off a tree.

" 'A leaf?' I said, surprised.

" 'Yes,' he confirmed.

" 'What am I supposed to do with it?' I asked desperately. He grabbed the leaf out of my hand again and said, 'Go back to the same position you were before and look through your camera.'

"I knelt down, captured the same frame as before. It was still way too exposed when, all of a sudden, a slight shadow covered the strong exposure through the sun. Granddad was holding the leaf above my camera to cover the sunlight. At the same time, the leaf had a tiny hole where one small sunbeam was striking through diagonally from the top right corner of the frame all the way to the bottom left. All of a sudden, the way too exposed picture turned into a unique piece of art with the right settings, colours, contrast and brightness, and on top of that it was full of texture and started to tell a story."

Emma's jaw dropped. She was speechless. "What happened then?" she asked.

"We kept going and tried to find all sorts of things on the street and at the beach to achieve what I would normally cover up with expensive gear. At the same time, I started to understand why certain techniques were utilised. Questions I had never asked myself. My granddad could feel my mood changing.

" 'You know Beth, I've met so many people in my life who were craving to become someone in order to be happy. They were trying to compensate for their lack of discipline, patience, creativity and some-times even passion with material substance, but you can have all the gear in the world and still have no idea about something. The flashy football boots don't make you a better player. The newest surfboard doesn't make you surf better, and the best camera gear doesn't make you a photographer. My point is to go out there with just your camera, take pictures and solve issues that you are facing no matter how long it takes or how you do it. These are the things in the end that will make you, honey, a photographer.'

"His words are still etched in the back of my head to this very day. I couldn't be more thankful for our moments together. On the way back, I put all my equipment in one bag and decided to sell it all. While I was sorting all that out in my car, I turned around and saw him sitting in front of his front door, staring at the ocean. I took my camera, knelt down, took the same leaf and hit the button."

While she was saying that, her eyes were looking no longer at us. Beth was looking between Emma and me, staring at the picture behind us. It was her granddad sitting in front of his house staring at the ocean. Once again, Emma and I were blown away.

"I'm really sorry, Ben, that we've ended up talking about me again. So sorry. So tell me, how does this whole painting thing work out with your visa?" Beth asked. "Aren't you working full time as a barista?"

Her change in topic came quite suddenly while I was still trying to process her mind-blowing story.

"Yes, I do. I mean, I guess there shouldn't be any issues. I might get a couple hundred dollars for my paintings. But I'm very far away from properly making a living off them."

"Yeah, that's true. She'll be alright," Beth said.

While I was trying to figure out who she meant by "she," the girls had already moved on to the next topic.

# Boy Oh Boy, T.M.A, Eleonora - She'll Be Alright

I turned around one last time and was staring once again at the picture of Beth's granddad. The stories Beth had told about him had just confirmed my initial impression of the picture, but now I saw an even happier, more fulfilled, wise old man, looking back on a life full of ups and downs, wins and losses, but simple and totally worth living. A man who was truly in balance with himself. A man who had found happiness within himself.

# Boy Oh Boy, T.M.A, Eleonora - She'll Be Alright

# 34

# SHE'LL BE ALRIGHT PART 2

It had been a few months since we attended Beth's event, and afterwards I started to notice a change in Emma. I'd never seen her taking so many pictures and being so happy at the same time. It almost felt like all the pressure was gone, but not today. Today the pressure was back, but this time for a different reason. It was her day. We had everything prepared and we were just waiting for the final call.

Emma's dream was to get her New Zealand residency. Not necessarily to live here forever, but at least to have a backup plan. She'd never set any goals for her photography, instead focusing on something else. Her short-term goal was to achieve residency in this beautiful country on the other side of the world. Even the little "I don't need a plan" Emma was striving for some resemblance of security in her life. She started working on this before I had even met her. I very much liked the idea of not worrying about visa situations, even though we had to talk about how long we actually might want to stay here. Occasionally, the thought arose of leaving our beautiful paradise together to go on a different adventure, but with the beauty of a New Zealand residence would come the obligation of staying in this country for a finite amount of time in order to turn this residence visa into a permanent one.

"What are you thinking?" Emma asked me while we were having coffee at home waiting for the magic phone call.

"Just thinking of how the next two years might look," I admitted to her.

"And how do they look?" she responded immediately.

I started laughing, "Well, this is what I was trying to figure out, babe."

I think Emma sensed a bit of insecurity here and was trying to dig a bit deeper. "Are you afraid you don't see yourself here in the next two years?" she asked.

I don't know if she was right or wrong. This place had given me so much that I didn't want to leave it just like that, but the commitment that comes with her visa was a bit intimidating. I felt the pressure of coming up with a response.

"Fear of commitment?" she tried to guess.

"There isn't any fear, Emma. I'm excited for you and for us. I know how badly you want this, and I know how hard you've been working for it. You've been unconditionally supporting me in my dreams, and so will I gladly support you in yours."

She smiled and grabbed my hand as if to say, "thank you." I felt the need to elaborate a little bit more though.

"If that means for the next two years you will be here, then the next two years I will be here. There will be enough time for us to go on more adventures together."

"Thanks, Ben, I appreciate your support. First things first though—I have to get my visa, then I can finally get rid of my job."

In order to get her visa, Emma needed to stay in her shitty office job. It's just not her, and it wasn't much dissimilar to my life in Germany before—the main reason I escaped to the other side of the world. Seeing her in a similar position facing the same struggle did upset me. You might think that it's not possible to face the same issues over here, because for so many people it's paradise and it truly is, but believe it or not, people are facing a similar struggle here as well. At least some of them. Emma was part of it, and she had been suffering from it quite a lot. Her job situation clearly had contributed to her mindset of escaping in the past. I tried to support her as much as I could, but the goal of her residency was tied to this job.

Suddenly, we heard a knock at the door. Emma jumped up, thinking immigration might bring the relieving message in person. She ran to the door, opened it and saw Francis standing there. I had invited him over for breakfast. We hadn't seen each other in ages and he wanted to congratulate Emma.

"And?" he said so loud that I could even hear it in the kitchen. I finally introduced them to each other at one of my previous exhibitions. Francis had been my very first friend here. He was a major reason why I started painting, and also why I climbed through Emma's window that fateful day. So it was important for me that they both would get along. They came back into the kitchen, as Emma was telling him that we were still waiting for the magic call. He could sense the tension.

"Are you guys okay?" he asked after greeting me with a classic Kiwi hug.

"Yes, we were just talking about how this whole dream of Emma's visa is tied to her unpleasant job situation. Everything will be a big relief once it's over," I elaborated.

I poured Francis a coffee without asking. He grabbed it and started talking right away. "Thanks, mate. Yes, I totally get that. Unfortunately, quite often we get ourselves into situations where we build up dependencies and can't get rid of the main source that is causing the pain. In Emma's case, it's the job that's tied to her visa. In other cases, it can be a relationship that is tied to various restrictions, like my and Grace's," he said.

It's true their relationship was very dependent on Grace's dream and passion. Sometimes we might underestimate what we have to sacrifice in order to follow our passion. My mind wanted to go deeper down that road, but Francis continued and presented his solution to this dilemma.

"There are two ways to go about it. Either you make sure the foundation you tie your dependencies to is solid and makes you happy in the first place, or you restrict your dependencies to none. The second option looks a bit harder but can be totally worth it and liberating. Either way, you come to the point where you must ask yourself, is it in fact worth it to reach that goal when it is tied to something that makes you so upset on a daily basis?" It was a very valid point he made here, and it felt like exactly what we were dealing with right now.

I was amazed how Francis would always enter a scenario and connect the dots straightaway. Emma's smile turned into a more worrying expression. Francis could sense it once again. "Don't worry, guys. You'll be totally fine. I guess I was just referencing more to me and Grace here."

I wasn't quite sure if it entirely was just related to their problems, but at the end of the day, I was pretty sure Emma would get her visa and everything would be okay.

"She'll be alright, as we say here in New Zealand," Francis said.

"I've heard that before, even though I still don't know who 'she' is," I admitted. Francis and Emma both laughed.

"You played it pretty cool in front of Beth though," Emma smirked. She was right about that. I was hoping someone would help me out here, but it looked like it would remain a secret as to whom "she" is.

I was still trying to figure out what this could all mean now for Emma and myself when suddenly the phone rang. There was a high chance that this would be the call from the immigration office. Emma jumped up again, ran to the phone and answered. Instead of saying her name, she was so nervous that all she could say was, "Hello."

We couldn't hear what the person on the other end was saying, but after Emma said, "Yes that's me," it was almost clear it was the call we had been waiting for the whole morning.

A few seconds passed, but her facial expression was still blank. Francis and I tried to guess until we heard a loud "Thank you so much."

It was pretty clear that could only mean one thing. She followed up with a "For sure. Thanks a lot. Have a good day." She put the phone down, looked at us and the big scream that we both expected came.

"I got my visa!" she screamed through the whole house. We both jumped up, let out a big "Yes!" and ran over to embrace her. I just wanted to give her a big, long hug. Emma's joy was limitless. I don't know if I had ever seen her so relieved and happy at the same time.

We opened a bottle of bubbles for the occasion and threw a spontaneous brunch. I peered down at my glass of bubbles, took a sip and then looked over at Emma. She smiled from one ear to the other.

"I have to tell Mum," she said super excited as she picked up the phone to call her.

The moment she called her mum, a thought came through my head, more unexpected and as fast as a lightning bolt. *The next two years are set in stone now.*

# 35.
# STUCK

"Goodbye, see you tomorrow," I said to my boss in the café at the end of my shift. I turned around and stepped outside through the front door. It had been a very long day, but my shift was finally over. I jumped onto my bike and there was only one place where I wanted to go, to my little studio. The place where I spent most of my time recently.

Emma and I were at the peak of our life together in New Zealand. She was so relieved about her visa, got a new job and just got more and more into her photography. On top of that, we moved in together just a few months ago. Sam and I decided to rent our own studio space together. Therefore, the heartbreak of our time as former flatmates wouldn't be so hard and we would still see each other on a regular base.

I sped up as fast as I could, not necessarily because I was in a hurry, but because I hate slow bike rides, especially when I'm by myself. It's different if I am riding with someone else and there's no real place to go to, but if I know where I'm going, I just want to get there as fast as possible. I crossed the last intersection, turned left and could already see Sam's car parked in front of the gate of our studio. He mainly uses the studio space when he needs to escape from his new flatmate to do some art collective planning.

I locked my bike next to the gate and went inside. I opened the door and could already hear him shouting across the room, "Hey mate."

The studio was in the shape of a square with big open windows facing west for some proper afternoon sun. It for sure had some real loft vibes.

We had a couch in there to chill, a little desk for Sam to get some work done and obviously a lot of painting tools and equipment. If you think of a cliché, urban Berlin art studio of two guys in their twenties or early thirties with no real plans in place, then you probably have a good idea of how this studio looked.

When I entered the studio, Sam was sitting at the desk preparing for the next exhibition at the Auckland Art Gallery. It was a big one. I wanted to prepare my best paintings for it because I had a feeling that this could be a big chance for me as an artist. I tried to keep our conversation short in order to start painting straightaway.

"Yo bro," I said and tried to put on my best possible Kiwi accent.

"Aye, how was your day?" Sam asked.

"Alright, I guess," I said, already able to sense that he would pick up on this. In the same way that he motivated me to be upright and stand up for myself, he picked on my tendency to complain. In his ideal world, I would say that every day is amazing, but that seemed impossible to me.

"What made your day just alright?" he asked.

"Everything is fine, mate." I tried to correct myself. Yes, I said everything feels like it's in place, but there was still just one thing that I couldn't quite let go.

"But?" he continued to ask as if he would have sensed already that there was something on my mind, as always. I wasn't quite sure whether or not I should talk to him about how the thought or feeling of getting stuck had evolved in my head.

"I guess it's the usual topic of self-doubt and the fear of getting stuck?" I tried to explain.

"Stuck?" he shouted, dropping the pen in his hand that he was using to calculate the budget for the next exhibition.

"I mean, as you know Emma's visa situation is pretty tight, and I feel like the next two years are planned out without me having any influence on them. That makes me feel a little stuck," I said.

"Stuck?" he shouted again and stood up as if he were about to get angry with me for real.

"You start repeating yourself, mate." I tried to play it cool, but that was just the last bit that set him on fire.

"Dude, tell me one more time you are stuck and you can look for a new studio," he said.

"Ehm, I am the leaseholder of this place," I said.

"You know what I mean," he said and couldn't keep a serious face anymore. "Stop complaining or looking for the problem in your perfect world when there is none, okay?"

I was relieved that this was rather a life lesson of his and that he wasn't seriously angry with me.

"A couple of years back you actually had real problems. Look at what you have become now."

After almost three years of living in this place, I still hadn't gotten used to how supportive people were over here. Complaining was not an option and Sam felt the need to dig even deeper.

"Look how far you have come," he repeated. "You were a little boy who knew shit all. You came to wonderful Kiwiland to change your life! Now, a few years later, here you are telling me that your day was just alright and that you feel *stuck*?" he said and emphasised "stuck" again.

I was seriously trying to figure out if this was a rhetorical question or if he would expect an answer. The fact that he made a little thinking pause gave me the feeling that it was the first option. The moment he continued to talk I knew I was right.

"You live with your beautiful sweetheart, Emma, you have friends such as Matt, Francis and myself, you became a decent artist, you have your own studio and Francis told me you can almost stand up on a surfboard! You have everything you have asked for a few short years ago. So soak it up, mate. I mean how amazing is that? Just relax, enjoy it and be grateful!"

When he said it like this, I started feeling like an idiot. Maybe that was his intention. It definitely started to work, and all of a sudden I started reflecting and thinking about how crazy this journey had been up until now. I mean, my entire life had flipped upside down. From crazy heavy rocks in my stomach to a painter in New Zealand with the best life partner and friends possible.

"Remember that time when you asked for all the things that you currently have?" Sam asked.

"Yes," I said completely timidly.

However, somehow it almost felt like everything was too perfect, and I wanted to attract some trouble or action. I wanted to prevent myself from the feeling of getting stuck. One question was on my mind that I needed to ask out loud.

"What would you do if you feel like you have achieved everything here?" I asked Sam.

"Have you, Ben? Have you?" he said and got a little more serious. "I understand the need for constant growth and constant movement, but just because your next achievement, goal or whatever, might take longer this time around, it doesn't mean you are stuck. Ben, you've created your own world, your own little paradise, and just because now you have everything you've asked for, doesn't mean you need to reach further or for something else. Enjoying or embracing is also an option."

He was totally right. I just needed to find a way to convince myself about it. I really didn't know what to say.

"I need to continue with those paintings," I finally came out with, which was true. I had been holding a brush in my hand for the entire conversation.

"All good, I won't hold you back any longer mate. I have to leave now anyway, but maybe have a think about what I've said. Being grateful for the things you have is so much better than always reaching for the

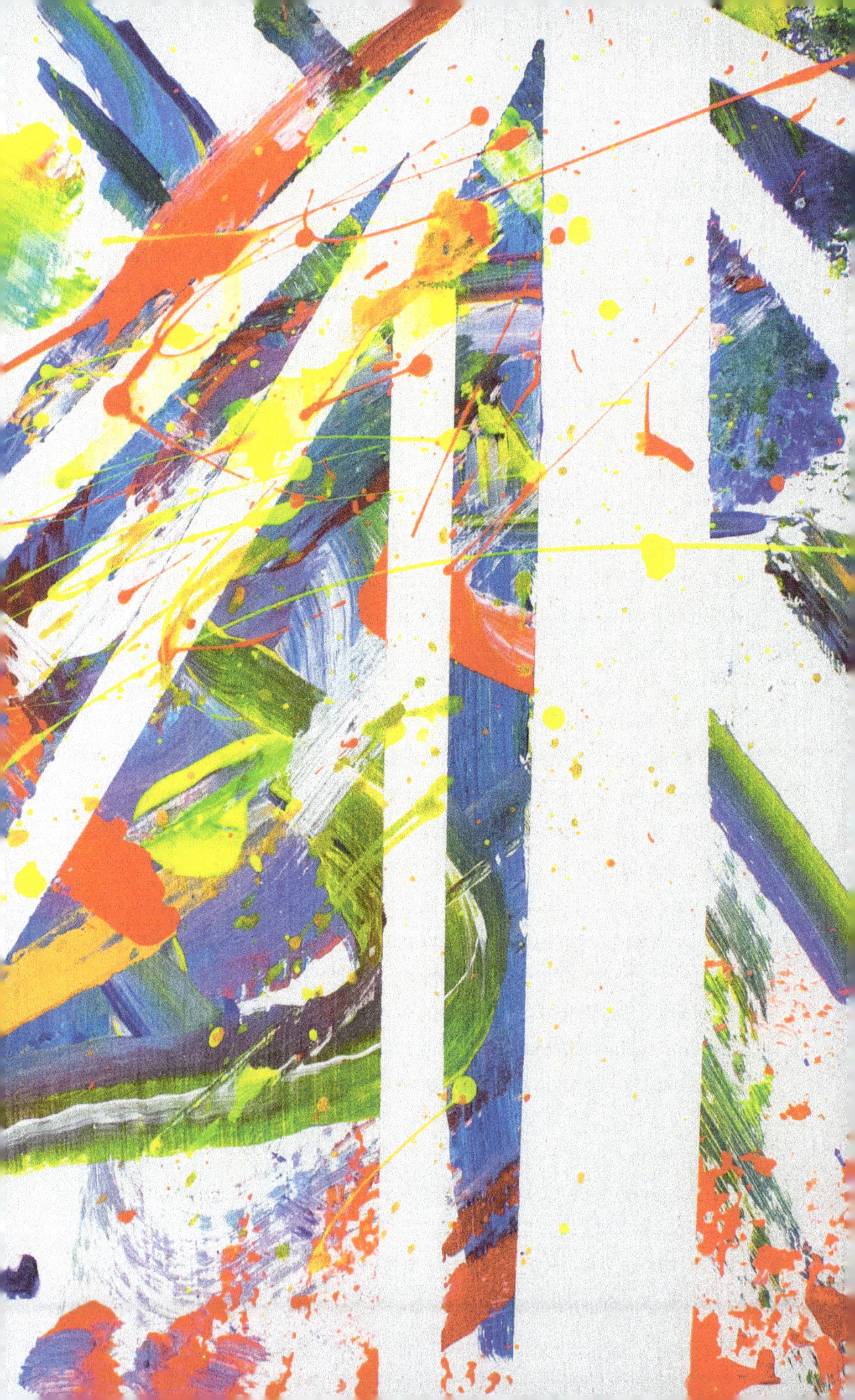

next big thing. You would notice that right away if somehow you were to lose the things you have right now."

"I know, Sam. I know you're right. I have definitely nothing to add to this. My brain just needs to understand that," I replied.

"Alright, I'll see you soon then. Make sure you get the best of the best for the exhibition next week. This event might actually be the next big thing for you and change your life. You never know," he said and shut the door of the studio behind him.

I wasn't quite sure what he exactly meant by changing my life. Maybe he was just teasing me based on my stupid feeling of being stuck. On the other hand, I knew that he saw every exhibition as an opportunity for every artist he takes care of. I decided to stop figuring stuff out for today, turned around and started painting.

# 36.
# THE BIG DAY

I was super excited about today. The past few weeks and months had been the most productive time in my life as an artist. I totally soaked up all the energy and advice from Sam, Matt, Francis, Emma and all the other beautiful and nice people around me. I loaded the last pieces of art into my car. I literally can't remember the last time I was so happy and proud of what I'd created. It's been an amazing feeling, and I couldn't wait for this exhibition to happen. A lot of people said they would attend tonight. You never know what will happen, but one important thing I learned from Sam is that you should look at every exhibition and every little step as if they could be your big chance, your life changer. One day in your career as an artist, it could be the case that one exhibition, one piece of art, or one Instagram post would change your life and would make your dream come true!

"Are we ready to go?" Emma asked.

Once more she had been a massive support in the last few months. I spent countless hours of my time in the studio and less with her. Quite often, Emma ended up eating dinner by herself while I tried to squeeze the last bit of creativity out of my brain. I could feel that I was coming closer to realising my dream of becoming an artist who is finally able to live off selling his paintings. It felt even more unreal having someone in your life who respects that and supports you, even if that means you have to put yourself and your needs in second place.

"Yes, that's it. Let's go!" I said.

We both jumped in the car and drove off towards the Auckland Art Gallery, exactly the same location where we first met. Emma noticed that I was more nervous than usual.

"Why so nervous?" she asked kindly.

"I don't know. I just have a feeling that tonight could be a big turning point. I don't know why. I just want everything to be perfect."

"There will never be a perfect, remember?" she said raising her eyebrow.

"Yeah, I know," I confirmed.

Just a few minutes later, I already slowed down the car and started looking for a parking spot as close to the entry as possible. I'd never had so much art for one exhibition, and especially none that I had been so proud of.

"There's one!" Emma spotted a gap by the door.

"Perfect," I said and turned right into the spot. Emma was about to leave the car and I grabbed her hand.

"What's up?" she said

"Thank you," I whispered.

"For what?" she chuckled.

"For everything. I can imagine it's not the greatest time with me spending so much time in the studio painting, coming home late for dinner and not giving you a lot of attention. I'm really happy to have you on my side," I smiled, and a little tear almost left my eye.

"Oh Ben, don't you worry. You have been inspiring to me since the first day I met you! I'm happy to have you! It's exciting sharing my life with you. I would do it again and again, every single time."

"Thank you," I whispered once more and tried to hold back my emotions.

We jumped out of the car and unloaded the artwork right in front of the gallery's entry. Sam and the other guys weren't there yet. It had never happened that I'd been the first one to arrive at an exhibition. This time Emma grabbed my hand. "Just calm down Ben. Everything is going to be alright!"

I was playing with my fingernails to distract myself from the nervousness that was controlling my whole body and causing a little stomach pain. Then from afar, I saw two lights, and as they came closer, I recognised the shape of Sam's car. He pulled up on the opposite side of the road, jumped out of the car and shouted across the street, "Hey guys!"

I don't know why every time I see him he makes me laugh. He grabbed two paintings and jogged across the road.

With both paintings under his armpits, he tried to reach for the keys in his pocket. After a gymnastic performance, he managed to reach the keys with the tip of his little finger. Emma assisted him, grabbed them out of his pocket and opened the door. Sam looked at us with his red face, sweat rolling down his forehead. "Thanks. Today is going to be a good one! I can feel it."

We went inside and Emma helped me set up my area in less than no time. Meanwhile, Matt and all the other guys had arrived. Within a half hour, the room was full of art and people that had something to tell the world.

"It looks great," Emma said as she passed me a glass of bubbles. "Here's to you, Picasso!"

She's called me that since the second date we went on. Technically the first one, because the actual first time she had a boyfriend. I reached for the glass and downed it to calm my nerves.

"Another one please," I said with a little smile, and Emma grinned back at me. The first people had come inside, and within the first thirty minutes, I had made two sales. That was already more than I'd usually sell in an entire evening at all previous events. Matt came over with another glass of bubbles. "Seems like your lucky day, Picasso." I don't know where he picked it up, and I swear he just said it for the first time. I didn't want to investigate any further and just took the compliment.

"Honestly man. You have made such strides in your work since the first time I met you. I always liked your paintings and your ideas, but within such a short amount of time they went through the roof."

*This was a bit too much*, I thought and didn't know what to say.

"Thank you, Matt, but you know I admire your stuff as well. If I'm honest, you have been a huge inspiration for me," I admitted.

"Ah come on, don't play the humbled guy. You are determined to go your way, so keep on swinging!" Matt said. I tried to laugh it away, but I wondered if he wanted to jinx something. Emma came back to me. She had been chatting away and looking at the other paintings.

"How are you doing honey?" she asked, smiling at me with her big, white, shiny teeth.

"Oh, from Picasso to honey." I laughed and continued, "It's going really well. People showing a lot of interest and…"

"Excuse me!" An older, serious-looking man interrupted us. I had noticed him ten minutes ago lingering. He was wandering around and didn't look like the usual person that would visit Sam's exhibitions.

"Yes, please?" I tried to be polite.

"Mr. Samson is my name. I'm an NZ Immigration Officer. Can I please see some ID?" I was very confused, and it took me a few seconds to realise what was going on.

I passed him my passport, which I always have on me, looked over to Emma and I could see the confusion on her face as well. He was looking at my passport and the piece of paper that was attached to it. It was my New Zealand Work Visa.

Sam saw that something was unusual and came over to us.

"Is there a problem, sir?" he interrupted. Samson looked at Sam, "I guess so, sir."

My heart dropped from my chest into my stomach, and I didn't know what was going on.

"I am the organiser of this exhibition. How can I help you?" Sam tried to intervene.

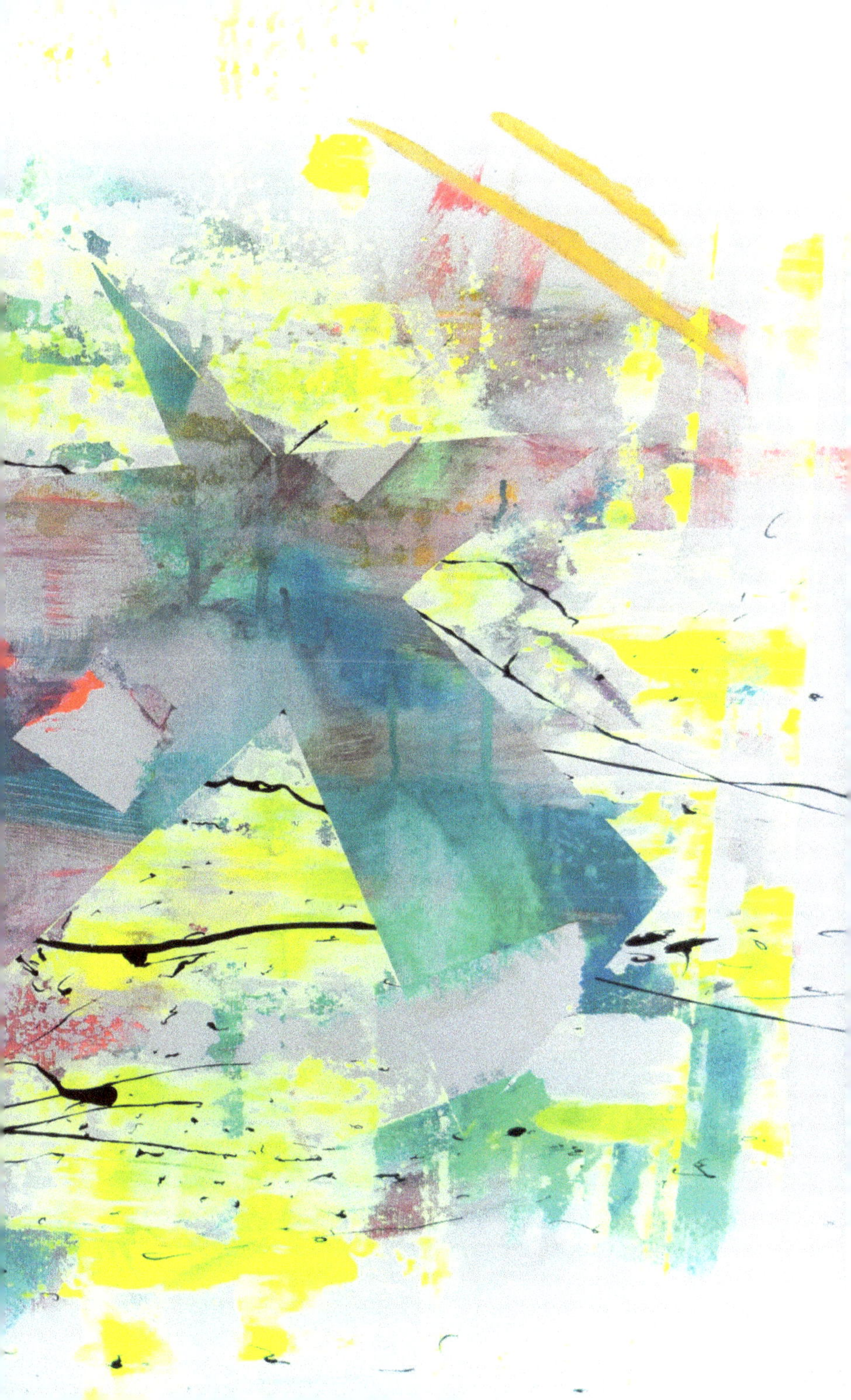

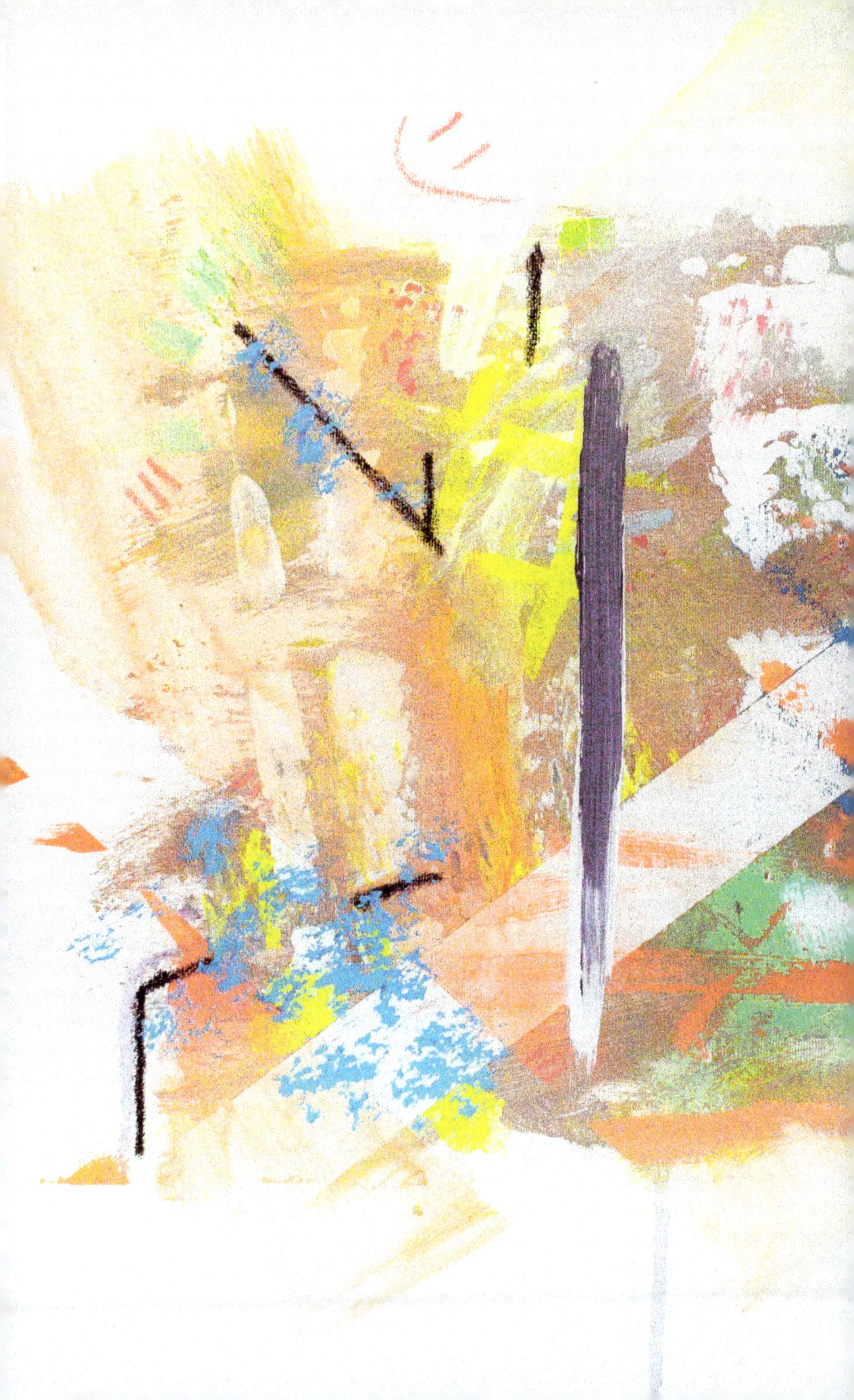

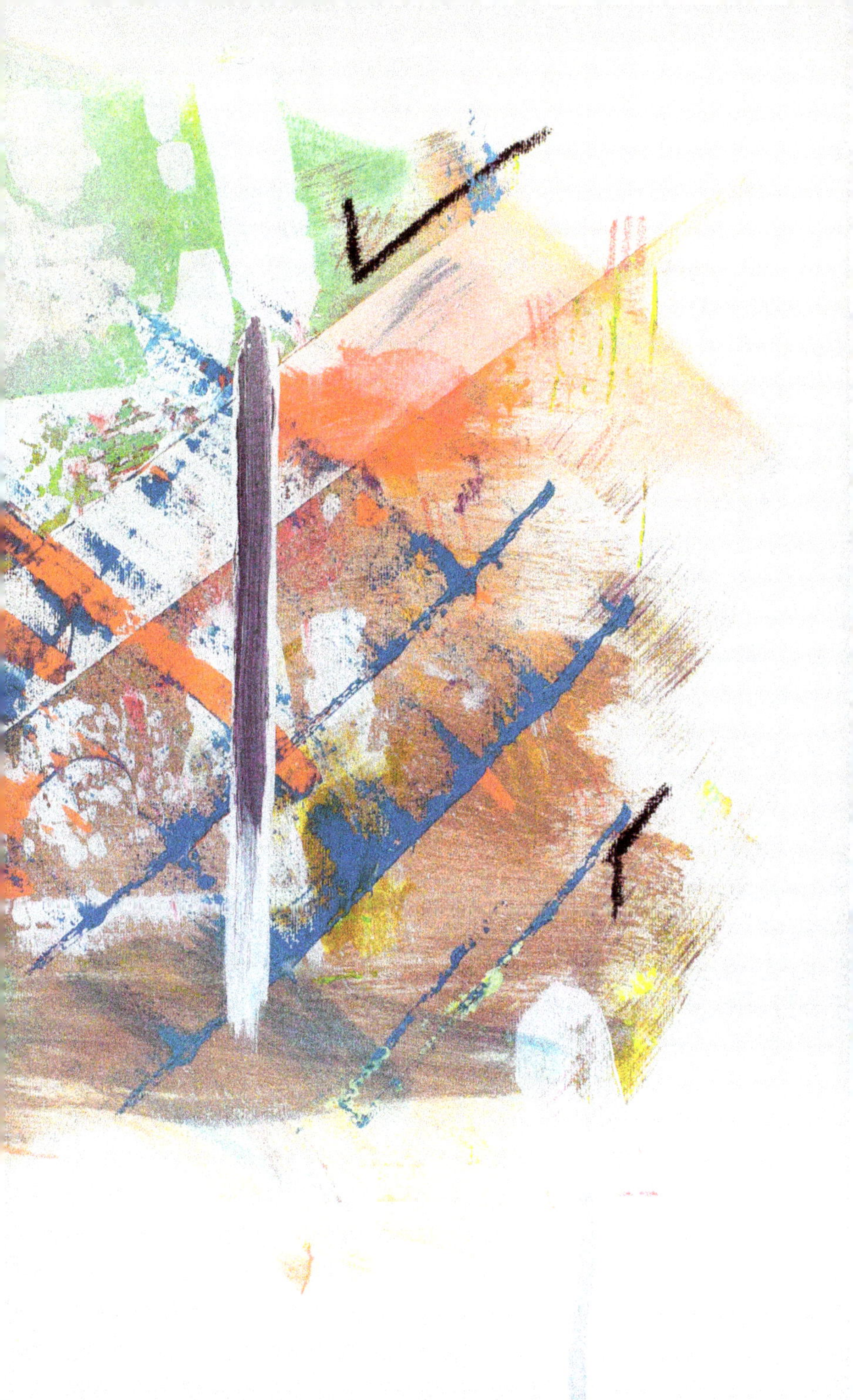

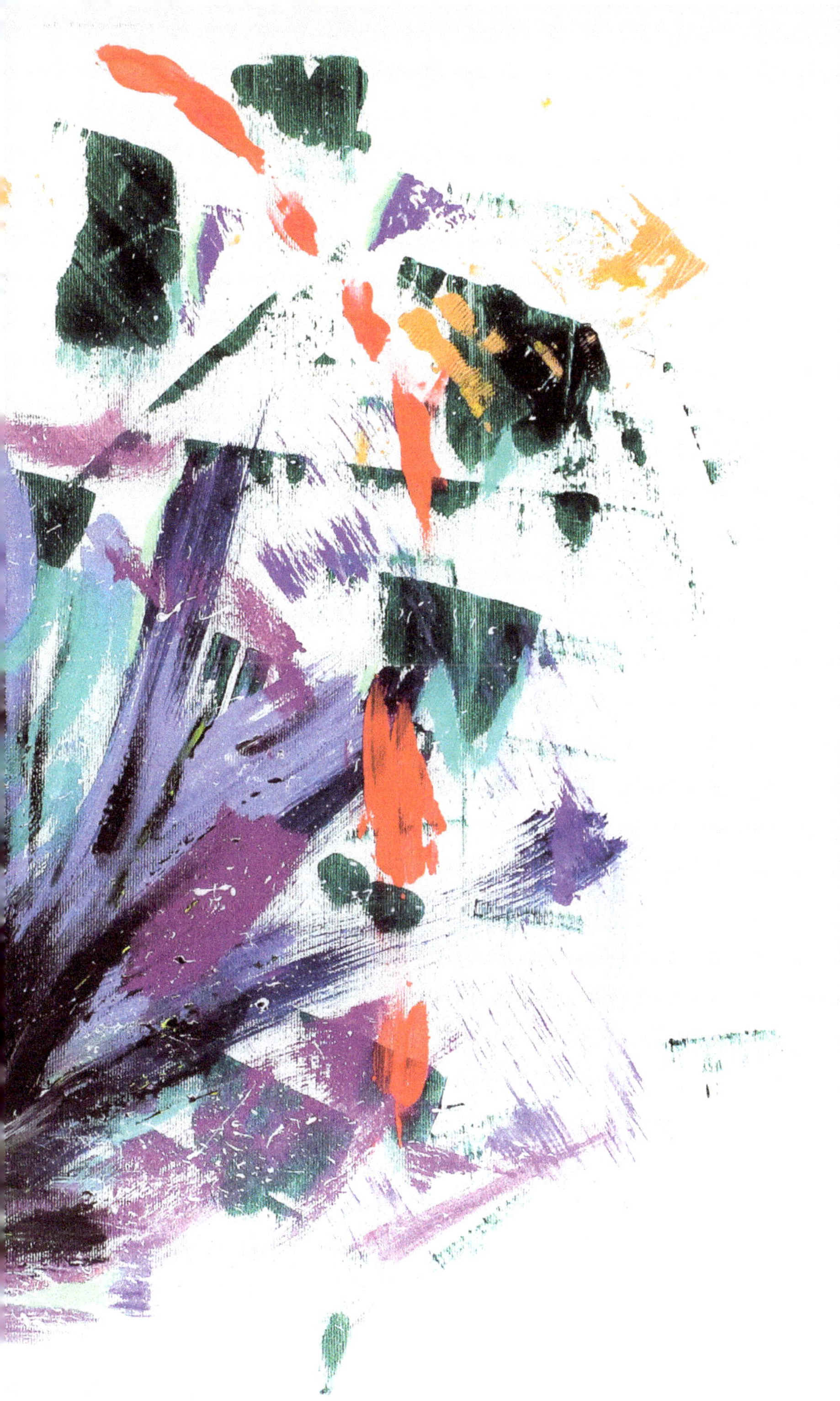

"NZ Immigration, Mr. Samson the name," he repeated to Sam, and then he turned back towards me. "Did you sell any pieces today sir?"

Sam tried to signal me not to reply, but I didn't know what to do. I was standing in front of my painted pieces with my names literally written all over them, and with two big gaps on the wall where the artworks that I'd sold had been hanging at the start of the night. I looked at Sam, then at my wall of art, then at Emma, and somehow I sputtered out.

"No, I haven't. Would you mind telling me what's going on officer?"

"I'm afraid, sir, that we've received multiple indications that you've been breaching the conditions of your work visa. Please follow me to the car. We will have to take you to the office to ask you some further questions."

My facial expression went blank. I was unable to understand what was going on.

I heard Emma saying, "What? You can't do that!"

I was paralysed and didn't know what to do. Sam put his hand on my shoulder and said, "All good bro, just go. Emma and I will take care of it."

"I'm coming with him," Emma jumped in front of me.

"Not happening," Mr. Samson said. "Please, after you," he commanded and guided me to the exit.

I turned around and saw the whole exhibition room in complete silence witnessing what was going on. Everyone had stopped talking and was staring at me and Mr. Samson. I saw Emma's face and could see the fear in her eyes. Mr. Samson escorted me outside and I jumped in the car, which was parked almost right in front of the entry next to mine. I looked back one last time to Emma, who was waiting at the gallery's entry, and I whispered to myself, "Everything is going to be alright."

# 37.
# WHAT'S YOUR RELATIONSHIP TO ART?

## Jordan Rakei - Imagination

I was sitting in the back of Mr. Samson's car, staring fearfully into the dark sky outside the backseat window. He didn't say a single word on the way to the immigration office. I didn't even dare to ask anything. A million thoughts were running through my head. Had I done anything wrong? What was going to happen now? I still had Emma's face in front of me, which I felt was already telling me that this wasn't going to end well.

Mr. Samson stopped the car, opened the back door and pointed at the door of a building straight ahead of me. "Please follow me inside," he said, without showing any kind of emotion. He guided me into a room that looked like one of those rooms where the police interview the murderer and put them in jail afterwards.

In the exact same room was an elderly looking lady already awaiting my arrival. She wasn't showing any facial expressions either. Samson pulled the chair away from the table and gave me the order to sit down. I took a seat and put my hands on my legs. I could feel how sweaty they'd become. The atmosphere in the room with Samson and that lady fuelled my belief that this was really not going to end well.

The lady took some papers out, put on her glasses and started talking.

"So, Mr. Schenk, do you know why you're here?" she asked. I didn't know if it was a trick question or if she was awaiting an actual answer.

"To be honest I have no idea," I replied as I looked down to the floor.

"My name is Mrs. Rodgers, NZ Immigration. What is your relationship to art, Mr. Schenk?"

I didn't quite get this question in the first place. I was so confused and scared at the same time. Is this whole thing going to affect my visa?

"Eh, excuse me, Mrs. Rodgers. It's my hobby. I like painting."

*It's the truth*, I thought. It definitely is just a hobby, a hobby that I really love and would like to turn into a living. Right in this second, I clocked on and she continued with her next question.

"Just to get the facts straight. You do work at Muriwai Café, correct?"

"Yes." I could feel the fear rising in my body. I got nervous and started to understand how serious this situation actually was. This was going to be about my future.

"As what?" she asked.

"As a barista, Mrs. Rodgers," I said.

All of a sudden, I became aware of where this was leading now, and I waited for her next question. Even though I now understood what was going on, I didn't know what to do or how to react.

"And did you ever sell any of your paintings in exchange for money, Mr. Schenk?"

I started to panic. What should I say? I just thought, *Just say something, Ben!* What if I lie? I just want to get out of this situation. I didn't want to leave this country, my whole life is here. How could I have never checked whether it is permissible with my work visa? *It's a hobby*, I thought. *It's just a hobby!*

"No, I haven't," I heard myself saying. I just wanted to get out of there as soon as possible and thought this will be the quickest and only way. However, I reckoned without Mrs. Rodgers.

"You do know that holding back information or giving false or misleading information to an immigration officer is strictly prohibited. So, I'll ask you one more time. Did you sell any of your artworks?"

"No," I said again. I knew that it was a lie, and so did they. Things were way too obvious given that Mr. Samson had picked me up from an exhibition that was full of my artwork, but I totally panicked and was hoping for a miracle that would relieve me from this situation.

Mrs. Rodgers answered non-verbally with a little head nod.

She noted something done in her papers, stood up, looked at me and Mr. Samson and said, "Please remain seated here. We will be back soon."

Her definition of soon was longer than anyone else would consider soon. After an hour, I was still sitting there alone with my thoughts, and neither of them were back. I felt pretty bad for lying, but I feel like I didn't have a choice. It seemed like my only way to get out of here. I feared that the truth would make them deport me and would rip me from my life. My friendships with Sam, Matt, Francis, my relationship with Emma, my spirit for painting, my reputation as an artist and my dream of making a living from it one day.

After nearly ninety minutes, I saw the door handle move and only Mrs. Rodgers came back into the room. The atmosphere was even tenser than before. She sat back down on her seat and looked at me with her serious face again, which looked even more serious now.

"We have evidence that you lied to us, Mr. Schenk. So, I'll ask you one last time. Did you ever receive payment for selling your artwork?"

The situation was unbelievably obvious now, and I started to realise that there was no way I would get out of this with my stupid lie, but the consequences seemed even scarier and out of my mouth came the word "No", once again.

The room remained silent for a few seconds. Mrs. Rodgers nodded once more.

"Do you have your phone on you, Mr. Schenk?" she asked.

"Yes," I said.

"Please be so kind to open your online bank account for me," she said.

That was the final moment when I became fully conscious of the fact that I was not going to get away with my naive lie. That was the moment everything clicked in, and I realised that this was 100 percent going to end badly for me.

I tried to get my phone out of my pocket. With my hands shaking, I tried to unlock it. I missed the numbers to unlock the screen multiple times. I knew even my last client at the exhibition paid via online transfer straightaway.

The tension in the room was no longer bearable. My fear was eating me up from the inside and I threw the phone on the table. Mrs. Rodgers remained silent for a second and looked at me. She knew exactly what was going on. She knew she was in control and asked in a sarcastic manner, "What's happening, Mr. Schenk?"

I spluttered out, "I'm sorry. If I open my bank account, you'll find payments I received for my paintings."

I jolted and recoiled as up until this point in time I had totally ignored the fact that I wasn't supposed to receive any other income than from the job in the café. The job that got me my work visa. The job that gave me permission to stay in the country.

"So, you did get paid?" she insisted.

"Yes, but only a few times. I didn't really make much money at all.

It really is just a hobby, really!" I tried to apologise and make her understand. "You need to believe me," I added desperately.

She completely ignored what I had said and only acknowledged the one thing she wanted to acknowledge. "So, you have lied to an immigration officer, Mr. Schenk."

It felt like she was just a robot, working off a checklist. She had no emotion and made not even the smallest effort to understand my situation. I knew it's not her job to understand my situation, but I was just so afraid I would lose everything.

"Yes, and I am truly sorry," I said. You could see in her body language that she didn't care at all.

"Okay, I will go back and report this to Mr. Samson. Is there anything you want to add to your statement?"

*Yes, there is a lot that I want to say,* I thought. "I'm very sorry that I lied. I know that it was a mistake. The whole thing was a mistake really, but I hope we can find a solution where I can pay a penalty or something. My whole life is here, my girlfriend, all my friends, my belongings, literally everything. I've been living in this country for such a long time. Please don't send me back. Please let me stay!"

She didn't reply anything to this. She dropped the pen after taking my statement, stood up and said, "I'll be back shortly with a decision, Mr. Schenk."

Fifteen minutes had passed since she had left, but it felt way longer as I was alone with my thoughts and fears. After another five minutes, she came back into the room.

"So, I've discussed your case with Mr. Samson and I will let you know the official decision now."

I just answered with a nod and a little "Okay."

"You've received payments for drawing and selling your art. In this case, you have breached the conditions of your work visa, which clearly states that you are not allowed to receive any other income other than from your job as a barista at Muriwai Café. That means your visa is immediately terminated and you have to leave the country within the next twenty-four hours. As a German citizen, we will take your right to a free tourist visa away from you. Mr. Samson will escort you home now to pack your personal belongings, and then we will hold you here and send you home on the next flight."

She paused for a second, but just to give me the final death blow.

"Mr. Schenk, you're officially deported from New Zealand!" were the last words that resonated in my head.

# 38

# GOODBYE EMMA

## Boy Oh Boy, Lophelia - Goodbye Emma

opened the door to our apartment. Emma was sitting on the couch, turned away from me. As soon as she heard me entering, she jumped up, spun around and ran to me. She kissed me passionately. While she hugged me, she opened her eyes and over my shoulder saw Mr. Samson lurking in the hallway.

"What's going on Ben?" she asked.

I didn't know what to say. It sounded unreal, and I felt like it would be real if said it out loud, but I didn't have a choice.

"I have to leave the country by tomorrow morning. Mr. Samson is just here to look after me while I'm packing my belongings."

"I don't understand Ben. Why?" Emma started crying.

"Because I breached the conditions of my visa by selling my art. I officially have been deported from New Zealand."

I actually tried to smile. I touched her cheek and tears ran down her face. I wanted to stay strong, but I couldn't. So I gave in. I held her as tight as I could and started crying as well.

"I don't want to interrupt sir, but we don't have the whole night. Please go and pack your stuff."

I couldn't really believe what he had just said. I turned around full of anger. "I tell you what, Mr. Samson. You can deport me. You can take away my life, but you won't take away five last minutes with the person that I love, okay?" I shouted.

Before Mr. Samson was able to reply Emma snapped in, "What do you mean you have to go?"

"I'm not allowed to stay here. They will take me to the airport, and I have to stay in the transit area until my flight departs."

Her tears started to run faster and faster until she started to scream "No, no, no why? Ben, that can't be real!"

"I know Emma, we have to stay strong now. I don't know why this is happening or why anyone deserves this, but I tried everything that I could. I have no rights and no chance and I can't afford a lawyer right now," I said desperately.

Emma sank down to her knees. I bent over her and tried everything to calm her down while inside I raged.

Mr. Samson came towards me, "I am really sorry, but we only have ten more minutes so please pack your things."

This was the first time that any of these immigration officers showed some sort of emotion, but it was clear to me that it wouldn't last for long.

I helped Emma up. She tried everything to hold it together. I grabbed the biggest suitcase I could find and started packing some stuff. Just anything I could get. Deep inside, I was expecting to be back soon, but I didn't know when, so the majority of my stuff was just clothes.

Emma helped me and chucked more things into the suitcase. She put in a picture of us that was standing next to our bed, and again more tears started rolling down her cheeks.

"We need to go," said Mr. Samson while standing in the doorway of our bedroom. I closed the suitcase, and we went back to the front door. Again, I held Emma as tight as I could. I didn't know what to say or what else I could do. I just couldn't believe I would have to go back to Germany just like this.

"What's gonna happen now?" she whispered. I pulled her head against my chest and whispered into her ear, "I'll be back soon, I promise. I love you. I'll be in touch as soon as I can!" Mr. Samson's grabbed my arm. I turned around and looked at him like I would hurt him if he'd try it again. Even though he was probably in the position to hurt me right now.

"I'm coming," I said loud and clear. I kissed Emma on her forehead and whispered one last "I love you" before leaving the apartment with my suitcase, followed by Mr. Samson.

# 39.
# A LONG JOURNEY

There I was, sitting in a room with three other people, waiting to get deported. It looked like an old, empty storage room with three couches in it to sleep on. It totally felt like a jail as we were trapped in there, unable to do anything. At least they gave me the WiFi password—such kindness. I texted my family at home that I would be back in a few days. They couldn't believe it. I was texting Emma so we could emotionally support each other, and Sam, Matt and Francis to let them know what happened. No one could believe it. *The adventure is over*, I thought. Just like that. How is this possible? Surely, I did something wrong without a doubt, but how can they take away my life over something like this. The amount of money I received for my paintings wasn't even enough to make it a case of not paying taxes. All the money went into rent for the studio and materials. I never thought about it, that creating art and painting pictures could be such a violent thing that one day would destroy my life in a single second.

"What did you do?" I heard someone say behind me. I turned around and saw a young dude, roughly my age.

"To be honest, I don't quite know. How about you?" I asked him.

"That's interesting. How do you not know?" he asked, before continuing. "I was missing a document to legally enter New Zealand, so I just have to go back to France immediately."

"Well, that sounds even harsher than what happened to me, I guess. I received a second income that I wasn't allowed on my visa," I tried to explain.

We both were looking at each other quite hopelessly and didn't know what else to say.

"I'm Ben, by the way," came out of my mouth.

"Dave," he introduced himself.

"Nice to meet you, Dave," I said.

We were just sitting there without speaking. It took about two hours until someone appeared in front of the locked door. A male in the shape of a bear, dressed in the official uniform of New Zealand Immigration opened the door, looked at both of us and said, "If you both would please follow me."

We grabbed what little luggage we had and followed him.

He escorted us along the security queue to our personal security gate. Our suitcases already had been checked in by immigration. After our personal 360-degrees inspection, we headed to the boarding gate. Once again, we bypassed the whole queue. The officer handed our passports to the stewardess, and we got escorted to our seats in the very last row, with Dave on one side and me on the other. We looked at each other, and neither of us could find the right words to say.

Thirty minutes later the plane was ready to take off, and I took one final glimpse of the Auckland skyline. One tear started rolling down my cheek. I tried to wipe it away, but it was immediately followed by a waterfall.

It was a thirty-hour journey ahead of me, and I wasn't mentally prepared for it. I didn't have a choice. All the pictures from the last three years were running through my head. Every positive memory, every up and down. I looked over to the other side and could see that Dave was deep in his thoughts as well.

"What are you thinking of?" I leaned over with my face still full of tears and tried to strike up a conversation.

"I don't know. Maybe something like, how can you be dumb enough to forget this one document?"

"Why are you blaming yourself? Don't you think they could have been a bit more cooperative?" I tried to cheer him up.

"Why should I? It was my mistake man. There is no one else you can blame for your own mistakes. Otherwise, how do you learn from them?" he said.

I held back for a second and didn't say anything. Maybe he was right. He probably was right. He is right. The whole time I had been thinking that they'd been so harsh to me, but at the end of the day it was my own fault.

"Maybe you're right," I said in the end.

"I am right, man. Trust me, I am right."

We had a sixteen-hour journey ahead of us on the first flight, and there would have been a lot to talk about, but his last words were still on my mind. There's no one else I could blame in this situation, and even if I'd try, it doesn't change anything. The best way to get on with it was probably accepting it for what it was and learning from my own mistakes. How should I accept it, though, and how could I move on? I felt like Dave would know the answer since he seemed so mature and wise about his own mistakes.

I turned to the right to ask for his advice and saw that he was asleep. The screen in front of me was showing a little digital airplane that was pointing towards Australia and slowly distancing itself from these two little beautiful islands at the end of the world. The timer in the top corner of the screen was showing 15:45, which meant 15 hours and 45 minutes to go until the stopover in Qatar. I unpacked the airline survival pack, which contained a toothbrush, some toothpaste, thrombosis socks and the most important thing for me at that very moment, a sleeping mask. I put my headphones on, chucked on my favourite playlist and slowly closed my eyes.

# Spotify - BOB's Classics (Playlist)

A massive pain in my back woke me up, and I found myself in the most uncomfortable position to sleep in. I was crawled together like a little embryo with my legs on the free seat next to me. I pulled the sleeping mask aside and saw Dave on the other side munching on his dinner.

I jumped up, looked at him and said sheepishly, "Don't tell me I missed it."

"Oh, hey man, yeah it seems like you did. They served it fifteen minutes ago, but you were dead asleep."

"No, I'm starving," I said, holding my belly to suppress the craving.

"Sorry man, but I'm not sure if they'll still bring you some. Don't forget you're officially a criminal now," he said and laughed.

"What?" I said irritated and half asleep.

"You got deported man, already forgot?" he pointed out with a cheeky smile.

Really, why is he rubbing it in? He saw that I wasn't in the mood for a laugh and straightaway took it back.

"Sorry man, that was a bad French joke. Press the button and I'm sure they can sort you out some dinner."

I think Dave could tell by my reaction that my current mental state wasn't the best, and that I'd no clue about what was going to happen next. I was completely bemused. I did as Dave advised, and the polite and friendly stewardess served me my dinner ten minutes later. Halfway through my meal, I looked at Dave again. "You know what, man?" I asked.

"Tell me," he replied straightaway.

"I am afraid," I admitted.

"Afraid of what?" he asked.

"What's going to happen now. My whole life got taken away. My friends, partner, job, everything," I said desperately. I don't know why I said it, but I felt the need to talk about it to someone and he seemed like a trustworthy person.

Dave didn't reply at first. He stared at me for a few seconds, nodded, and then said, "I understand."

Wow. I understand? I wondered whether that was all he had to say. Maybe I was expecting a piece of amazing advice that would help me get rid of the pain that came with the whole deportation thing.

"But..." he followed up, "...to come back to what we started discussing earlier. You need to accept your own mistakes and the situation in order to move on as quickly as you can. It sounds very cheesy and maybe a bit too hippie, but such things happen for a reason, and there is a reason why you have to go back now, even though everything seemed to be in place. You need to trust the situation, and you need to trust yourself that something wants you on this path. As far as I know, you seem like a nice guy and not like someone who has done anything bad on purpose. So, trust yourself, and soon you will find out why this has happened."

When he said it, it felt right, and for a second the pain turned into excitement and curiosity before turning back into heartache and sadness a second later. However, it was a glimpse of positivity in this bleak reality.

"I don't know what to say, Dave. I just hope you're going to be right," I said.

"Trust me, I am right," he said again full of confidence.

I smiled and thought about what might be wrong with this guy. He seemed to have a lot of self-esteem, but I decided to trust his words. I just wanted to feel a bit better, and the more I thought about what he'd just said, the better I felt.

I finished my last bites and looked at the screen again. The clock was showing 8:45 left.

"What are you doing when you get back?" I asked Dave.

"No plan man, but I also think there might be a reason why I should be at home at the moment and maybe not in New Zealand," he said.

"Okay, but how do you feel about not having a plan?" I asked curiously.

"Well, I think it's very liberating, isn't it? I can go with the flow, do what I like and enjoy this one life I have, including all the ups and downs."

It sounded like something I'd already heard from someone else, when I first arrived in New Zealand, just under slightly different circumstances.

"Aren't you afraid?" I asked.

"Afraid of what?" he fired back.

"Running out of money, getting lost, being forced to go back to your old life and feeling obligated to do work or things you don't like?" I dumped all my fears onto him.

"Are we talking about my fears or your fears, Ben?"

Maybe he hit the sweet spot right there.

He continued, "I understand you're afraid, but your life is always in your own hands. I can't run out of money if I work, which I have done and which I will do. You have to define for yourself how much money is enough money," he said.

"How much is enough?" I asked.

"Depends on your perspective. Let me tell you a funny story. I used to work at a funfair before I planned on coming to New Zealand. One evening I was serving some crêpes. At some point, I saw two familiar faces. They were two guys I went to university with. We studied business administration together. When our studies showed me that I wanted to do something else with my life, it showed them that their logical next step was to get a promotion in their workplace and earn a lot more money."

"Yeah, I can kind of relate. Sounds very similar to my life before New Zealand," I told him.

"Anyway, I hadn't seen either of these guys in three years, and they came up to get some of my crêpes. Of course, they recognised me and asked me what I'd been doing since we finished university. I told them about my trip to Asia, my hiking adventure in South America and my surfing trips to Australia. I asked how they had been, and they told me that they got their promotion and were still with the same company. They have been doing the same thing the whole time and went on their three weeks' holidays every year. Then one of them told me that he had spoken to a friend, and both agreed on the 'proven' fact that you really need to earn a lot of money to put aside before you are in your mid-thirties, otherwise it's going to be very difficult in the future.

"Apart from the fact that it was very vague to say what he means by 'difficult', one thing was very obvious. I was the one working for a lot less money at the fair, and probably in all my previous jobs as well, whereas these guys had been making ten times the money I had made during the same time. Yet, who sounded more scared to you about the future and having enough money?" he finished by passing the ball back to me.

I had to think about this story for a second. Of course, the answer was obvious, but it was a very interesting point of view. While I was still processing his words, he continued.

"Don't get me wrong, I respect the people who believe in this and live this kind of lifestyle, but it's also not for everyone. Some people are meant to do something else, something different, and a lot of them carry a talent in them for their whole life without knowing it. This talent will probably never be acknowledged because they got discouraged by friends, family or society every time they tried to follow their feelings. You know, the kind of people who are afraid of themselves and occupied by the fears that get spread in the world. It's well-planted in their heads and for most people, it takes control without them even knowing. You know, if you have a purpose in life and you know that purpose and you follow that purpose, something strange happens. You don't think about the jobs you do as jobs anymore. You don't get discouraged, frustrated or depressed by your job anymore, because all of a sudden you do it for different reasons and not for having enough money or a secure future. Only God knows what "a secure future" even means, right? You do those jobs in order to spend more time with what you actually want to do with your life. You don't go to work thinking you have to do that for the rest of your life. It becomes a tool to achieve your actual goal. Everything else gets less important as well. All of a sudden, there's something else that drives you. You don't care about wearing the freshest clothes or driving the nicest car. Something else drives you now, and you just need a car to get from A to B, and you just need new shoes because your old ones are full of holes. That automatically means you will spend less money in your life, which then will also reduce your fear of losing all that money. If there is not a lot to lose you won't be afraid. You have something special inside of you, which is your purpose. The purpose of why you are here, for the sake of living a fulfilling life. This purpose will lead you to something that you can maybe call a plan if you need to. The most important thing is that you trust and believe in yourself. Take the opportunities that will arise from this fate and make the most out of them. Why are you worried, Ben?" he finished.

*Who on earth is this guy?* I thought. Seriously, I had goosebumps all over my body, and I felt so encouraged that I wanted to start painting straightaway. All the fear was gone for a few seconds and it felt like everything was still in the right place despite the circumstances. He touched me deep down in my heart without even really knowing my story.

"Tea or coffee, sir?" a kind voice interrupted this magic moment. I jumped a little bit, looked up and saw the stewardess. "Excuse me, tea or coffee?" she repeated.

"Ehm...tea without milk, please," I said.

And back I was from the illusion of being invincible, back to rock bottom in just a few seconds.

Dave watched my reaction, and he could tell I was bouncing backwards and forwards inside as to whether I should believe his words or just think that he was absolutely insane. It probably was not the first time he'd been confronted with such a reaction. The stewardess passed me the tea, continued down the aisle and I immediately went back to Dave.

"I know you probably think I took a little bit too much acid, but as far as I understand you come across as someone who has found his purpose. That means at the end of the day it's up to you, Ben. You choose which life you want to live, but never ever tell me you don't have a choice. There is always a choice. Trust me, I am right," he said once again.

I didn't know how to deal with such confidence.

"But where is the choice now? I lost everything and will probably not be allowed back into the country that I lived in for the last three years?" I asked full of doubt and complete despair.

"Well, New Zealand is not the only country in this world, my friend. You decide if you want to stay in Germany, live back up to your old standards or if you take on the past three years and choose to live a different life, in a different country. Did you surf in New Zealand?" he asked.

"Well, let's say I tried, and the few times I did, I enjoyed it for sure," I replied insecurely.

"See, come to France then, or go to the Mediterranean where it's nice and warm. There are beautiful beaches as well and nice places to live. I have heard it's a very similar lifestyle to New Zealand," he said.

*How random*, I thought.

"Why France or the Mediterranean?" I asked.

"I don't know man, that was just a random suggestion. If you don't have a plan yet, remember, that everything is possible. Don't forget how liberating this is," he pointed out.

I tried everything to shift my focus, but my emotions took over again and all I could feel was fear and more fear. I really tried my best though to hold on to his words as much as I could.

"I'll try my best man. Thanks for sharing your thoughts with me anyway. I really appreciate it," I thanked him.

"No worries, man. Pleasure is mine. As I said, you seem like a cool guy."

He took a tissue, grabbed a pen out of his pocket, wrote something on it and passed it over to me "Here's my number. I'll be jumping on a different flight when we get to Qatar. It was a pleasure talking to you. Feel free to text me whenever you want, my friend," he kindly offered.

"Thanks, man, I really appreciate the chat," I said, grabbed the tissue from him, pulled out my phone and added his contact. One more time I looked on the screen and it showed 8:25.

I couldn't believe how much time was still to go. I put my headphones back on and scrolled through the movie library and picked one called "Captain Fantastic." The movie started, and I decided to turn my face towards Dave one last time to say, "Thank you" again, but he was already fast asleep once more.

My feelings were all over the place, and even though Dave's stories were so encouraging, everything was still so fresh. The fear and pain regarding what had just happened took over again. I looked out the window, thinking about Emma and my friends, wondering what they would be doing right now. The tears were on their way back and the sun was blinding me when, all of a sudden, I remembered a quote that Sam used to say after he almost lost the collective. "Above the clouds, there is always sun! Always!" The moment I realised that, the heartache lifted for a tiny second again, and I enjoyed the insane view above the dark clouds.

"Cabin crew, please prepare the cabin for landing," I heard someone saying in my dream. Then I realised I had crossed the border to reality already, and it was the actual captain's voice that signalled the crew that we would land within the next thirty minutes. I was still tired. I spent the last eight hours with broken sleep, movies and thoughts about all sorts of things, but especially Dave's words.

He still had his eyes shut, and I didn't think he was going to wake up before we reached Qatar. The last thirty minutes flew by and before I had even noticed, the lights outside were shining right through the aircraft windows.

"Welcome to Qatar. The local time in Doha is 3:30 a.m.," the stewardess announced through the speakers. Dave slowly started to wake up.

"Had a good sleep, mate?" I asked him.

"Yeah, it was alright. A bit uncomfortable!" Dave smiled.

The plane jerked into its final parking position. Everyone jumped up and tried to get their bags like it was an emergency evacuation. Everyone apart from Dave and myself. We knew we'd have to wait until we got picked up and escorted to the transit zone.

"I really feel like a criminal," I said to Dave.

"Well, you are one." He smiled again.

A few minutes after the last passenger had left the plane, someone came to pick us up and guided us to the waiting room. Dave's flight to Paris was an immediate connection, whereas I had to wait two hours to board my flight to Frankfurt. In front of the transit room where I had to wait, we both knew it was time to say our goodbyes.

"Alright man, it was nice to meet you," I started.

"Pleasure is mine, my friend. I just remembered that I never asked you, where did you get your second income from?"

"Abstract painting," I said sharp and short.

"Oh wow, so you are an artist, right?"

Unexpectedly, his question made me feel very uncomfortable. Two days ago, I would have answered this question confidently and full of pride by saying "Yes," without a doubt. But now I felt that I had lost everything, including my identification as an artist, something I had worked so hard to call myself. It was the fact that I'd go back into a country where everyone only knew me as Ben Schenk, the depressed insurance salesman. No one would see me as an artist, and right at this moment, I didn't have the confidence to see myself like this anymore.

"No, not really," I said.

You could see that Dave was slightly irritated and surprised by my answer, but there was no time for him to question it—he had to catch his connecting flight. We parted with a message of hope.

"Okay. Trust me, things are happening for a reason. Maybe you don't know the reason yet, but there will be one that will tell you why you shouldn't be in New Zealand right now. Also, remember that you always have a choice," Dave said.

"Thank you, man. I really appreciate your words. Have a safe trip and we'll be in touch," I replied.

"Thanks, you too, and feel free to text me any time you want," Dave said as the security guard escorted him to the gate.

# 40.
# SOMEHOW...

I was sitting in the transit zone and, against the normal circumstances of being a lawbreaker, I had WiFi once again. I felt more like one of those prisoners who had extra luxuries compared to others, like in those movies where the rich guy who had led a drug cartel for decades finally gets to prison, but his cell has an ensuite, a TV and a PlayStation. That's me. I'm here locked up in a separate room watched by a guard, not running off without my passport. What a dumb thing that would be to do anyway. Why would I run off without my passport in a country like Qatar? So I stayed where I was, unlocked my phone and hit the FaceTime button to call Emma.

As soon as she picked up, a tear started to roll down my cheek.

"How are you?" she said, crying straightaway too. It was so hard hearing her that sad. I don't know if it was the right thing to call her, but I felt like it. I tried to downplay my feelings and told her about my meeting with Dave and his inspiring words. She started crying even more. I think she got the wrong end of the stick and felt like I meant that it was meant to be that we were apart. I tried to calm her down—definitely a bad idea.

"Emma, please, calm down. It's going to be okay."

"Stop telling me to calm down! You know that doesn't help," she shouted angrily.

I had forgotten about that. It actually does help me if there is someone who tries to tell me to relax a bit, rather than not saying anything or making it worse. Anyhow, keep in mind it doesn't work with Emma Wilson.

"I'm sorry, Emma. I was just trying to help."

"I know, but it doesn't help," she responded briskly.

*Okay, I got it*, I thought. Dave's words all of a sudden felt so small when I saw Emma crying. Sadness was the dominant sentiment here, and everything he said appeared more shanti shanti to me than anything else. It's easy to think about it and say stuff like, "You always have a choice," but the reality was that there were two people who loved each other, had chosen to live together and were all of a sudden forced to be apart.

"What are we going to do then?" she said.

"I don't know, Emma. I'm not even home yet, and I don't even want to think about what to expect there. I've hardly even been able to take in what happened. How should I know what to do?"

"I know, I'm sorry. My feelings are all over the place," she admitted.

"So are mine," I confided.

"There's just suddenly a big hole here. Sam was just at our place and dropped off all your paintings from the gallery. We are all in shock."

I didn't know how to feel about her words. Yes, there was a big hole, but at the same time, I was totally aware of the fact that the world will just keep spinning, whether I'm there or not. There might be a shock for the moment, but their lives will just keep going, and in a few days or a few weeks, someone might not even notice that I was there, whereas on the other side, I felt like my life was just on hold forever. Of course, the fact that I'd lost everything was very dominant, but the feeling of knowing that life would just continue without me was even worse.

"Let's see," I said.

"What does that mean, Ben?" she asked.

I knew that this could totally mean anything and nothing at the same time, but I felt so lost already.

"I mean, you guys still have everything, you'll be fine. I'm just facing the bits and pieces of what's left."

"Stop it, Ben. Don't say that. It's the absolute wrong way to go about it. I lost you here too. My life isn't the same either. We need to work on ways to fix it, but don't feel sorry for yourself. That's the worst that could happen now."

She was completely right. I was amazed by her words and wondered where she got the energy from to confront me with this. At the same time, I had no power left to cope with all of this now. Despite Dave's and her words, my mind and my feelings were dominated by the pain. The big hole that I left in New Zealand was also a big hole in my heart now, and I had no idea how to fix it. My life was on pause, and I somehow needed to find the play button again.

"Thanks, Emma. I know you're right, but right now it just hurts."

"I totally understand that, Ben. Let's make sure you get home safe, and we will talk after you have arrived, okay?"

"Sounds good," I said.

"I love you, Ben. Somehow, we will find a way out of this."

"Somehow...," I repeated.

"Please, Ben."

"It's okay. I love you too, Emma. Please don't worry about me. I'll text you as soon as possible. Stay strong," I said more desperately than anything else.

"Bye," was her last word before she hung up.

I looked up and stared at the guard who was watching me in the waiting room. He was just another robot, just like any other person that works for immigration authorities. They are here to protect the country's borders from badass criminals such as me—a serial killer with a brush and some paint who made a few hundred bucks on the side of his job. I kept staring at him, and I felt a little smile coming over my face, laughing about my own little joke. In the next second, Emma's last words repeated in my head. Especially one word, which was proof to me that we both had no idea how to get out of this situation together.

"Somehow," I whispered to myself.

# 41.
# WELCOME "HOME"

boarded the flight that would catapult me right back into a life I'd kind of forgotten about and pushed away for a very long time. What I'd encountered in the past three years of living in New Zealand was unique to me, a way to go about life that was unknown to my young, little self. I always thought that it was impossible to feel so much support from friends and people who were close to you. I would have never grasped that such people see potential in someone and push you beyond your comfort zone to grow and achieve goals that you set in your mind. That was something I'd never experienced before unless it had to do with my career as an insurance salesman.

Fear raced through my veins. *What if I fall back into old habits now*, I thought. Due to the fact that I hadn't entirely comprehended what had really happened in the last forty-eight hours, I was already worrying about the next few days.

The last time I had seen my friends and family was three years ago, when I'd walked through the departure gate. A lot had changed since then, especially on my side, but what about them? Confusion was slowly spreading all across my head. "I need to rest," I said out loud to myself. The person next to me on the plane gave me a slightly odd look. Well, technically the person in the row in front of me. Because I was still officially a felon without a passport, I still had to be separated from the normal travelling folk.

With this last thought, I slowly closed my eyes, sank more and more into the most uncomfortable plane chair ever and tried to sleep. I still had six hours to go until the Frankfurt Airport, where my dad and a handful of Skype calls were waiting for me after three years.

Do we want to get into father-son relationship problems now or not, I asked myself. Well, do I have a choice? Only a few hours separated me from this confrontation.

# Boy Oh Boy, Bar.ba - Welcome "Home"

The captain again gave the heads-up that we were approaching Frankfurt now. I was nervous for many reasons. For the first time in a very long time, I could see small German rooftops again, tiny gardens, and roads that looked like Autobahn. The plane slowly inched closer to the ground, and all these little things grew bigger and bigger. I wasn't above the clouds anymore, so I could feel how the painter and wannabe Kiwi, Ben Schenk, kept on fading while the old, little, fragile Ben started to surface again. As soon as the big Boeing 720 got its grip on the runway, hard brakes pushed me forward and I knew it was time to face the harsh, brutal reality.

We landed safely, and instead of relief I was feeling more and more tension. Since on paper I was still the most dangerous person on this aircraft, I had to wait again until the last passenger had left it. A friendly stewardess came up to me in the last row, and without putting me in handcuffs, she managed to escort me to the exit of the plane. There was already someone waiting for me. Probably, the most German guy I had seen in recent years. He had a little necklace with a card hanging around his neck saying, Hans, Dietrich, Frankfurt Airport. As I said, it's impossible to be more German than him.

"Welcome back, Mr. Schenk," he said. My first thought was, Welcome back? For real? Is he trying to be funny? The stewardess handed him an envelope. and we all knew what was in there.

Dietrich took over escorting me from the aircraft to the passport control. "How was your flight, Mr. Schenk?" he asked. Come on, really?! Cut the bullshit, I nearly said until I decided last second to play along with his little game. "Thanks for asking, really nice. Very pleasant thirty-hour trip halfway around the world. Amazing views, such a good time! Have you ever done it?" I asked him to heat up the conversation he had started. He looked at me with big eyes. I think we set the tone now. He clearly wasn't expecting such an answer from a totally jet-lagged, deported German.

"No, I haven't, but it sounds like I should," he answered.

Yes, you should and now shut up, I was whispering to myself. Unfortunately, it only took him just twenty seconds to come up with the next provocation.

"Hmm, deported I see, so I'm escorting a criminal to the passport control here," he said, unable to hide his cheeky smile.

*Honestly, what is Dietrich's problem?* I thought. Anyway, I tell you what. We will see who gives up first.

"Heavy drug dealing, sexual harassment and mayhem, I might have to go straight to jail from here," I said with an absolutely straight face.

He swallowed for a second and tried to look up in his documents if I seriously was a crazy killer and why I wouldn't be handcuffed. On the third page, he then found the reason why I actually got deported.

"I see what you're doing, Mr. Schenk. No worries, we can distinguish between a sex perpetrator and a hobby Picasso," he said. This was getting personal now. The word "Picasso" triggered the picture of Emma's face when Mr. Samson separated us in the hallway. I couldn't hold it any longer.

"I think, Dietrich, if you don't shut up any second now, I might actually end up in jail. For mayhem at an airport employee," I almost shouted.

If I thought that would stop him from being an angry, old, desperate German with no hobbies other than taking advantage of his little, tiny bit of power while he escorts deported people from the aircraft door to the passport control, I was wrong.

"Oh, are we a bit sensitive today, Mr. Schenk?" he continued.

In a snap of a second, I remembered the view I had when we breached the sky and flew over the clouds on my way back from Auckland to Germany. I remember how cloudy the day was, just like my mood, but the sky above was blue and the sun was shining bright like always. I took a deep breath and decided this time not to take his provocation but to turn the conversation around.

"Totally relaxed, Dietrich. I am very pleased to be back," I said sarcastically.

He looked rather confused, which was fair enough since my articulation jumped from active-aggressive to passive-aggressive within a few seconds.

We turned around the corner, and at the end of the hallway I could see a big sign saying, Passport Control. Since my emotions were all over the place for the last two days, I didn't feel anything by the time I arrived at the gate.

"Here is your passport. Welcome back to Germany once again," Dietrich said and handed the documents in my direction.

I missed what Dietrich said and was almost paralysed staring at the police officer in front of me. It was like a short-term déjà-vu from just hours ago, apart from the fact that this officer had to let me into the country regardless since it's my country of origin.

"Mr. Schenk, your documents," I heard a more energetic voice repeating.

I felt a little hit against my arm and turned to Dietrich. "Excuse me, sir, thank you very much. Until next time," I said without being entirely aware of what words were coming out of my mouth.

Once again, Dietrich was confused. "Well, let's hope there won't be a next time," he said and left.

"Your passport please, sir," the police officer in the glass box in front of me requested.

I handed my documents straight to him. I was curious about what he would say to me. I waited an eternity, which in real life was only thirty seconds.

He looked up at me and said, "Welcome home, sir!"

Really? No comment about my deportation? Nothing. I grabbed my passport and passed through the gate next to his glass box.

# 42.
# HI DAD

I mentioned it before. I don't want to say that I wasn't looking forward to the moment I'd see my family again, but to put it in a diplomatic way, it'd been a very long time. Some people would call it a disturbing parent-son relationship—for me it has always been like this. It was just normal. My parents never had a lot of interest in the things I liked. At the age of ten, I had to figure out for myself how to get to football training during the week and matches on the weekends. I would say it was a mixture of having no time and having no interest in my activities.

And now? Now they still don't have a clue about what I am doing. I'm drawing pictures? Creating art? How do I earn money from that and what do I do if I don't earn enough money to live from it? How do I live? Why do I even do it? Questions I have been hearing a lot in the past, but only from one side. Only from friends and family from Germany and Europe. I have never been asked these questions by someone in New Zealand. People noticed my spirit. I was doing something that I was passionate about. They valued the fact that I was brave enough to do what I loved regardless of status, age or money—something I already miss about the country and its people.

With those thoughts in my head, I moved closer towards the exit, closer to the door, knowing that my dad will be behind it waiting for me. I was so confused about everything that I wouldn't even know how to greet him. I surely supposed a hug after such a long time, right? He would want to do the same, correct?

I decided to step out of this tangle in my head. I took a deep breath and moved one step closer to the light beam that recognised my body and opened the final door to the exit.

When the automatic doors slid open, I encountered a group of people with signs in their hands. I was pretty sure that my dad wouldn't have prepared such a sign for me, and so I was helplessly looking for someone that looked like him. I tiptoed, tilted my head to the left and right until I recognised a face and a hand that was waving wildly. That was my dad.

I moved towards him, and while I was still thinking about how to say hello, he'd already opened his arms, and there was no doubt left that we were going to hug. It felt awkward, yet nice at the same time.

"Hey, how are you?" he asked me.

"Thanks. I'm alright. How are you?" I answered.

"I'm good, but I am not the one who got deported," he said.

*Bam, straight into it!* I thought. I tried to laugh it off, but it didn't quite work, even though I could tell he didn't notice.

He smiled at me, and we just stared at each other for what felt like forever. I wondered whether I had already run out of topics to talk about, or whether I was just overwhelmed.

"Okay, let me get your luggage and we will go to the car. You look like you could use some sleep," he said, ending the awkward silence.

"Yes, I actually could. It was a bit of a journey," I admitted.

"Do you want to talk about what happened?" he asked. This came unexpectedly. I wasn't quite sure what to say and how to feel about this question.

My dad is definitely the last guy who likes to talk about feelings and emotions. Did he really mean it? Or furthermore, would he even understand what I have been through? Anyway, I thought I will give it a crack since he came all the way to pick me up.

"Hmm, yeah, we can do that. I mean, I feel terrible, I lost everything

I had within a few hours." I looked at him craving for some magical words that would get me out of this terrible mindset.

"Yeah, I can imagine," was all he said.

Let's face it, was I really expecting more? I could somehow understand him. It's like me attending a funeral and coming up to the person who has experienced the loss and saying, "I'm sorry for your loss."

Don't get me wrong, when I've been in those situations, I have been sorry, but I know that it's also just a phrase that doesn't really help the person in the situation. The person won't feel any better just because one hundred people say that they feel sorry for their loss.

Is there a golden solution for this situation? Is there anything you can realistically do to make that other person feel better, right at that moment? How about you empathise on a different level, listen and pay attention to what's going on in order to say something more meaningful than just a phrase.

That might not work at a funeral for sure, and I'm aware of the fact that you sometimes have to accept the situation for what it is. In the interest of overcoming the pain, you actually need to feel it through. You need to feel it as part of being able to let it go one day.

I've almost always dropped the "Sorry for your loss" phrase if I couldn't bear listening to their story and how they truly felt in order to engage. I mean, that is what engagement means, right? Two people who connect and feed off each other because they listen and they convincingly try to relate to what the other person has been through. Even if they can't give advice or change anything about the current situation, at least they're present and listen. It seemed like the issue was way bigger than just mentioning the almost meaningless "Sorry for your loss" phrase at a funeral.

People are so distracted by their own problems in life that they've forgotten what it means for someone to properly listen and really engage with someone else.

People like my dad. To be honest, I didn't make it easy for him either. The way I started sharing what had just happened was not very descriptive at all. I didn't offer him a lot of input to engage with, but this was just based on my experiences in the past, and with just one sentence he confirmed what had been developing in my mind over the past few years. "Yeah, I can imagine," was the phrase that was on repeat in my head.

"Can you, Dad? Can you?" I blurted out.

Suddenly, it was silence for a second. Fuck, did I just say that out loud? He looked at me slightly irritated and then stopped for a second. I guess he was thinking about whether he should drop my bag or not. A few seconds later he decided to continue walking, facing straight ahead he said,

"Yes, I can, I guess."

My head just sank to the floor. For the rest of the long walk from the arrival gate to the car park, I was walking face down thinking about whether I should say something or not. Should I change the topic, or actually start a deep conversation that we ought to have started many years ago? I have to face the facts myself though. I'm not brave enough either. I hate confrontations, and this was also why there was so much unsaid between us, stopping us both from having something like a relationship. Extreme situations like me losing my entire life only amplify these things.

We jumped in the car and started driving towards home. For quite a while, there was the usual silence, drowned out by the car stereo. This was the scenario that I was already quite used to on long car rides with my dad.

## Boy Oh Boy, Conor Ef - So Insecure

After a while, he looked at me and asked, "So, what's your plan now?"

Seriously, was that what he had just asked me? Did I look like someone who had a plan, right now?

I don't know where I took this last piece of sarcasm from that was left in me, but for some reason, I heard myself saying, "I'll finish my masters now and then I'm back in the insurance game. I want to be a big fish and run my own insurance company."

You could tell by the look in his eyes that he had no idea how to take this. He literally couldn't tell if that was a joke or not. "Okay, ehm, okay, I didn't expect that if I am honest," he said.

*Oh man, he did take it seriously.* "Dad, I'm super sorry, but that ain't gonna happen."

I think this piece of information didn't come totally unexpected for him. I've been away for the past few years, and even he should have noticed that I was very happy with the massive turn my life had taken when I moved to New Zealand. I think this is another reason why it was so painful to sit here in the car with him and nothing else other than my suitcase. I felt very safe over there. I'd built up confidence and created my own new comfort zone. All this had gone within less than forty-eight hours. Facing how quickly such things can transpire made it extremely hard to stay optimistic. While I was thinking about that, I also thought that this was exactly what I should be talking about to the person sitting right next to me, who is meant to be my father figure.

"You should think about it though. It is important that you get yourself sorted as soon as possible, especially right now," he said.

I couldn't believe what I'd just heard, and before I could even say something he continued.

"Make sure first thing tomorrow you register as unemployed and sort out your health insurance."

I turned my head outside the window. It was a mixture of anger and astonishment. I wanted to scream out loud due to how unbelievably oblivious he was. How could someone be so ignorant and push through his own ideology of life in such a situation?

Then all the courage I'd attained in New Zealand rose inside of me. I was thinking of all the challenges I had overcome, the people I had met and all that I'd experienced.

"You know what?" I heard myself asking rhetorically. "Do I really need to tell you that I've lost everything that I'd built up over the past years in the click of a finger? I honestly don't think I need to tell you that. I know you've been living this monotonous life for a very long time, but believe it or not, there is a lot more out there. A lot more than you can imagine. Just because that's the only way you know how to go about life doesn't mean it's the right way. I don't want to be here. I didn't choose to come back myself. I have the woman I love sitting on the other side of the world, I have my friends and my passion for painting over there— everything that was driving me. And now I'm stuck here in a car with someone who is trying to tell me that the first thing I should think of is taking care of German bureaucracy, seriously?" I said and almost started crying again.

These words were a recipe for disaster. I was surprised that he didn't stop the car straightaway and throw me out on the side of the road. If I knew one thing about my dad, it was that he would never let such words just wash over him. Especially not such words that came from his son who his meant to treat him respectfully. His response came immediately.

"So you think you have soaked up the wisdom of life by living outside of Germany for a couple of years?" he said.

Okay, I didn't expect we would go down the nasty road now. I was trying to prevent this from happening, but I have to admit that my emotional breakout had set it off.

"What wisdom? I'm just telling you that there is more to life than just money, status and career. I am happy for you if that's the life you can identify yourself with, but I can't. It's nothing I want to pursue for myself. So again, I didn't choose to be here right now," I said full of anger.

After I emphasised that again, I became aware that this could also be misunderstood as I didn't choose to see him again (which was, unfortunately, kind of true as well).

"I am sorry, Ben."

What did he just say? Before I could process that he continued. "I only want the best for you."

"The best?" I responded immediately. To send another provocation, "Do you think that is the best for me?"

I straightaway realised that that might not have been the best thing to say.

"I'm sorry, I shouldn't have said that."

"It's okay, Ben," he said thoughtfully.

That was the first time ever I saw my dad being reflective, which made me even more upset. I thought I'd be relieved by saying all that, and that I could reach him with my words, convincing him that he was wrong, but seeing him like this just made it worse.

"I am sorry, Dad. I shouldn't have said any of that," I repeated.

"It's okay, Ben," he said, and I could tell he was just resigning.

I turned my face back to the side, looked out of the window and watched the trees passing by at such a magical speed that it looked like a fast-forwarded slide show. I zoomed in on the sound of the engine, driving 160 km/h, and we continued on our way home to whatever was expecting me there.

# 43.
# HI MUM

A couple of hours and no more spoken words later, we arrived at a place that I used to call my home for almost twenty-five years, minus the four years when I moved outside the village into the city—the big city that never really fulfilled me either. I stepped out of the car onto the footpath that was still the same as it was the last time I'd been here, three years ago. Something was different though. The colours weren't as strong as they were before. Everything appeared much more faded, like someone had put a grey filter on my vision. It was a huge difference compared to the pure colours and nature I was confronted with in New Zealand. It was hard for me to hide my sadness about everything that had happened most recently, and I'm not even talking about the last few hours in the car with my dad.

My first thought was that it's going be a long and rocky road to recover from this. It was something that happened within what felt like a millisecond, but which would mark me forever.

I was looking up at the grey sky while my dad was unloading my luggage when I heard the front door of my parents' house opening and someone running with big steps towards me. Before I had the time to take my eyes from the moody sky, I could already hear her voice.

"Honey!" she said gleefully, and I could already feel her arms around me, pulling me as close as possible to her. She pushed her head as tightly as she could onto my chest, and the moment she looked up at me, I could see a few tears running down her cheeks.

My feelings at this point were all over the place. Of course, I was happy to see my mum after such a long time, and clearly so was she, but at the same moment, I couldn't get over the fact of how much I hadn't chosen to be here right now in this situation. In the end, the feeling of being able to have my mum in my arms again won overall, and I said with a slightly wobbly voice, "It's okay. I'm here now."

Her face, full of tiny little tears, turned into a smile. My dad had taken care of everything else in the meantime, so there was nothing else for us to do other than go inside.

After we entered the house, I found myself facing a fully set table with breakfast. I had already forgotten what time and day it was, and I surely didn't know what kind of meal I should eat next. It probably was breakfast time here, at least it was according to how my mum set the table.

To be honest, I wasn't feeling like having food at all. My mind was with Emma, how she would be or what she would be doing right now. I wanted to reach out to her as quickly as possible when I also remembered at the same time that she might be already asleep. That was also the one thing I indeed needed the most right now, sleep.

"Sit down, honey," my mum said and pulled the chair away from the table, so I could take a seat.

I sat down and it didn't even take her three seconds until she passed me the bread.

"I'm not really hungry, Mum," I said.

She nodded.

"I understand Ben. I don't want to overwhelm you. I can imagine how you feel right now," she said.

*Here we go again*, I thought. Is this going to be another version of what went down at the airport and in the car? Let's be honest, I wasn't necessarily hoping that my mum would come up with anything smarter than my dad, but when did it become acceptable to just always say, "I can imagine how you feel," when only one thing was for sure, "You can't!"

Again, I said it out loud and not in a less aggressive manner compared to when I said it to my dad.

He was sitting at the table with us. He reached for my mum's hand and was trying to signal to her not to take it personally. That actually should have been my part. I know I was heartbroken, frustrated and in an extreme situation, and even though I highly disagree with the "I can imagine" sentence, I had no right to reply so disrespectfully to the people who love me regardless of how few times I'd reached out to them in recent years. Especially now that I was forced to be back, I could rely on my dad to pick me up from the airport and my mum to prepare a massive breakfast, have my bed made and fully take care of everything else.

"Guys, I am truly sorry. I know you only want the best for me, I know you really do, but I myself can't even comprehend or wrap my head around what has happened in the past two days. How can a life get taken away just like this? This seems surreal to me, and I don't understand it myself. So, how can you?" I thought I might have hit the sweet spot there.

I looked into two faces that were either upset or avoiding looking me in my eyes. It was just a matter of someone making the first step here in order to accept that it might be easier to admit that you can't actually imagine how someone else feels when you've never been in such a situation.

"I think you're right Ben, I'm sorry. I was just trying to make you feel better because I feel sorry and helpless," my mum admitted.

I was very surprised by her answer and had to admit that I didn't expect it. I still wasn't quite sure if she was just saying it to escape this awkward situation for all of us, or if she seriously meant it. I didn't know what I would expect them to say anyway. I think all I wanted was to be by myself and process the impossible. Before I went off to bed, however, I decided to apologise for my outbursts.

"Mum, Dad, I'm sorry. I said a few things today that I shouldn't have said. I guess nothing you do or say can make the pain I feel right now vanish. I guess no one can at the moment. The best thing is that I just get some rest now, and maybe tomorrow the world will look different," I said in reflection, but also desperate at the same time.

My mum nodded and said, "Your bed is made. Everything is like always. Like you were never gone."

*Bless her*, I thought. By now, I had already given up on convincing them of my point of view, but "everything is like always" was definitely the last thing I wanted to hear at that moment. However, without further ado, I left the table and went straight back to the room. I opened the door and all I could see was the bed. My mind and body were completely run-down. It was still super early, but I didn't have a choice—all I needed was a long and deep sleep.

# 44.
# DON'T LET IT TAKE OVER

I woke up from what felt like a twenty-four-hour nonstop sleep. I checked my phone and saw a few text messages from Emma asking how I was and if there were any news.

*Any news?* I thought. The big news was that I'm feeling like a human being again after several mental breakdowns, a thirty-hour journey and several arguments with my mum and dad.

I wanted to reply to her, but all I had to say wasn't very cheerful. I definitely wanted to try everything to not let myself get dragged down by the situation. It was so obvious and predictable that depression was waiting around the corner. My aim was to absolutely avoid the obvious. After rearranging all my thoughts, I decided that the best way to go about it was to take all the energy I had left and focus on a way to get back to my beloved place that I used to call home.

The first and best option I could think of was hiring a lawyer to try to find a way back in. Realistically, I was so far away from living off selling my paintings because it was just a passion. Without the job in the café, I wouldn't have even survived a single week over there. I know I had breached the conditions of my visa. I was totally aware of it by now, but I didn't feel like someone who had any bad intentions to do harm to this beautiful country or anyone else. On the other hand, does a person with bad intentions ever feel like a person with bad intentions? I doubt it.

I grabbed my phone and started texting. There was a high chance Emma was already asleep again, and I didn't feel like calling because this was the first time after three days that I was mentally in an almost stable position, able to cope with the situation.

"Hey babe, how are you? I hope you are doing okay despite the circumstances. I am relatively okay. I will try everything to get back ASAP. I will reach out to lawyers today to see what's possible and what isn't. I'll keep you updated. Love you."

As soon as I hit send, I could feel fresh optimistic energy arising inside me. I threw my phone in the corner, got out of bed, walked over to my desk, opened my laptop and started googling German immigration lawyers New Zealand.

The initial optimism I wanted to take advantage of quite quickly faded, as things turned out not to be as promising as I thought. I collected a lot of phone numbers and reached out to several lawyers. I read up on my rights and the consequences of my behaviour. It might look like the consequences seemed blown out of proportion compared to what I actually did, but that doesn't change the situation I am in right now.

I read an article about a famous foreign boxer who got busted importing drugs into New Zealand, but after paying the right amount of money, he was allowed to stay. Come on seriously? What kinda world do we live in?

This fed my initial reaction regarding how unfair it was to take away my life for creating art, being creative and spreading strong messages to other people that had an effect on their lives in a positive way. It just didn't feel fair at all.

Why was I here and Emma over there? Why was this drug dealer there and not me? All I wanted now was to be with Emma. For all these questions, it seemed impossible to find a logical answer. My brain just did not want to accept the fact that I was in this position. By now, the initial enthusiasm had faded away entirely. I felt so low on energy again that I acted paralysed. Everything felt slow and my motivation was at the bottom of the bottom. I was here in my old room where I grew up, at my parents' place with nothing left other than a suitcase full of clothes and a picture of Emma and me, while the life I used to have continued somewhere else without me. The last time I had felt so misplaced was before I resigned from my last job here in Germany, and back then I was already very close to being diagnosed with depression. Some might say I actually was depressed.

The whole process started to turn into a real struggle. For days, I was on the phone at night with German immigration lawyers based in New Zealand. The outrageous fees, the long waiting periods, the close to 50:50 success rate—I had it all covered! I was finally and officially out of energy. This whole process started to eat me up from inside.

It was 1:22 a.m. here in Germany, and I had just come off the phone with another lawyer who made me the promising offer of guaranteeing me a 50:50 chance to win the case if I pay him 3.500 New Zealand Dollars and I only had to wait between two to three months for him to be available to take on my case. That was too much. I grabbed my phone and sent a text to Emma.

"I'm going to do it myself! I'm coming back!"

What I meant was that I decided to reapply for a new visa myself, with character references from all my friends and a bit of luck.

I didn't expect an answer back any time soon, but it only took a few minutes for her to reply. Obviously, for her, it was the middle of the day. I still wasn't used to the massive time zone difference. It felt like we were living in two completely opposite lives. The only reason I was still awake was the drive of me trying to come back as soon as possible.

"What do you mean? When will you come back?" Emma texted back.

It was a message full of hope and confusion. I knew my initial text had contributed to it and it was rather more euphoric than rational, but I just wanted it to be true.

I asked Emma to write up a character reference for me, and I started sending out the same request to all my friends in New Zealand, full of hope and optimism when at the same time I was absolutely drained from the last few days. I hadn't done much, but I could feel my body and brain starting to process what had happened. All this was triggered by meeting people such as Dave, being confronted with the child-parent relationship issue, or the unfamiliar situation Emma and I had been forced into.

It felt like a protection mechanism of the brain, wanting to prevent me from facing the real damage. It looked like I wanted to use hope as an escape and to throw myself into those options that I thought could bring my old life back, rather than facing the reason why my old life had been taken away and how my new life could look like.

"How long do we want to live in the past before it gets too much?" I whispered to myself while lying in bed trying to sleep. My body was fully exhausted, but my mind was running at 100 mph, and it wasn't thinking about slowing down any time soon.

As a follow-up to my self-talk, I could feel a numbness rising in me. I really wanted to stop it, but I didn't know how to. All I could think of was, don't let it take over, just don't, and the next thing I heard was my alarm going off.

# 45.
# SAME, SAME BUT (NOT) DIFFERENT

Every day felt so similar and monotonous to me. I got up, replied to a couple of messages from Emma and then waited for the day to end.

However, I somehow did manage to make progress in collecting tons of character references, and my reapplication was slowly coming together. Today would also be slightly different. I was going to meet Paul, one of my oldest friends here. I hadn't seen him for the entire time I was away. Obviously, he promised to visit me many times, but he never did. Neither did anyone else. Now that I'm back anyway, I thought it would be a good idea to catch up with him and distract myself. I was on my way to the café, where we were supposed to meet, listening to music on my headphones.

# Christian Löffler - Ry

Right at that moment, I received another text message from Emma.

"Don't worry about it all, I will come back soon, and we will figure it out together."

It was already the middle of the night over there, which made the whole message more questionable, when at the same time I was very happy and relieved to receive it. I missed her so much that, no matter how long it would take for my reapplication to get accepted, I would still want to see her as soon as possible. I needed to reassure myself and texted her back straightaway. "Are you sure?"

It didn't even take a minute for her to come back just to confirm, "Yes, I am. Very sure."

I pushed the phone to my chest and looked up to the sky. This must have looked like I was praying to God, but I didn't care. I had so many questions in my head, but at the same time I didn't want to overwhelm her, because I think the decision she made was already big and intimidating enough.

"Let's talk on the phone tomorrow babe. I'm meeting Paul now. Have a good night. I love you," I quickly texted before I reached the café.

I was in front of the entrance, opened the door, walked inside and saw Paul already sitting in the corner. I went up to him and checked my phone one more time and saw Emma's reply popping up as a notification.

"I love you too. Don't worry, we are gonna make it."

I took a deep breath. Put my phone away and smiled.

Paul stood up gave me a hug and said, "You don't look too unhappy for someone who got deported!" The deportation topic seemed to have become a running joke now for people over here.

"Thanks, buddy," I said and we both sat down. We ordered shitty German coffees and Paul continued his deportation introductions in a more serious manner. "No seriously, what are you smiling about?" he asked.

"Emma," I said.

"You guys are okay? How's she coping with the situation?"

*That was surprisingly a very good question*, I thought. The whole time it was all about me so far, but we are in this together, and I feel like just because she is in the place I want to be, it's not as bad for her as it is for me, but her life is not really the same as before either.

"We are trying our best Paul," I tried to be as precise as possible.

"That means?" he asked.

That was a proper Paul question. He wouldn't stop asking until he got a precise reply to his question, almost like Francis. The difference, though, was that Francis always had a magic plan in the back of his mind to help you push yourself out of your comfort zone and into uncomfortable situations, whereas Paul was just curious and always wanted to get to the bottom of it all.

So, I knew I didn't even need to look for excuses, because he wouldn't give up asking anyway until I gave away more details. Therefore, I tried my best to explain myself.

"Well, I'll reapply for my visa, but it looks like she will also be coming back soon anyway."

"Coming back as in living here?" he asked surprised.

Good question, was the immediate reaction in my head. I felt like at the moment I just assumed that she would come back forever and we'd just live here. That's why I felt relief when she told me, but I mean, she still had almost the entire two years of her visa requirements in front of her, so why would she do that? She needed to be in the country for at least more than six months a year for the following two years in order to fully get her permanent residency.

"I don't think so," was my answer when at the same moment I realised that I had gotten way too excited about it all too early.

"Okay, but at least you guys are going to see each other again soon," Paul tried to be as diplomatic as possible.

He was right. "Yes, that's true," I confirmed.

Before he would ask me how I felt about the past few weeks and everything that had happened, I decided to turn the tables to ask him how he had been doing. We'd been talking on and off during my time in New Zealand, but it had been a while since he gave me a detailed update about what was happening in his life. At the same, I strongly didn't feel like talking about my recent weeks.

"So...what's new in your life Paul?" I started to change the topic. You could see he was a little bit surprised by the sudden plot twist in our conversation, but he ran with it and started talking.

"You know, not a lot. Mia and I are having the odd arguments. I'm still working for the same tech company and we're currently saving up to buy a house, plus Mia won't stop talking about us having a baby."

*Wow! That's some serious innovative plan right there*, I thought. I knew about the arguments between him and his partner Mia. He kept telling me and complaining to me about them. The few times we spoke on the phone, he would leave the apartment in order to talk openly with me and vent about his relationship issues.

Fair enough, Emma and our relationship also had its ups and downs and it hadn't been the smoothest start either. Right now, we were facing a massive crisis, though it's not our fault. We got forced into it, and generally I would never complain about the way she was, whereas Paul continued telling me about the silly arguments they had.

"...you know, I just placed the coffee can on the kitchen table and she got annoyed and started a whole argument about it. She even shouted at me!"

I tried to relate and just thought how Emma would laugh about this stuff. We had bigger fish to fry, and we never shouted at each other. Not even close to that. I wanted to say something without comparing his relationship to mine. I tried to help myself and not compare Mia with Emma, but I at least needed to ask him one honest question.

"Are you sure you guys want to buy a house together?"

"Sure, why not?" he said straightaway, not reflecting on what he was telling me before.

The whole thing just made me sad. I was back here, many years later, and it felt like nothing had changed. My best friend still worked in the same job, went on the odd holiday and wanted to buy a house with the person that constantly shouts at him for unreasonable stuff.

There were so many red flags popping up. The same red flags I used to ignore many years ago. The old Ben would sit here and probably contribute something to that idea of buying a house. The new Ben couldn't help himself but intervene.

"Paul, how many times have you been arguing with Mia and complaining about her?" I asked him.

He seriously had to think about it. "Hmm, a few times maybe?" he said.

I could feel that I'd slowly started to turn into the friend that Francis and Sam once used to be for me.

"Stop lying to yourself," I said when I realised the surprised face he made to deal with my newfound directness.

"What are you talking about Ben. You have changed!" he replied immediately and desperately, but he was right.

"Yes, I have indeed and I don't want to continue watching you dig your own grave. That's why I'm trying to do what a real friend would do and tell you my honest thoughts, rather than covering the truth just to make you feel better."

I knew he would take it personally, so I felt the need to continue. "If you are with someone who doesn't get the best out of you, someone whom you complain about on a daily basis, it's worth considering taking a step back rather than creating more dependencies such as building a house or becoming parents just because you think that would fix the problem when in fact it makes it worse." I tried to finish off my little rant, but I still had to ask him one more question.

"What have you done the past few years other than work?"

"I went on holidays Ben, with Mia," he said very angrily. I feel like he knew what I was aiming for.

"Yes, you told me about it. How she ruined it in your eyes by just complaining and making you feel like you ruined the trip by not meeting her expectations. Paul, believe me, nothing has changed since I left. Don't you think it's time to face the truth and do something about it? It's okay that some plans don't work out the way we imagine them to."

I could tell he was about to explode.

"I'll tell you what Ben, just because you travelled to the other side of the world and did a little bit of colouring here and there doesn't mean you are the guru of life now and have figured out how it all works. My life is fine the way it is. I have a plan, and as you can see right now, it's kind of worked out, because at least I can be together with my partner and have everything I need here," he blurted out.

It was total silence at the table. Paul didn't touch his coffee at all.

"I think it's better if I go now," he said.

"Yes, I think it is," realising how much his parting words had hurt me.

He put a ten euro note on the table. "Here, for the coffees. Talk soon," and then left the café.

His words did hurt indeed, but for some reason, despite my very fragile mental state, I could somehow see the truth behind them. At least what appeared to be the truth for me. His reaction reminded me a lot of my dad's when we'd had our little confrontation on the way home from the airport. There were just two worlds crashing into each other. For one fleeting moment, I felt proud about my experiences over the past few years, the people I met and the person I had become. For a rare glimpse of a second, the whole deportation ordeal just became so small next to it, almost a feeling like it was totally worth it. I wouldn't swap not getting deported for the amazing experiences I had. However, my thoughts brought me back to reality right away, and I once more became conscious of how much I don't want to be stuck in this place right now.

So many years had passed for Paul and all the other people I had met here—it was just the same, the same but (not) different.

"Another coffee, sir?" a kind voice asked me. I looked up from my chair and saw the waitress.

"I think I'm good for now. I need to leave soon," I replied.

She nodded her head and left.

Once again, I ended up in this mismatch of optimism and depression. The feeling was somewhere between being grateful for the experiences but feeling depressed about being back here at the same time. The only thing I could think of for protecting myself from being overwhelmed by the sadness was to keep on taking action.

# 46.
# FINGERS CROSSED

I set my alarm super early in the morning so Emma and I could speak to each other on the phone. One of us had to break the early morning cycle in order to make time and room to hear from each other. Since she was working and I'm not, I thought I would bite the dust here.

She picked up the phone. "Hey, honey."

My breath stopped for a second. It felt like an eternity since I had heard her voice. I took a deep breath and answered very slowly. "Hey, babe." Emma sensed the situation immediately.

"I know it's super weird, right? I'm not used to it," she said.

"Yes, I feel slightly overwhelmed right now if I'm honest," I admitted.

"Okay, let's try to be normal. How was it with Paul?" Emma asked.

She had never met Paul, but she was present many times when I was talking to him on the phone because, unlike him, I didn't need to leave the room in exchange for being able to talk openly and honestly to my best friend.

"Let's not talk about it," I said.

"What happened?" she asked.

"We got into a little argument because our lives have become drastically different over the years." I tried to be as generic and diplomatic as possible.

"Okay, I understand," she said.

Emma was about to further question me regarding my argument with Paul when I decided to intervene with the topic that was dwelling on my mind.

"So, when are you coming?" I blurted out. You could feel I took her aback a little bit by being so direct.

"Okay, Ben. Yes, I started looking into it."

I remembered Paul's question about how Emma was coping with the situation, so I tried to show a bit more understanding without hiding my excitement too much.

"I'm sorry babe, I don't want to overwhelm you. I'm just so excited that you're coming. What's the plan?" I heard myself asking.

"There is no plan, Ben. When did I ever have one?" she said.

*That is true*, I thought.

She continued, "I head back to England for a few weeks. Big Nan is not really well and I really want to see her again and obviously you. I thought it might be good if you could make it over. This way we can spend time together with my family and figure stuff out together. How is the visa application coming along?"

I already knew that my initial thought of her giving up her dream in order to be with me somewhere else was a bit too ambitious, but I felt like my initial euphoria had shrunk to the bare minimum—basically, down to me visiting her in England for a couple of weeks. I tried to cover my doubts as much as I could, so I straightaway jumped onto her question.

"It's almost done. I'm just waiting for the final character reference from Francis and then I will submit it in the next couple of days. Fingers crossed." A bit of luck was indeed exactly what I needed in this case.

"Okay, I will book my flight then as well. I'm excited to see you again soon, Ben." I was happy as well, but it got harder and harder to hide my slight disappointment regarding the circumstances. I don't know where the expectation would come from of her giving up her goals in favour of being with me, especially after everything she'd done for me and my dream.

All of a sudden, I remembered the last conversation I had with Sam in my studio and the fear of losing everything that just made my day "Alright" back then. My worries of getting stuck now feel more vivid than ever before. I felt like I already lost most of it and Emma was the one thing that was left. I wanted to hold on to her as much and as tightly as I could, without realising that she might need air to breathe and figure stuff out herself again. It was just like someone ripped me out of paradise, because I didn't appreciate it enough, and now I had to suffer in order to learn.

"Okay, I'm looking forward to it as well," I managed to say. She could tell that I was deep into thoughts.

"How is everything else then? Are you okay?" she asked.

"What do you think?" I snapped and tried to apologise immediately. "I'm sorry. I'm really sorry, Emma. I'm not okay. I am trying to be okay. I try everything to be okay. I try to be as proactive as possible, but I can't do anything about it. I am honestly not okay."

"I know, Ben. Everyone misses you here. I saw Matt the other day and he was asking about you."

*Do you actually know, Emma, how it is to lose everything?* was the thought I had in my head, but this time I resisted saying it out loud. Telling me that people in the place I want to be, but can't be, miss me doesn't make it any easier.

"Emma, just come back soon and hold me tight, okay?" was all I could say at this second. My emotions completely took over.

"I will, Ben. I'm going to bed now," she said.

"Okay. Keep me posted with any updates. I miss you."

"I miss you too, Ben, a lot. Have a good day and make the best out of it. Love you."

Before I could say that I loved her back, she had already hung up. Her last wish repeated in my mind "Make the best out of it." I was trying as much as I could, but it didn't seem that easy. I sat on my bed for a little longer. I had no energy or motivation to get up or to do anything whatsoever when, in the next minute, an email notification popped up.

It was an email from Francis.

Subject: Character Reference Ben Schenk.

It was my little wake-up call for the day. I had received the final missing piece in order to submit my application. I jumped up and opened the email on my laptop. I skipped his kind and cute words about him missing me, which were just an obstacle right now in order to submit my application. I downloaded the file and then uploaded it to the server of the New Zealand immigration office. Within a couple of minutes, I wrapped up everything, scrolled down to the bottom of the page and hit the submit button.

"We have successfully received your application," was the message I saw on the screen. I looked outside my bedroom window and whispered to myself, "Fingers crossed."

# 47.
# LET'S HOPE AND SEE

"What time are you going to arrive?" was the message I was waiting to receive for the past few weeks. Finally, I woke up this morning to this exact message from Emma. My stuff was already packed, and when I opened my eyes, I knew today would be the day I would go to England and finally see her again. She had already arrived back home a couple of days ago. Even though I wanted to see her as soon as possible, I also wanted to give her some time with Big Nan and also some time to recover from her jet lag.

However, now I couldn't wait any longer, so I quickly got up and made myself a coffee. My dad was already in the kitchen and kindly offered to drive me once again to the airport.

The most recent weeks with my parents hadn't necessarily been easy. No matter how much I did enjoy the tiny breakthrough we'd had at the breakfast table on my first morning, it still remained a fact for me that you can't change other people's opinions and views in such a short amount of time. Especially not such well-planted ones lived by for so many years.

My parents didn't hesitate to signal to me that they didn't put much hope in my reapplication and thought that I should rather apply for jobs and earn some money again. In their eyes, I needed a plan and that was obviously not living from painting abstract art one day. The undefined time frame of "one day" would trigger them a lot. For my mum and my dad, "one day" basically means no security or guarantee that this desired scenario would actually become true.

I didn't want to hear any of that. Nor did I want to think about applying for jobs, nor had I thought much about painting since I was back. No one would ask me about it anyway.

Regardless, I had to admit that, despite all these arguments and the emotional issues we had had between parent and son, they've still been there for me and have expressed their love through little things such as my dad driving and picking me up anywhere since I'd been back.

"Are you ready?" he said while I was quickly finishing my coffee. My mum was waiting in the hallway to say goodbye, and everyone seemed a little more relieved today, including me. My parents had never met Emma, and I hadn't told them much about her, but all they knew is that she was very special to me and that's all that matters, at least for me.

Unfortunately, I only packed a little suitcase and a backpack. As excited as I was about seeing her, I was as much scared by the fact that the moment might not last long since she would only be in England for a few weeks. I put all my hopes into getting my new visa application accepted in time so that I could travel back to New Zealand together with Emma.

My dad was already waiting downstairs with my suitcase in his hand. I quickly hugged my mum and off we went to the airport. The car ride was the usual, as always. We didn't speak much, but as opposed to the last time I was rather optimistic. Everything went super quickly. My dad dropped me off at the airport and within thirty minutes I was in front of the gate that would bring me to London.

I grabbed my phone to check if I'd received any messages from Emma.

"How far are you, babe?" was the notification I could see.

Emma was as impatient as me, and it'd been a very long time since we could both feel something like hope, but a hope that was entangled with the excitement of seeing each other again—thanks to her, sooner than expected.

"At the gate, boarding soon," I texted back. Within a few seconds, she replied, "Can't wait! Safe flight! Love you." I grinned and awaited the call to board the aircraft.

A few hours later, the plane arrived at London-Gatwick Airport and I couldn't wait to get off the aircraft. I tried to calm myself down, but it was almost impossible. I jumped out of my seat and grabbed my backpack plus the little suitcase that I had smuggled on board as a second hand luggage just to be quicker at the exit gate.

As soon as I got off that aircraft, I started walking faster and faster until it finally turned into running. *Fuck it*, I thought and sprinted towards the passport control. Everything happened so fast that I almost forgot about my little immigration déjà-vu when I passed the official border to the United Kingdom.

There was only one split second when I was facing the British officer in his glass box, where I thought about what could possibly go wrong as someone who got deported from another country. He scanned my passport, gave me the all-clear and I just kept running towards the arrival area.

There it finally was, the exit sign. I ran up the light beam and the door opened. I looked left, and then straight to the right, when suddenly I could already see those shiny, big white teeth and the massive smile of Emma. I ran to the right, jumped over the fence and opened my arms. Emma pounced on me and I tried to hold her as tightly as possible. For one brief moment, everything was perfectly alright. For one moment, it was just the beauty of reconnecting and all our worries and fears were forgotten for this tiny blink of a moment.

"Hey, Picasso," she said as she stroked my cheek and gave me a big kiss.

"Hey, babe," I whispered as I kissed her whole face multiple times.

"Stop it," she laughed. "People are already looking!"

"I don't care," I said as I continued kissing and hugging her. We were like little teenagers freshly in love, not being fully aware of what kind of situation we were actually in.

She grabbed my hand and said, "It's chaos here. Let's get out of here."

We started walking towards the car park. On the way there, we just kept smiling and couldn't stop touching each other. It just didn't feel real for both of us. The last time we hugged was when Mr. Samson was waiting in the hallway to escort me to the airport.

It felt like we didn't want to say much, or perhaps we were both just utterly overwhelmed by our own feelings for each other.

"I'm so happy," was pretty much all I could say and kept repeating. We arrived at the car park, jumped in the car and before Emma started the ride back home, we just looked at each other again and laughed.

"This is crazy," Emma said.

"I know. Very hard to believe." We touched and pinched each other to convince ourselves that this moment was real.

"Let's go, my mum is already waiting for us."

I had never met Jay before. Emma had been staying at her place during her time in England. I had only heard about Jay. Sometimes I ended up being part of their FaceTime calls, but more accidentally than on purpose.

It was late afternoon, but as winter approached it was getting darker earlier and earlier. We found ourselves in this almost classic "RY X—Howling" car ride moment, where no one needed to say a word.

# RY X, Frank Wiedemann - Howling (Âme Remix)

All I could see were the car lights that were blinding us and the dashboard lights inside the car. The sky outside was a mixture of dark pink and black. I watched Emma while she drove and I smiled. I didn't want this moment to end. I just wanted to hold her hand whenever she didn't need it to switch gears. She noticed that I was watching her the whole time, so she tried to shift my attention.

"Nervous to meet Mum and the rest of the family?"

"Actually no, I've only heard good things about them and I'm more than happy to meet them," I said. Emma's family bond was intimidating and admiring at the same time. Especially, given my family background, I knew I would embrace the feeling of being surrounded by people who understand and encourage each other on their way through life.

The car lights kept passing by, and almost an hour later we found ourselves in front of Jay's house. We got out of the car, grabbed my luggage and went inside. Her mum was already waiting for us. Emma opened the door and Jay, who was sitting on the couch, jumped up straightaway and came towards me with open arms.

"So nice to finally meet you, Ben!" she said as she gave me a hug.

"Likewise, Jay. Thanks for having me," I replied.

It was the predictable warm welcome. Jay had prepared some dinner and we ended up having a great time, talking about all sorts of things. I could tell that she was trying to avoid one topic for sure—a topic that was on all our minds during the entire time sitting at the dinner table.

"It's okay, I'll do it," Jay said as Emma started collecting the empty dishes.

"No, Mum. You already cooked," Emma said. I wanted to be polite as well and interjected, "Yes, we can do it!"

Jay looked at both of us and said, "No, you guys go upstairs, arrive and catch up on things. Come on, you both deserve it."

Emma and I knew that any kind of resistance was pointless, so we gave in and walked up to Emma's room.

"I'm so full," Emma said as she let herself fall onto the bed. I sat next to her and didn't want to waste any more seconds talking about what was on my mind the whole time.

"So, how are we going to go about it?" I asked.

"Go about what?" she tried to pretend that she wouldn't know what I was talking about.

"What if my application doesn't get accepted? What's going to happen to us?" I asked more precisely. I knew it only had been a few hours since we had been back together, but the time we would have together wasn't much, so I wanted to get it off my chest as soon as possible.

"Ben, I don't know," she said.

*That wasn't very helpful at all*, I thought.

She could sense that and followed up. "Let's just hope that you get accepted and we go back together in two weeks, okay?"

Hope was all she had to offer, which was very disappointing.

"Let's think positively," she added.

Unfortunately, that wasn't what I wanted to hear. I don't know why I was still expecting her to solve this issue by deciding to stay here with me. For some reason that seemed like the only solution to me. She grabbed my hand and said, "Let's have a good time here. You get to meet everyone and we'll stay optimistic that immigration will accept your application. Come on."

She grabbed my head, pulled it towards her and gave me a kiss. I wanted to kiss her back, but I didn't know how to feel about it and my gut feeling was telling me, "Let's hope and see" seems way too naive. In the end, it seemed like I didn't have a choice and gave in. I kissed her back and said, "Okay, let's hope and see."

# 48.
# FAMILY TIME

The first few days back with Emma were nothing short of amazing. Most of the time, when we managed to suppress the fear of what could happen to our future together, we were just fully in love. Eventually though, the rose-coloured glasses cracked and the fear of not being able to go back loomed over me. I then ended up worrying and overthinking again.

However, today there was no time to worry. We arrived at Uncle Joe's and Aunty Anne's place. It was about time to finally meet them, as they had invited us over for dinner. We parked the car in their driveway, walked up to the front door and rang the bell.

When Joe opened the door to his house, he couldn't hold back and started with, "Ben, *Herzlichestes Will-kommen. Freut mich Dir kennenzulernen.*" He smiled and followed up with an English, "I hope this was correct." His German was hilarious.

Emma had warned me beforehand that he had picked up a few words on his work trips to Germany and would try to impress me with it when we finally got to meet each other.

I thought it would have been a weird first impression if I would have corrected him. I definitely didn't want to be that guy and just said, "Very good. Nice to meet you as well."

Jay couldn't hide her laugh about Joe's introduction and Aunty Anne followed up with, "Nice to finally meet you, Ben. We've heard a lot about you."

A sentence no family member of mine could ever say to Emma, was my thought.

After that entertaining welcome, we entered the house with the dinner table already set. Joe offered me a beer and gave me a quick tour through the house while the girls were sitting and chatting at the table. He showed me all his stuff. His man cave, including his guitar, his brand-new barbecue, his herb garden, his electronic helicopter and so much more. I'd never seen so many things and evidence of hobbies all in one place. It seemed like he was trying to learn how to play the guitar while learning another language and three other things simultaneously.

"You paint, right?" he interrupted my thoughts.

For some reason, this question caught me off guard. It was literally the first time that this topic came up since I was back in Europe. No one had asked me—not Mum, neither Dad, Paul nor any other of my friends. I hadn't even thought about it myself. Dave was the last one who confronted me with this topic, and already then I had massive self-doubt. I felt that, by crossing the border into Germany, I morphed straight back into the broken guy I used to be, almost like I took on my old identity. Obviously, the reason and the circumstances why I was back played a massive part in it, but it was still very weird that nothing of that self-confidence I had gained through my adventure was left.

"Yes, I do."

"Nice, that must be pretty tough to be an artist over here, right?" he asked.

I simply had no answer to this. The last thing I felt right now would be that I am an artist and especially not over here. It seems like, when you lose almost everything, you are desperate for some sort of security that would give you something to hold on to in your life. The path of an artist, the journey and the dream of living off it, was already risky enough—in a situation where everything is up in the air, you definitely don't want to think about yourself as an artist.

All of a sudden, I blurted out, "To be honest, I mean, I just painted a few pictures. Nothing big. I'm not really good at it anyway."

Why? Why the fuck would I say that? What happened to the guy that would sell his own artworks at exhibitions, and who was happy to have his own studio, and who called himself that most privileged thing—an artist? I was shocked by my own answer and surprised by how naturally it came out.

"Ah, okay," Joe said. "When Emma talked about it, it sounded a bit bigger. So, you are looking for a job in Germany then, or what's the plan?"

I could feel the pressure adding up. He wasn't the first person to ask me that. My parents got on my nerves beforehand and Emma's "Let's see what happens" strategy seemed pretty risky to my fragile inner me. I felt like people wanted me to have a plan when all I wanted was to go back as soon as possible, but the fact that people kept asking me and the possibility of not getting my application accepted was totally getting into me and resulted in a big mess of fear again. That fear caused an emergency lie.

"Yes, I am currently looking for a job."

This was everything, but not true. I had the feeling though that this answer would serve his and any other people's expectations.

"That's good, and I guess you can still paint at the same time as a hobby?" Joe said.

His words were toxic to my soul. The word "hobby" in combination with me painting triggered my anger. I didn't want to say anything else when Anne's "dinner is ready" shout saved me from this awkward and uncomfortable situation.

When we returned to the dinner table, Emma's sister, Ally, and George, had arrived as well. They'd gotten a babysitter to look after the kids to be able to come over to meet me for the first time as well. A "nice to meet you, mate" and a handshake was George's welcoming gesture, while Ally gave me a big hug and greeted me in the same welcoming way as Jay had done a few days ago.

We all sat down at the table while Anne was serving dinner for everyone. We had some nice chats about all sorts of things, but I could feel that everyone was trying to avoid the topic of New Zealand again, just like days ago when we had dinner with Jay. I feel like everyone wanted to know what was going on now, but no one de facto dared to ask. This created an awkward silence at one point, a silence that everyone noticed and Joe tried to break by saying, "So, Ben is looking for a job now."

This made the whole situation even worse and more awkward.

Anne confirmed Joe's sentence with a small "Nice, I guess it's good to have a plan, isn't it?" I didn't know what to say and just nodded. I looked over to Emma and could see her confusion. She knew that I explicitly wasn't looking for jobs and wouldn't want to.

Then it was George's time to shine. "I have some connections in the sales world. I can hook you up if you like, even with some German-based companies."

I know they were just trying to help, but it seemed like people do not understand that's just not the path I want to go down now. If I'm honest, it kind of was my own fault. I was too scared to tell the truth and led them down this route.

Emma could sense my frustration level rising, so she decided to reply on my behalf.

"I think Ben is okay. He decided to also reapply for a new visa. We are just waiting for an answer and we will figure it out," she said and everyone stopped talking for a second.

I guess Joe and George especially figured that it was time to stop talking about jobs and the topic in general.

"Ben, do you want to come outside for a second?" Emma asked. I know that this meant in her language "we need to talk." I nodded and followed her outside like a little boy. When we left the table, you could sense a slight feeling of surrogate shame. Emma's family tried not to make it too weird and continued to talk.

We went outside and in front of the door, Emma didn't waste a second. "Ben, why would you say that?"

"I don't know. I just felt like that is what everyone expects from me. I'm so scared that the application won't go through."

"One thing that doesn't help for sure is lying to yourself. We both know that you aren't looking for jobs and that you don't want to do it. What happened to the guy I met at the Auckland Art Gallery?" she asked looking right into my eyes.

That was the main question here. When she said it out loud, I became even more aware of the fact how much I had lost sense of who I truly am.

"I'm not an artist, not right now. Not anymore. All I want is to go back." And my head sank to the floor.

"Ben!" Emma shouted. "Look at me. Remember what I said. You are good the way you are."

"Emma, it doesn't seem like it. Over here I am a no one. Everyone expects me to provide a life plan. Everyone else around me has one, and I'm here with literally nothing. Everyone wants me to have a job and goals that evolve around that. It feels impossible right now to be creative and to do something different."

"Go on then, apply for jobs. I guarantee you it won't make you happy if you keep ignoring who you truly are. A wise man once said to me that I am an amazing photographer. Back then, I didn't want to hear it and ended up being frustrated and escaping from my fears. That same man made me believe in myself, and without following that career as an artist or photographer, I can now say that I'm a good photographer, and that I face fear and failure; I don't need to run away from them. Just that feeling itself is worth it."

I don't know why, but it seemed like Emma managed to resist everything that had happened and was still able to live by the mindset offered to her or me in New Zealand, but maybe that was the point here. She would go back either way next week, whereas my future was still completely unpredictable.

"I don't know, Emma," I resigned, desperately shrugging my shoulders.

Now she could tell that I was the one shutting down. My mind was overrun with too many questions and expectations.

"Can we go back inside, please," I requested.

She just nodded and could tell that there was no way we would come up with a solution until I would finally hear back about my visa application. For now, we would return to the dinner table, where the whole family thought that looking for a job was the perfect plan. At the same time, I was a bit relieved that they also knew about the application and my wish to go back.

When we returned to the dinner table, everyone was chatting and kept on taking to prevent another awkward moment from happening. I sat back next to Joe and tried to pay attention to his conversation with George. They both were talking about their jobs. They complained about how stressful the last few weeks had been, and that they had no time for their families or anything else. I shook my head and could only think, "Why do you do it then?"

# 49

# SO, WHAT'S YOUR PLAN?

"Why do you do it then?"

This sentence lingered in my head for a while after that night. Why would you restrict yourself to a life where everything revolves around work and a job that soaks up so much of your time and energy that you have nothing left in you for the things that really matter in your life? Like your family, your passion or chasing your own fulfilment.

Despite these little ups and downs, it had been a great time though. A few days later after dinner at Joe's and Anne's, I also finally got to meet Big Nan on a nice walk through the forest with Ally and the kids. Nan was a nice, empathic and wise person with a lot of love for her daughters and granddaughters.

It was so heartwarming meeting Emma's entire family. They managed to make me feel at home within just a few days. I had never felt so welcomed into a new family. They had accepted me as one of them straight from the start and created a trustworthy and honest environment for me. It made me feel like I have always been a part of their amazing bond. They were all a lot more open-minded than the people I surrounded myself with in Germany, but even here the desire for financial security and a successful career was clearly not something to simply dismiss, especially not with George and Joe. To be fair, they were also the only people who had confronted me with my passion and the guy I used to be in New Zealand.

In the end, it was a mixture of feelings. It looked like everyone kinda seemed to understand the situation, but it just made them feel worried about Emma and me. They all wished us the best of luck that the application would get accepted, even though sometimes I couldn't lose the feeling that some might want to see me looking and applying for jobs again. "Just in case." That's probably something Aunty Anne would say and something she would have in common with my mum.

Emma's time in England was almost coming to an end already, and we didn't have much time at all to figure things out. We were both just hoping and expecting that my visa would get accepted and we could get back to normal. If we were honest with ourselves, we knew that we didn't really have a "plan B." Some people might have expected us to, but we definitely didn't.

It was a Saturday night and uncertainty was rising in me once more. I hadn't heard back from immigration, and I was set to go back to Germany on Monday. What was even worse, Emma would go back to New Zealand the following day. Our initial "Let's see what happens" strategy clearly didn't work out for us.

"What's on your mind, Ben?" Emma asked.

We were both sitting on her bed watching a Netflix movie that was based on a true story. Emma loves any kind of movie that is based on true events. The fact that this story might have happened to someone in reality allowed her to get fully drawn into the movie. She noticed that my mind was somewhere else, but not with the film we were watching.

"What are we going to do?" I asked, looking at her hopelessly.

Emma straightaway knew what this was about. It just felt like another desperate attempt of mine to get something out of her.

"I don't know, Ben," she replied.

Something I'd heard about ten times in the past few weeks. This time, I aired my honest thoughts.

"Well, that doesn't help us," I blurted out.

I was hoping that she would come up with a suggestion herself. Something along the lines of her offering to stay a bit longer or not head back at all, but once again I knew that would be just too much to ask for.

Ultimately, we should have both just admitted that we don't have an answer to how we would deal with the situation if my only avenue to return to my personal paradise would be declined. One thing was for sure, it wouldn't make things any easier. In our minds, there was only one solution, and that was that New Zealand immigration would show mercy, and we would return back to our old lives as soon as possible.

Emma gave up on this conversation before it had even started, and her eyes and mind had returned to focus on the screen. I couldn't concentrate at all and wanted to punish my brain by coming up with something that would end this waiting game.

Just then, an email notification popped up in the top right corner of my laptop screen while Emma was watching the movie.

"Ben," she said, grabbing my arm with one hand and pointing the finger of her other hand at the screen.

The sender information showed "NZ Immigration" and the subject line was "Your Work Visa Application."

Both of our hearts stopped beating for a second. Emma hit the pause button and passed the laptop over to me. I was paralysed and couldn't move. The laptop was on my lap, but my whole body was frozen.

"Come on, open it," Emma said.

"I can't," I replied.

Emma took my hand. "Ben, this is the one thing we've been waiting for this entire time. Come on, open it and everything will be fine."

I was so scared, but obviously, she was right, and I needed to check it. I opened my mail app and clicked on the message.

I tried to skip the blah blah blah, and scrolled straight down to the attachment, which would contain the final decision. I took a deep breath and double-clicked on the document.

While the PDF file was loading, Emma squeezed my hand harder. The document opened and what I read pulled the ground out from under my feet a second time within a couple of months.

The laptop slid out of my hands onto the floor. I didn't show any reaction at all. Emma was fully aware of the situation and no questions were needed. Without reading the document, she knew that our relationship was about to get tested again, but this time to an even bigger extent.

She tried to hug me, but my body showed no reaction at all. I was just sitting upright and couldn't feel anything. No sadness, no anger, nothing. Inside of me, it was completely empty.

"Say something, Ben," Emma said as she tried to delicately shake me. After I still didn't show any responsiveness, she started to shake me harder. "Please, say something," she said, getting louder and almost beginning to cry.

"It's okay," I whispered and laid down. I pulled the blanket over me and turned to the side.

There was nothing anyone could have done at this moment to make the numbness I was experiencing go away. It was the second devastating message within just a few months. A second defeat, one that I beyond any doubt couldn't handle at that point.

Emma did the only right thing she could have done. She got up, picked up the laptop, shut it down, switched the light off, came back to bed and held me very tightly. I took her hand and tried everything to refrain from bursting into tears.

Many hours had passed, and I was still in the same position. Emma was already in a deep sleep. I could hear her breathing very heavily. It was impossible for me to sleep. I thought it would help me to forget the numbness and the emptiness in my body, but it clearly didn't work. I got out of the bed and looked outside the window. The moon was super bright, shining into my face. I wanted to distract myself, so I reached for my phone plus my headphones and hit play.

# Boy Oh Boy, Eleonora - Off the Emptiness

I didn't know if the song that had started playing would make it better or worse, but while I was staring into the dark sky, so many vivid memories passed through my inner eye. The last time this happened was above the clouds on my flight from Auckland back home. This time it was different though. The memories were clear and defined. So many details appeared. The moment when Francis and I painted our first painting. The moment when I served Sam a triple shot flat white, the moment Emma talked to me the first time and our first night together. All the good and of course some of the bad things as well. Suddenly, there was this accumulation of pictures, pictures that were mine and no one in this world could ever take them away from me. The empty space in my body slowly started to fill again with those little memories of that amazing adventure. With those memories, the initial numbness turned into bitter sadness and disappointment.

It was finally over now. There was no chance of going back. The message was crystal clear. I will never be able to go back. I turned around and watched Emma sleeping. This was truly the worst outstanding battle I had to fight now. I felt like I would somehow be able to get over the deportation itself, but I didn't have any solution to handle the fact that I will be separated from the woman I love so much for an undetermined amount of time. My fear of losing her was bottomless, but at the same time, I knew there was nothing I could do about it. Especially not right now.

I decided to crawl back into bed. I stroked her hair and kissed her forehead. Then I pushed my body against hers, and once again I tried to fall asleep.

When I woke up, I wasn't quite sure if I'd managed to sleep at all, or if I'd just had a very long snooze. My body and brain were drained. I opened my eyes and the space next to me was empty. I turned around and Emma walked into the room. We both looked at each other and froze for a second. She sat down next to me, stroked my head and said, "It's okay."

*What is okay?* I thought. The fact that I fly back to Germany tomorrow and we have no idea what's going to happen next? Or the fact that I have no idea what to do with my life now at all.

It almost felt like Emma was trying to acknowledge how I felt, but also trying to prevent herself from not getting drawn into it too much and not second-doubting her decision. It was pretty clear that the pressure was on her now.

"Are you going to join us for a walk in the park?" she asked.

"Was she really just going to ignore the fact that our only hope of being together had just been taken away?"

"Come on, it will help distract you," she continued.

I didn't have the energy or strength in me to kickstart this conversation with her now. I just nodded and stood up.

"I'll quickly get ready," I mumbled. I still had the clothes on that I had been wearing last night. I brushed my teeth and went downstairs. We put on our warm coats, jumped in the car and drove towards the park. Jay didn't know yet what had happened last night, and no one made an attempt to tell her about it. We were just chatting about the cold weather and the roast dinner that would follow tonight.

When we arrived at the park, Emma's whole family was already awaiting our arrival, apart from Big Nan. She'd stayed at home to rest a bit. The kids were already running around the car. I jumped out and

Uncle Joe greeted me with a good old "Hallo, *mein Freund*" in very broken German.

I had no clue how I'd be able to hold it all together. I tried my best to pretend that everything would be fine. Either way, everyone knew that I'd got deported, but no one knew about the latest developments yet. We started walking and I didn't feel like talking at all. George and Joe were walking in front of me talking about work, plans and goals again. Emma, Jay and Ally were deep in a conversation as well. The kids kept playing and running around.

My mind kept drifting off; I was knackered. I had to think deeply to determine how this all had begun. How did I end up in this situation, where a declined visa application could destroy me just like that? Everything felt like it did before I had left for New Zealand. Can I even compare that feeling? My whole thought process was interrupted by one stupid question.

"So what's your plan, then?" asked Aunty Anne.

# 50

# SUNDAY ROAST

"Ben!" I heard Emma shouting again. By now, I was familiar with what had just happened. While Big Nan was still sound asleep in her chair in front of me, I grasped that I'd once again drifted off to the max. After I opened my eyes, I shouted back to Emma, "Yes please!"

"The door, Ben! Can you please open the door!" Emma shouted again when in the next second I heard that someone was ringing the doorbell (probably for the second time). This time it woke up Big Nan as well. "Got it," I shouted, jumped off the couch and ran towards the door.

When I opened it, the whole bunch of Emma's family were there. Joe, Anne, Ally, George and the kids had arrived all at once and were smiling at me. "Sunday Roast," Joe said and lifted up the dish he was holding in his hand, which resembled something like a pre-roasted chicken.

It was already pretty late, and we had all met again at Big Nan's house. As much as the Sunday walk was a tradition, so was the Sunday roast. Everyone participated.

The whole family was there now, ready to chip into the preparation process of the roast apart from Joe, George and me. I don't know if we were supposed to look after the kids, or just meant to sit around and leave Emma, her mum, her sister and Nan to their own devices in the kitchen. I felt a bit useless and started setting the table. *At least it counted for something*, I thought. The roast was almost ready. George tried to get the kids to the table, and I sat down next to Joe.

"Luckily, I got my Irish passport on Friday," Joe said out of the blue.

"Ah really? Congratulations!" I replied.

Joe was half Irish, and if one thing divided the dinner table in two, then it was Britain leaving the European Union.

I had figured out by now that Joe and Anne leave nothing to chance. Be prepared for the worst—always have a plan B! That's the sentence they would put on their gravestones. Or at least I'd do it for them if no one else would. To be fair, Joe worked in Germany and travelled back and forth every week. Britain not being in the European Union would definitely affect his life, so good for him for taking initiative.

"Can't wait for the Schnitzel," he said.

His German made me laugh again. I tried to ignore the fact that the ladies wouldn't be putting "Schnitzel" on the table today, and especially not a traditional German one, so I jumped back to his icebreaker.

"So, that means you can travel into Germany and back to Britain without any trouble, no matter what will happen?" I said.

"Yes, exactly. I don't want to rely on politics finding a resolution on its own, so I tried to guarantee my own luck."

*Sounds about right to me*, I thought, even though after being back in Europe for nearly three months now, I still was struggling to adjust to this fully planned and secure lifestyle.

"And you? What do you want to do now?"

*There it was again*, I thought. Why on earth do people keep asking me this?

"I don't know," I said helplessly. Joe didn't seem to notice my cry for help.

"But you should have a plan just in case New Zealand doesn't work out."

He started to push my boundaries of coping with the situation. I didn't respond, so he continued. "So, have you looked for jobs? What's your plan, Ben?" he asked.

I felt like I had heard this question a million times in so many variations by now, and I started to feel ashamed for not having all the answers. Something gave me the feeling that it was my responsibility and my duty to present something that sounded like a goal and the perfect plan to reach it. Even though it wouldn't be what I really wanted to do, at least it would be something that others would acknowledge with a "That sounds like a plan!" The perfect acknowledgement for pretending that you have a clue about your life, for knowing exactly what's going to happen next.

It doesn't matter if you actually don't have a clue. At least you can make other people believe that. They'll probably get jealous, which will then make them insecure, so they'll try to catch up, double-check their life plan and everyone will end up in a never-ending race until their last heartbeat. Then, we might look back and ask ourselves, "What were we trying to chase the whole time?"

I could feel my old life and previous patterns of thought starting to catch up to me, despite my amazing time in New Zealand. Unexpectedly, a memory of Sam and I popped into my head. I remembered back then, Sam had come up to me when the collective was at its bottom. Things didn't go as planned because he had no money and was completely broke. We were sitting at an Asian restaurant, and I had invited him for dinner. He was munching on his crispy duck and said something super interesting.

"Weird, I always thought life is over when you're broke, and now I'm sitting here eating duck and drinking beers," he laughed.

"What did you think would happen? You thought you would just vanish the next second after your bank account showed zero?" I said.

He smiled with the sauce around his mouth as he grabbed another piece of duck with his hand.

"Actually, yeah, something kind of like that. Everyone tells you that if you run out of money your life is over, but look at me; I'm still alive and

I have my friends, all the people from the collective. I'm pretty confident life goes on and I'll be able to turn it all around again," he said.

It's weird because it was exactly that, what everyone used to tell me in my early twenties. I heard my mum saying, "Ben, remember to always keep a good credit score. It's important, you don't want to obstruct your future." My parents always judged people who were broke or in debt without knowing what had happened to them or how they might have ended up in this position.

To be fair, I always had taken pretty good care of my finances, but it's not about spending all your money, not worrying about paying it back and carelessly ending up in debt. That should never be the case. However, it's important to know that life would go on, and that there are unexpected situations that could take all you had. You have to be aware that there is momentum, and that it can change as quickly as it came. You can't protect yourself from those situations with insurance or a secure job. Technically, your job is never secure, so why not take the risk and not worry about not having a plan?

"At least I took the risk," Sam said as if reading my mind.

"I know, and I think that's something you can be very proud of. Look at what you've created. The fact that you're broke doesn't mean the end of the collective, and it doesn't mean that you're a bad person!" I said, not merely just to encourage him. I meant it. "Who said it's over now, mate? Winners never gonna quit." Straightaway I thought what a dumb thing to say. Of course, it's true, but it was very cliché.

This memory triggered the thought in me of not giving a fuck, what other people in society would think of me being twenty-eight and not having a clue what tomorrow, the next week, the next months and maybe not even the next few years will resemble.

I repeated Joe's initial question in my head. "What's your plan?"

It finally came how it should have come a lot earlier.

"To be honest, Joe, I have no idea. Not even a little," I said with a clear and slightly raised tone but still in a calm and considerate manner.

I could feel how fed up I was having to justify myself in front of people such as my parents, Paul or now Joe. I had been bottling it all up for the past few weeks, but now I was about to explode.

He looked at me, very surprised, and I could tell he definitely didn't expect such a clear and honest answer. I didn't even know where that came from myself. All I knew and noticed at that moment was a feeling of adrenalin and satisfaction hitting my body. It was triggered by one thing—saying something that I meant one hundred percent. I decided to continue.

"And you know what, Joe?" I said it so loud that I caught George's attention as well. Emma had entered the room with a plate of roasted potatoes. She placed them on the table and focused her eyes on me as well.

"I am sick of making something up just to get your approval. I'm proud of you and happy for you that you've got everything sorted in life. I really am. Even for you, George," as I turned my head towards him.

"You have my total respect, but I can't compete with that and I don't want to, guys. There's no plan and there won't be one for a long time." I got more and more into an emotional rage. I looked behind me and saw Jay, Ally, Nan and Aunty Anne next to Emma. Everyone was silently staring at me, even the kids. I decided to use this moment to finish off my little emotional breakout.

"You can think what you want. I might be a loser in your eyes, or I might not be. I don't care. In the past few years, I discovered a life that doesn't follow all the rules, one that isn't laid out for the next ten years. Not every step is set in stone, and if one step doesn't work out the way it was meant to, there's another route lined up. My life got fucked over, but even if it wouldn't have been, it doesn't really matter. Stop judging people by their plans. Stop comparing and stop showing off. How about you all try to live your life for once and not worry about what bad things could happen next and how you could prevent them from happening to you. For a long time, I thought I was the sick one. I was the one who was wrong, but only because you are the majority doesn't mean you are right. So would you all please do me a favour and stop asking me this stupid question! It's annoying and I'm tired of thinking about possible solutions I could present to you that I don't even want for myself."

A little tear started running down my cheek. I was full of anger by now, but also so relieved at the same time. It felt like the last three months, including what happened last night, had finally found its breaking point right at this particular moment. I totally underestimated the liberating feeling of telling the truth. But I didn't think it would be a good idea to attend that Sunday roast any longer. In the moment of anger and liberation, I jumped out of my chair, ran towards the door and turned around for one last time and said with tears of anger and relief on my face,

"And just for the record. I don't have a plan!"

I turned towards the front door again, grabbed my jacket, stumbled into my shoes and fell out the door. The total silence behind me hinted at confusion and a few speechless people.

# 51.
# ACCEPT IT

I ran outside just to be alone with my thoughts. It didn't even take thirty seconds for Emma to come running after me.

"Wait, Ben, please wait!" she shouted. I was still so emotional and irrational that I kept running.

Emma shouted again. "Please, wait Ben!"

I stopped and turned around. Emma stopped as well ten metres behind me and we looked each other in the eyes.

My face was still full of tears and anger. For a few seconds, we were staring at each other, then she came closer, and her face turned into a big smile.

"Wow," she said and continued after a few seconds of silence. "I'm proud of you. That was quite unexpected, but it seemed like something was bottling up and you needed to spill it from your heart," she said.

"It looks like it," I grimaced while tears of relief now rolled down my cheeks.

"I love you, Emma, I really do, and I wish the situation would be different now. I wish we would have our old life back in New Zealand." Emma stopped me right there. She came up to me, put her finger on my mouth, pulled me close, gave me a big hug and said, "It's okay, Ben. It's okay. We are here now. Together. That's all that matters."

# Boy Oh Boy - All That Matters

I knew the day when Emma would go back to New Zealand was rather close, but for now, for this tiny moment, I was just content to be in her arms. I could feel how my heartbeat was slowing down and synchronising with hers.

"I might have to go for a stroll," I said to her. Immediately she replied, "Well, would you mind if I join?"

I quite quickly sputtered out a "No" and we were off.

"I have to say, Ben, they were all a bit shocked, but you truly spoke from your heart. I think you've opened their eyes."

"You think so?" I asked critically.

"Maybe. Joe looked a bit angry, but also very pensive when I left."

All of a sudden, it felt like the moment had arrived to finally air my honest thoughts to Emma too.

"Well, I didn't want to blow up, but it all came out at once, and it's not just the fact that I'm lost in life and that I lost my life. It's also the fact that you'll be going back very soon and I don't know how to handle it. I don't want to be without you and I can't be without you, Emma. When will we see each other again? I'm scared," I said all at once.

"Don't be. Everything will be okay," she replied.

"Yes, you keep saying that, but there is no way for me to ever go back to New Zealand. So why don't you stay here with me? We can live together somewhere in Europe, anywhere else in the world, wherever you want."

"Ben, you know I need to go back. I have my job there, my friends, my life is over there as well."

"I know Emma, but I thought our life was ours together? What's the point of living in the one country I can't bear to be in?" My voice quivered with an air of desperation.

She stopped walking and glanced up to the sky. You could feel that the mood had slightly shifted and now she was about to start crying. She took a deep breath and said with a slightly broken voice.

"Don't make it too hard for me, Ben. You know I have to go back."

"Do you Emma? Do you?" I asked her.

I took a deep breath. No response from her, so I continued. "I think this is a decision against us. Don't you think so?" I said.

Now Emma raised her voice. "This is not just about you Ben. Yes, you got deported, but I have a life there too. It has always been about you and your paintings. You as an artist. This was your main goal. I have supported since the first day that we met, and I still support you. But now I just can't leave everything behind because you can't come back," she stopped.

This sounded very different from just a short while ago. "What just happened there?" I asked myself.

"I think this is a fundamental question for us, isn't it? We aren't seventeen anymore. You have to decide if you want to be with me or if you want to live in New Zealand with someone else."

Immediately, I regretted the last part of my sentence "with someone else."

Emma was gasping for her breath. "I can't believe you're saying this, Ben. Not now. Not in this situation."

I felt like apologising at least for the last bit.

"I'm sorry, but I am serious Emma. I can't go back. It's impossible and I thought what we had was something that was meant to last. Something special. How are we supposed to live eighteen thousand kilometres apart? Give me at least something I can cling to and don't just say you'll go back."

I knew I sounded very desperate saying this, but this was truly how I felt. I wanted at least some light at the end of the tunnel, but it didn't look like Emma was going to give it to me.

"I don't want to talk about it right now, Ben."

"When else do you want to talk about it then? You're about to leave and I have to go back tomorrow. You are telling me I'm the one you want to be with and spend the rest of your life with, and yet you're heading back to the one country in the world I'm not allowed to enter. I mean, how am I supposed to feel? What am I supposed to think Emma? You say one thing, but your actions suggest something entirely different."

I could tell that she was just shutting down. That's what she would do when she felt attacked or couldn't cope with a situation. She would go completely quiet and not say a word. Her face tilted downwards for a moment, then she lifted her head and our eyes met.

"I think it's better if I go back to the house. Feel free to come back whenever you want," and without blinking her eyes, she turned around and went back to Nan's house. We had roughly been walking for ten minutes. I was speechless.

By the time I was able to say something, she was already around the corner and out of sight. I didn't know what to do when right in that second my phone rang. I pulled it out of my pocket and looked at the screen. It was Francis. I really didn't feel like picking up, but I'd been putting him off for a while now. This obviously wasn't the right time, but for some reason, I picked up anyway.

"Hey, Francis," I answered.

"Hey, mate, how are you doing? What's happening?"

"Yeah, alright, man," I said. "How are you?"

It was pointless to say that because I knew he would pick on it right away, like always.

"Okay, just tell me what happened instead of pretending."

I'm still amazed how this guy can have such a good radar for people. I have to admit I didn't make it very hard for him, but he also had the knack of always reaching out to me in the moments I was struggling the most. I decided not to fight it any longer. I told him about my declined application and gave him the breakdown of the past hour, or at least what felt like an hour to me.

"...and now I am here outside and don't know what to do," I finished summarising.

"Ahh, man, that sounds harsh. I'm super sorry," was his reply.

It felt like after all the conversations we had, I was almost expecting that master answer that would touch me deep inside and solve all my problems. When it didn't come, I was disappointed. So, I just followed up with a simple "yes, I know," because I didn't know what else to say.

Suddenly, Francis cut straight to the heart of the matter. "What can you do about it?"

"About what?" I asked.

"Emma wanting to go back, others expecting you to have a plan, not knowing what happens next?"

"I don't know, Francis. I was hoping you would know the answer."

"Accept it," Francis said curtly.

I wasn't sure if he would follow up with an explanation or not, so I didn't say anything for a few seconds.

After a bit of awkward silence, I tried to follow it up with him. "That's it?"

"Yes, that's it, Ben." It seemed as though he wanted to provoke some sort of reaction.

"Would you mind explaining it a bit more?"

"Sure," he said with a big-ass grin that I could almost hear through the phone.

"As simple as the answer may be, as simple is the explanation, my friend. What can you do about Emma going back to New Zealand?" he asked.

I tried to think for a few seconds and then answered. "Nothing. That's the problem."

"Exactly, so accept it!" He raised his voice and continued "What can you do about others thinking that you need a plan?"

Straightaway I thought and said, "I should tell them that you don't always need a plan."

"No," Francis said. "That's way too much effort. It's not your place to tell them that. So just accept it and let them think what they want to think."

"Okay," I acknowledged.

"Last but not least, what can you do about the fact that you don't know what to do now or what will happen next?"

"Tough one," I said. "I guess just accept it?"

"No," he said. "Oh, hang on, actually, yeah, you were right," he corrected himself as we both burst into laughter.

"Of course, you could try and do something about it now, but it's also fine to accept it for what it is for now. You've been through a lot. Some people suffer from such trauma for a lifetime. So just accept it for now. Let time guide you on the right path," he finished.

"Ah Francis, I mean I can't say anything about it. I guess you're just right once again."

"Ben, it's not about being right or wrong. People care too much and they want to control situations that they can't control. The easiest way to live a happier life is to accept the things you can't control. The things that are meant to happen will happen either way, and you're not some magical boy who can stop or change this. You can only decide if you force yourself to fight against it and end up complaining about what life has done to you, or you're the one accepting it and taking things as they are and as they come. This, my friend, is the main foundation for happiness and satisfaction."

"How though?" I asked

"You wonder how? Well, if you take things as they are, nothing can really ever get you down. Of course, bad situations shouldn't be sugarcoated as good ones, but if nothing can shock you and you follow the way life has prepared for you, you can make big strides towards living a happier life including all of the rollercoaster rides it has prepared for you. On top of that, you need to understand that life is vivid, a constantly moving journey. Things that feel impossible today might be possible tomorrow and the other way around."

"Oh man, why do his words always sink in so much All of a sudden, I listened, I believed and I followed what he said. The insecurity that had evolved from the argument with Emma had eased up and I was a lot calmer. Francis sensed that my breathing was slowing down and that it was silent for a little while, so he took the initiative to give me one last piece of advice.

"Man, you've tried everything to come back, but now it's time to accept what happened. If something is that obvious and clear, the universe is definitely trying to tell you that you should not be in New Zealand right now. So please go back to the house and tell Emma that you love her and that you accept her decision and that you will trust that the future will provide the things for you and her."

I felt like I'd heard these words before and for a tiny second, I remembered Dave, the French guy I met on my flight back to Germany. He advised me to accept the situation for what it was as well and that there was a reason for it all, but the pain was too present and fresh for me to follow his advice back then. Francis turned it up a notch, and his words made it right into my heart. Apart from one very worrying question which was left on my mind.

"But what if that means that Emma and I will be separated?" I asked frightfully.

"You want the honest answer, Ben?" he asked.

"Of course," I confirmed.

"If this is going to happen, accept it."

# 52.
# CAN I HAVE A PUFF?

"Accept it" was all I had in my head now. Shortly after his advice, we hung up and I was on my way back to the house.

It was brutal to face reality and to accept it for what it was. I think I was always trying to protect myself from getting hurt or feeling pain. I had forgotten pain and sadness are just feelings like any other such as happiness. Both are feelings that make us feel alive. The other option would be not feeling anything, and that can't be the solution either for any of us. Feeling out of control is the worst, but one thing was for certain, I couldn't control other people, and I didn't want to. I can't control what they think or what they'll do and I don't want to do it. I repeated it over and over to myself while I was getting closer and closer to facing the mess I had left almost an hour ago.

I arrived at the front door and Emma was outside smoking a cigarette. The last time I saw her smoking was a very long time ago. When I first met her, she always told me that she wanted to stop on her twenty-seventh birthday, which she did up until now.

"Can I have a puff, please?"

She had noticed me coming from a ways away and luckily enough for me, she stayed and didn't wander away.

She looked me in the face and passed me the cigarette. I took a deep puff and coughed as if I had just gotten diagnosed with bronchitis. Emma smiled because she knew that I hardly smoked, especially after she'd quit. I almost never really smoked, only when we started dating or in extreme situations, but I felt like this was definitely one of them.

"I think I have to fix a few things," I continued.

"Yes, I think you should," Emma said and exhaled her cigarette. I wasn't quite sure if she meant our argument or the whole situation at the dinner table. She'd said I'd done the right thing and then we started fighting.

"First of all, I'd like to apologise to you, Emma," I started. Her face looked down at the ground. It felt like she didn't want to face me and didn't want to go through it again.

"I accept your decision, Emma. We don't have a choice. We have to put ourselves in this position and need to take the risk."

"Which risk?" I could notice that tears started to build up in her eyes again.

"I don't know, maybe the fact that we are facing a very long-distance relationship in a situation where I, under no circumstances, can't be where you want to be. I've never faced such a situation, babe. All I know is that I want to be with you, but it's easy to say for me because everything I had got stripped away from me. Your life is still there, and your big goal is still there. In order to get it, you need to go back. There's nothing I can do about it other than accept it," I said and paused for a second.

"I always said that I appreciate your unconditional support for my dreams. I guess now it's my turn to pay it back, even though I feel like I'm going to hurt myself by letting you go. A relationship is also about personal growth, and there is no growth if we don't push the boundaries. Who knows what would happen if you give up your dream because of me. If we only play safe, we might end up in a situation of missed opportunities and regrets. At the end of the day, we both want to sit in front of our house in Portugal, face the ocean and look back on our lives and say to ourselves that we both lived and made the most out of it, am I right?"

I wasn't quite sure if she got my reference to Beth's granddad, but I could tell Emma was again hesitating between being grateful and painfully crying. The heartache was pretty obvious for both of us. She gave me a hug and whispered in my ear, "We are going make it. I promise."

I didn't want to say anything, because I could sense that a weird feeling was telling me that this sentence stemmed more from hope rather than conviction. I pulled her even closer and held her very tight, while I could feel the tears returning to my eyes as well.

We were holding each other for a very long time and I didn't want to let her go. After what felt like forever, she looked at me and said, "Let's go back inside."

"Wait," I said and pulled her close to give her a long kiss. My thumb touched her cheek to wipe the remaining tears off her face.

I looked into her eyes, smiled and said, "Now we can go."

# 53.
# WHO WANTS DESSERT?

When we opened the front door, you could hear people chatting in the room next door that sharply veered into an abrupt hush. We took off our shoes, and it was dead silent. It felt like the whole dinner table was awaiting our return. I didn't know what to expect at all. To be honest, my feeling was more leaning towards a lot of angry faces and eyes that wanted to kill me instantly. I tried my best to put up a very humbled face. I mean It was the truth, I did feel very sorry for my outburst. I thought that this was a good starting point for an apology. Emma took my hand and started pulling me towards the dining room. Holding her hand and her going ahead of me gave me that little bit of confidence that I needed.

We entered the room and, as I expected, all pairs of eyes were staring at me. I wasn't quite sure if I should say something straightaway or find my way back to my chair first. I thought it might be the right thing to clear the air, to begin with.

"I just wanted to say something…," I started to say just as Joe raised his hand. I thought, *Oh my God, here we go.*

"Please have a seat, Ben."

I thought it might be better not to interrupt him since I had caused enough trouble here. So I just followed his instructions and found my way back to my seat.

"I wanted to say something first, Ben, if that's okay."

"Of course," I said instantly.

"I'm sorry Ben, I think I took it a little too far. You were totally right. I have no idea how you feel right now, or how someone feels who loses everything within just a few hours, and is then forced to head back to a place that you've been trying to avoid. In fact, I think, if someone can learn something from someone, it's George and me from you and not the other way around," he said.

"I didn't say anything," George said with a cheeky smile.

Joe gave him a look to shut up. He continued quite unexpectedly, "Who the fuck needs a plan if nothing goes by plan in life anyway?"

All of a sudden, the room went absolutely quiet. I could feel my emotions rising towards something like "Finally."

Then, Aunty Anne gave him the look. Joe noticed it straightaway and it didn't take him a second to react to it. It felt like he had just gotten started.

"Seriously, who needs a plan? If nothing goes to plan anyway...," he repeated and continued, "...three days after I booked my flight to go to Australia for a year I bumped into Aunty Anne. I know that this is a bit off topic."

"Yes, it is," Aunty Anne said fully blushing. I couldn't believe that the vibe had changed without me even apologising.

"What I wanted to say...," Joe continued, "...is that if I would have known that I would meet the woman of my life just three days after I had decided to go to the other side of the world for a year, I would have never done it. In my head, everything was planned out. I was in my mid-twenties, and I didn't like the job my parents had chosen for me. So, I was ready for an adventure," he said.

I didn't know what to pick on first—the parallels I started to see between his life and mine, or the fact that Aunty Anne and he made it work in the end.

I didn't want to interrupt his flow, and neither did anyone else. I slightly twisted my head around and could see everyone drawn to Joe's lips. Jay was smiling, while Emma continued to hold my hand.

"So what happened to you and Aunty Anne then?" I asked. Jay started to smile even more as if she had heard this story already many times.

"Well, Ben, when you know, you just know. I had a few more weeks left before my flight, and the more time I spent with her, the less I wanted to go on that trip, but I made this decision and I knew that I was going there. No offence, darling," he said and looked at Aunty Anne. "It's okay, go ahead," she replied, acknowledging the fact that he'd checked in with her.

"Okay," he continued to get even more clear with the message he was actually going for. "Never expect that a woman or a relationship will fix your problems," he said.

It felt like a little lightning. I guess he was totally right, but this was a side of Joe that I hadn't encountered thus far. I'd had a few good talks with Jay in my short time there, but in my eyes, Joe and George had always been a little bit like my dad. Without any doubt more open-minded and empathic, yet they were career-driven and focused. Just like always having a plan.

"I feel like you need to elaborate on this a bit more," Jay said, seeing the little shock in Emma's eyes.

"Don't get me wrong here, guys. Anne is an amazing woman, and she has of course taken my life to another level, but also and maybe only because I fixed myself first by going on this trip. What looked like meeting each other in such an inconvenient moment in time, paid off in the long haul, because I was convinced of two things. First, that I just met the woman I'd like to spend a big chunk of my life with..."

"A big chunk?" Aunty interrupted him, half angry, half laughing.

"A very big chunk, darling," he laughed and continued to his second point.

"And secondly that I needed to go on that trip to fix myself in order to be ready for this woman, and guess what Ben, none of this was planned. The opposite was the case, I freed myself from what made me unhappy back then. When you had your little emotional break out it reminded me of how narrow-minded I'd become. So before you apologise, I have to apologise first. Just in case you were actually thinking of apologising," he laughed.

"Yes, I actually was about to," I said with a smile of relief.

If there is a situation where you can say that someone found the right words, then it was definitely Joe with his Australia story.

"However, Joe," I surprised everyone as it seemed as though I was about to provoke the situation again. I could feel the curiosity in the room drawn to me and what I was about to ask. "Why did you end up in the job that you are in right now, planning out your career in order to get a better pension?" I asked him.

It didn't take him a second to answer.

"My friend, because I have everything I need in life, and an old man needs some goals in his last few years, doesn't he?"

"I think he does," Aunty Anne said, patting his hand as the entire table broke into laughter.

I guess he was right; I was wrong and just too judgemental in the first place. I felt even worse now, making such a show of it all.

"See, I didn't even know that," George said. "I guess I can learn something here as well," he pondered.

I wasn't aware and didn't know that I would have kicked off a proper chain reaction. Emma could feel the relief as well and the emotions in the room changing to something greater. She grabbed my hand even harder, pulled me over to her side and gave me a kiss.

"And one thing I might want to add," Joe started off again.

"These are the stories that shape you, *mein Freund*. This might feel like the roughest moment of your life, and you might have just hit rock bottom, but everything you have is here." When he said that, he pointed his finger at my chest.

"It's all within you. The stories and moments you've created are something that no one is ever going to take away from you again. On top of that, you have a beautiful woman that is on your side, and you can get through this together."

I knew he wasn't aware of our argument outside, but he wasn't wrong either. I was so happy she was here with me and still so afraid that she would be gone again very soon.

"If I might say one last thing and then I am finished, I promise. I want to correct myself. It's totally okay to not have a plan sometimes. I might not be a good example for it, and neither is George."

"Eyy!" George's fist hit Joe's shoulder.

"But I was a good example of it twenty-five years ago, and you just reminded me of that. Thanks, Ben."

"No worries, mate," I said grinning.

I was taken aback by his story and the new sentiment at the table. It felt like instead of apologising, it was about time to let everyone know what happened last night. I felt I needed to finally air it in order to find a way to deal with it. I wasn't quite sure how Emma would feel about me using such an occasion as this, but at the same time, I'd been completely closed up and lost in my head ever since I'd received the bad news last night. It was about time to jump out of it and arrive back to reality. Face the situation, accept it and find a way to deal with it. "I'd like to say one more thing," I started.

"You really don't need to apologise," Joe interrupted.

"It's not about that Joe," I continued with a wobbly but determined voice. "I just want you all to know that last night it became official. I will never be allowed back into New Zealand again. My reapplication got declined. They think I'm not trustworthy enough because I lied when they asked me if I got paid for my paintings."

I stopped for a second, and once again I felt like I had ruined the dinner. Everything went dead silent once again, but it felt like a weight had been lifted off my shoulders when I said it out loud. The whole day, my mind had been drifting on and off; I was just sick and tired of it.

"This means that I'll be going back to Germany tomorrow. Emma will head back to New Zealand on Tuesday, and we will have to determine how to deal with this situation. It might be a while until we see each other again, but I'm very sure we will. I'm very happy that I got to meet you all. I really am."

I stopped there again because I could feel how wobbly my voice had become. The silence turned into shock. Emma was still holding my hand while Joe started to grab my other hand. He looked at me and whispered, "I'm sorry, mate."

Jay came over to give Emma and me a big hug.

The news was obviously devastating, but the family bond was making up for it, and it felt good to feel respected and understood.

"I'm sorry that I ruined the atmosphere again, but I just wanted to honestly tell you why I've been so caught up in my head today."

Everyone nodded when suddenly Big Nan took the floor and said, "Ben, Emma!"

We both looked at her, and so did everyone else. "Allow me to say one thing. I'm very proud of you both. You two are a prime example of why it's important to take risks and leave your comfort zone in life. You pushed boundaries that no one else at this table dared to push. So do me one favour and don't let those circumstances ruin your spirit and your bond. I love you both, and even if the time ahead might look difficult, make the most of it, and in a few years' time, you'll both look back on it and laugh about today," she concluded, tugging on our heartstrings.

I pulled Emma close to me, and it felt like there was nothing left to be said.

Before I was able to process what just happened, Jay shouted, "Who wants dessert?"

# 54.
# BACK TO THE UNCERTAIN

## DJ Koze, Kurt Wagner - Muddy Funster

I was walking along the beach and could feel the sand between my toes. Suddenly, it felt special again. Every little grain of sand caused a sensation under my feet and tickled my toes. I licked my lips with my tongue and could taste the salt, my hair floating in the wind. Under my arm, I was carrying a surfboard. I'd just caught the perfect wave—my first proper wave and probably the best wave of my life. And it was long one too! Francis would have been very proud of me. It had carried me all the way back to shore. While I was walking along the beach back to my car, I could hear a ringing noise. It got louder and louder until it started to hurt my ears. It was so repetitive that I thought it must be an alarm or something. I heard a voice from behind.

"Ben, Ben, Ben!" It became louder and louder until it reached a level that could be classified as a shout!

"Jesus! Ben, wake the fuck up, we need to leave!"

I opened my eyes, jumped up and looked into the eyes of the person next to me. It was Emma. "We missed the alarm! Hurry up, we need to go to the airport. You gotta catch your flight!" I turned my head to the other side and was staring at the alarm clock. 3:15 a.m. I just thought, *Oh my God, I don't want to get up.*

"Okay, okay, okay, I'll just brush my teeth and then I'm ready," I said in an apologetic tone. I mean, it was very nice of her to drive me all the way to the airport at such a ridiculous time, just so I could catch the cheapest flight of the day back to Germany.

My dream felt so real and got me thinking. "Why can't it always be like in our dreams? Why do we not always live the life that we dream about?"

I quickly brushed my teeth, grabbed my backpack and jumped in the car. It was an unpleasant feeling I was carrying around with me this morning. Not just because of today, but on this particular morning it felt pretty strong. It partly had to do with leaving Emma's family and also leaving Emma.

We weren't going to see each other for at least six months now, most likely even way longer, and neither will I see her nor her family in the meantime. She was going to head back to New Zealand—a very strange place to choose to live in due to the distance, but very beautiful and unique at the same time. We were facing two years of uncertainty, two years where we would most likely be apart for most of it until Emma would receive her permanent residency. So, what should I do in the meantime? This uncertainty was mainly responsible for the unpleasant feeling in my belly—not knowing what was going to happen in the next few days, weeks and months. The fear of not having a plan had returned.

It didn't have to be so difficult; it could be so easy. I could go online, type in something like "jobs in sales/finance—Germany" and would likely find hundreds of job opportunities all over the place. Each of them held the possibility for me to earn money, which I could use then to get a flat, a place to live. I could save it or spend it on new clothes, parties or nice holidays to take some time off the job I just searched for. All this would definitely contribute to the fact that the fear of the uncertainty would go away, and I could slowly make my way back up from rock bottom. That means that the unpleasant feeling would vanish just because I would have a plan in mind, something I could tell my parents. They could look at me proudly and probably say my favourite sentence, "That sounds like a plan."

"What's up?" Emma said.

I was pretty quiet in the car, looking outside the window into the dark, totally caught up in my own thoughts. I guess she was very used to it by now, but she would never stop asking me "What's up" even though she knew exactly what was up. "Nothing" would be my usual reply, but since that might be the last time I was going to see her for a long time, I thought it might be worth it to get some more things off my chest. "I'm just thinking about the near future and what I'm going to do and what I want to do," I said.

"What do you want to do?" she asked.

She kind of knew the answer to this already, but by now it was crystal clear that we wouldn't spend the near future together, so I tried to focus on the rest that I used to enjoy. "I'm not sure yet. I'd like to live near the beach, learn how to surf properly and work on new art at the same time, maybe go to some exhibitions, sell my work, make some money and go back to learn surfing." I said it in an almost dreamy voice. Listening to my own words already implied that I wasn't even convinced myself about what I had just said.

"Go and do it then," Emma encouraged me. If someone understands my situation, then it's her. I think sometimes I underestimate how many people not even at my age, even younger and older, are suffering from the same draining thoughts. I have to say that Emma was right about what she said, but it almost seems impossible at the moment to just go and do the things I'd like to do. Too many things had happened in the past three months. Too much of that was out of my control. It felt like something kept holding me back from chasing the things I desire.

Since I was forced back, every time I'd focus on the thought of living at the beach, going for a surf and living off creating new paintings, a feeling came up. It was like a heavy rock that sat in the middle of my stomach and made me feel a few kilograms heavier, stopping me from moving.

It was that unpleasant feeling again, triggered by fear. The fear of failing, the fear of not being good enough, the feeling of things not working out, the fear of not having a plan, the fear of running out of money. For some strange reason, I thought that the only thing that could smash this rock into a million pieces and make it disappear would be having a strong, secure plan in mind, one that would result in a "proper" job that most likely would provide me with a secure income and a pension, so that I wouldn't need to worry about my life when old. *Great*, I thought. At least I could be sure that the feeling would go away if I just got a "normal" job, like George or Uncle Joe. While it seemed like I had the answers to all my questions, I remembered that I already had this "normal" job and a secure income. I also had a flashy car and the latest iPhone paid for by my company. I didn't have to worry about money. I had enough to buy new shoes and clothes once or twice a month. I kept thinking about that time roughly four years ago, and I remembered something that had to do with that pebble as well. Yes, there it was again. Hello, little rock, back again. Hang on though, my mum, my dad, my grandparents, my old boss and even some of my friends used to tell me that I needed this mysterious plan that will take away all my fears of financial issues and not feeling good enough.

What if it wouldn't? What if it's still going to be there? Different rock but same feeling? The feeling of being just a functional robot that does the work someone else tells him to do. The feeling of having a day off and still thinking about how much you don't want to go back to work the next day.

For now, it seemed as though this unpleasant feeling will always be there, no matter which way I go.

"Great chat," a grumpy voice said next to me. Damn it, it had happened again—I had drifted off.

"We're here now," Emma said. I looked out through the window and saw the airport. *Here we go*, I thought, *off to my uncertain future*. I gave Emma a long hug and a kiss on her soft lips. A little tear ran down her cheek and two little ones down mine, and again I reminded myself of how much I fucking hate goodbyes. No matter how long, it was always a pain knowing that you won't see someone you care so much about for an uncertain amount of time.

This time it seemed like the biggest and toughest goodbye of my life. So many questions remained unanswered. So many thoughts on my mind and so much fear about the upcoming future. I really didn't want to let her go, but the past few days had made it clear that this was my only chance to be able to hold her in my arms again one day soon.

In my arms, I was holding the last remaining thing that was left of the beautiful life that I used to have, a life that was too good to be true. I embraced the moment as much as I could before we relieved the pressure of our hug. I kissed her forehead once more and whispered one last time, "I love you." By now we both were crying again.

Emma said with a wobbly voice "I love you too," and then the moment had arrived. I grabbed my luggage, turned around one more time and walked up the stairs. Above me was a big sign saying, "Departures," behind me my girlfriend, the person I love so much, who would fly back to New Zealand the next day, and in my stomach was a rather heavy rock that had since joined me on my way back to Germany.

# 55.
# THE MOST VALUABLE THING

**Boy Oh Boy - Coisa Valiosa**

Where is the hope in all this? Have I taken absolutely nothing I've learned on board over the past three years? All the advice, all these amazing people, people who taught me and showed me different ways of looking at life? Why doesn't it want to fully sink in? Why does everything feel so hopeless? Why is fear the dominating factor here?

For a long time, being an artist and living from selling my paintings was my dream, my goal and sometimes something that other people would interpret as my plan. Since I'd been forced back, I haven't touched a single brush. I haven't painted a single dot. It felt like my momentum, including my creativity and my passion for painting, was gone and still stuck to my old life over in New Zealand—the one thing that was a life-saver and made me the guy I am today.

I never had a proper plan in New Zealand either, but since no one ever truly cared about it over there, I also never really felt like I needed one. All I was focused on was my goal of becoming an artist. I spent my time and energy on my passion for painting. That in itself was enough to make me feel safe and fulfilled without ever having a proper plan to present to anyone.

I couldn't believe that I had gotten so caught up in fighting the things that I'd experienced since the deportation. I put all my energy into finding a way back into a life that once existed, instead of accepting the facts for what they were. I wanted to build a new life based on the beautiful foundation of memories, pictures and life lessons I have learned in the past few years.

It was time to leave the pain behind me. It was time to grab the brush again and look into a bright future. It was time to show the people in Europe, my parents and my friends that a life without a plan was totally possible even over here. It was time to show everyone that everything was possible, and that there are opportunities to live a fulfilled and happy life, no matter what happens. That's the least I could do. That's the least I owed Sam, Francis, Matt and Emma. If I didn't do it for myself, then I could at least show the people that matter to me most, and who have made my last three years unbelievably special, that their words, time and life lessons had a real impact on me.

Right at this moment, I felt something push on my right upper leg. Something pushed my wallet straight into my butt cheek. I took it out of my pocket and opened it. Instinctually, I reached into the side pocket of the wallet and pulled out a little note that was folded back into a tiny envelope.

It was Grace's article. The page that I had once ripped out of Francis' magazine. I unfolded it again, read through it and looked at her work.

It was the reminder I needed in this situation. A reminder of who I've become, a reminder of who I truly was.

I took a deep breath, washed my face in the sink of the airport bathroom, looked up in the mirror and said to myself, "My name is Ben Schenk. I'm 28 years old and I'm an artist."

# ABOUT THE AUTHOR

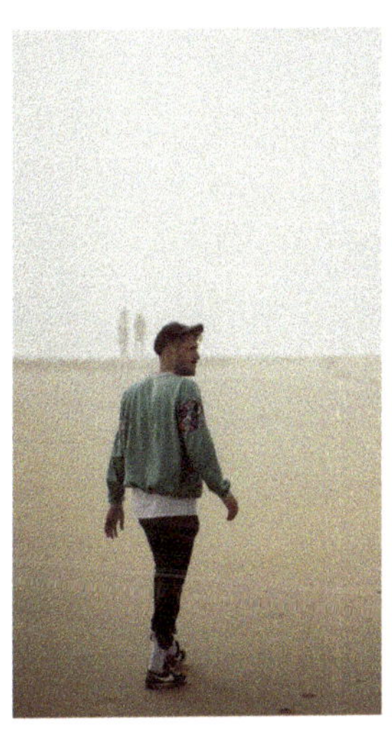

Marco Wagner is no award-winning New York Times author who has written multiple best-sellers. He is simply a young German music producer who found peace by the seaside in Ericeira, Portugal. Together with his musical partner David, they mainly produce deep-melodic electronic music under the alias of Boy Oh Boy. They bumped into each other in New Zealand in 2017, where Marco spent over three years of his life.

When unpredictable circumstances took place, Marco's only way to cope with this situation was by writing. He hopes that anyone who encounters similar scenarios, thoughts, doubts or frustrations will find inspiration in this book to accept and overcome what life has thrown at them, no matter how harsh or brutal it might appear.

Marco's aspiration was that this story be heard one day and will help someone else out there to gain the power of moving on, letting go and striving for fulfilment. The output from all this is his first-ever book and Boy Oh Boy's first-ever musical album, "So, What's Your Plan."

# THANK YOU

## So, What's Your Plan? (Album)

1. Boy Oh Boy – Hitting Rock Bottom
2. Boy Oh Boy, Nairobi D – Do it, Bro!
3. Boy Oh Boy – Meeting Emma
4. Boy Oh Boy, T.M.A, Eleonora – She'll Be Alright
5. Boy Oh Boy, Lophelia – Goodbye Emma
6. Boy Oh Boy, Bar.ba – Welcome "Home"
7. Boy Oh Boy, Conor Ef – So Insecure
8. Boy Oh Boy, Eleonora – Off the Emptiness
9. Boy Oh Boy – All That Matters
10. Boy Oh Boy – Coisa Valiosa

I'm very grateful for the people who were part of this crazy adventure in New Zealand and clearly, without you this story would not exist today, but I'm also incredibly thankful for the amazing artists who played a major part in bringing this project to life.

<table>
<tr><td>Nairobi D</td><td>Conor EF</td></tr>
<tr><td>T.M.A</td><td>Bebetta</td></tr>
<tr><td>Lophelia</td><td>Le Palf</td></tr>
<tr><td>Eleonora</td><td>Anne Veiser</td></tr>
<tr><td>Bar.ba</td><td>Aldo T. Ventresca</td></tr>
</table>

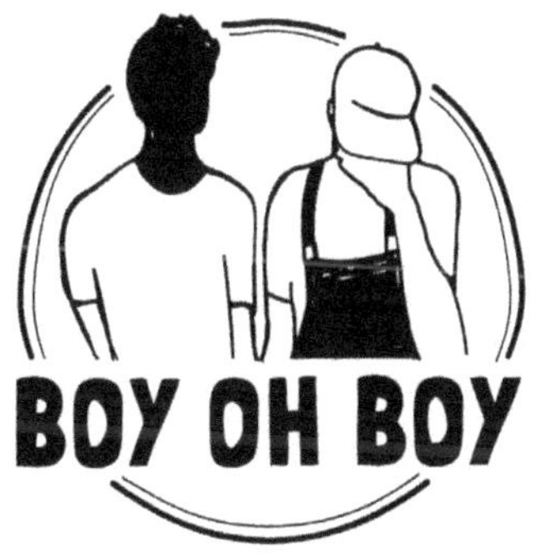


Thank you very much with all my heart!

Yours,
Boy Oh Boy

Milton Keynes UK
Ingram Content Group UK Ltd.
UKHW020613310723
426070UK00009B/53